D1098116

CHEROKEE STRIP

CHEYENNE-ARAPAHOE LEASED LANDS

DODGE CITY

BEAVER CITY

CAMP SUPPLY

MOBEETIE

Chickasha

Medicine Lodge

Coldwater

Ashland

Englewood

Commanche Pool

Great Salt Plains

Cimarron River

Cimarron River (1878-79)

OLIVE BROTHERS TRAIL

DODGE SUPPLY TRAIL

WESTERN (TEXAS)

WASHITA

Sweetwater Cr.

Rath City

RED RIVER

JONES (RATH TRAIL) (MOBEETIE TO DOUBLE MTN)

· Legend ·

Old Trails ----

Streams

Ranch Brands

Towns-Forts ▪ Ashland

LOST TRAILS

of the

CIMARRON

Harry E. Chrisman

LOST TRAILS

of the

CIMARRON

Harry E. Chrisman

SAGE BOOKS, *Denver*

Copyright 1961 by Harry E. Chrisman

Library of Congress Catalog Card No: 61-14370

LIBRARY

NOV - 8 1977

UNIVERSITY OF THE PACIFIC

337291
Western
Americana

F
702
N6
C55

Sage Books are published by

Alan Swallow, 2679 South York, Denver 10, Colorado .

Dedicated to my Mother

BERNICE GERTRUDE (HUNTER) CHRISMAN

Pioneer : Musician : Writer

"I think everyone should leave
a mark of some kind along the
Trails they travel."

> —OLIVER M. NELSON, 1861-1957
> Cowboy and camp cook
> along the Cimarron.

Table of Contents

Table of Illustrations

Introduction

The nature of pioneer life along the Cimarron, whether that of the buffalo hunters or of the cattlemen in the 1870's and 1880's, was not one to produce writers or artists with the time and talent to document their deeds with words and with pictures. As a consequence, the broken and twisted trails left by them are now almost entirely wiped from the face of the earth, their stories forgotten. With the hope that a book of anecdotes, reminiscences and folk stories might again help to reveal these Lost Trails of the Cimarron, this book was compiled and written.

The author regrets its serious inadequacies as a history of the region and can only wish that the anecdotal material had not been so sparse. But the day is too late and Time has waited on no one to put the available material together for the reader. Fifty years ago Richard B. (Dick) Quinn made an early attempt to record the history of the region directly from the pens of the men and women who had lived it. Realizing how fast the frontier was fading, he sent out written requests to the several old timers still living in the Hardesty, Oklahoma, region to jot down their *reminiscences* of the southwest cattle range. Be simple, he urged them. Just tell what you thought about in the range cattle days and bring your notes to the *Hardesty Herald* office, which Quinn was then publishing at the now ghost-site that was Old Hardesty. Quinn then sat back and awaited results.

A few days later a genuine old-time cowboy of the '70's appeared at Quinn's office. The old timer was past middle-age, stiff-legged and dressed in the familiar faded levis and worn boots. After a friendly visit the old fellow left, handing Dick Quinn a worn piece of foolscap paper upon which was scribbled his story of the "pioneer days." Quinn was elated and as soon as the visitor closed the door opened the folded paper and read:

11

The mercury stands at 68 degres today with som wind clouds rolling in fum the nawth towad the Texas panhandel. We huv hed a dry open winter but awful cold since November. Grass is shawt. With early moisture we can expec a better year next year.

The lesson learned by Dick Quinn, pioneer editor, fifty years ago, goes doubly for western researchers in pursuit of easily-accessible material today. If it is easy to obtain, then it is "old hat" and has probably been published a dozen times before.

The material for this book was collected from many sources, oral and written. Chief among these sources have been pioneer cattlemen such as Bernard H. Lemert and Burris Wright, both of whom have recently passed on to the Other Range. Bernard Lemert had been an Inspector for the Southwest Cattleman's Association and probably knew the range cattle business as well as any man living at the time. Mr. Wright punched cattle in the Cimarron region as a boy, later in Arizona and New Mexico and owned a lovely Cimarron valley ranch and other farm land in his later years.

Other sources have been the newspapers of the area, the files of the *Guymon Herald,* very considerately loaned the author by Warren Zimmerman of Lawrence, Kansas, former editor. The *Hardesty Herald,* and files of the *Fargo Springs News* and later Liberal, Kansas, papers have been searched, as have been the files of the *Beaver Herald-Democrat* and other newspapers of the Cimarron region.

Among other old timers who have been of great aid to the author in preparing these stories are the late Al Olive of Dodge City and his helpful and cheerful wife, Ida. The newspaper clipping files of the late F. A. Hobble of Dodge City, made available to the author by Herbert Hobble of Liberal, Kansas, provided much factual material. The late Oliver M. Nelson of Muskogee, Oklahoma, who loaned his original manuscript of "The West and No Man's Land, 1878-1889," to be studied and who made a tape recording of an hour's duration telling of the old days in No

Man's Land, deserves great thanks. Mr. Nelson's valued correspondence of five years' time has also been drawn upon for factual material and clarification of his personal story in the Neutral Strip as well as for the feeling for the Old West which it gives.

The late Merritt Beeson of Dodge City gave the author great help in the compiling of facts for this book. He gave cheerfully and from a full storehouse of knowledge about old Dodge and the Cimarron country, and his genial countenance is forever engraved on the author's mind.

Gary Walker, of the Liberal High School faculty, is to be thanked for reading and criticizing the manuscript; and I should also like to mention the help on pioneer matters always willingly given me by Jess McCoid of Liberal, Kansas.

Many other old pioneers deserve great thanks for their helpfulness, including Andy Myers of Dighton, Kansas, old-time cowboy, city marshal and probate judge. To others who have assisted me in many ways, librarians, friends, relatives—my thanks.

Appendices at the end of the book are offered to further aid the reader in an understanding of places and events in the open range country between the Arkansas and the Canadian—the Cimarron Country. Appendix I is a complete roster of the 116 members of the Western Kansas Cattle Growers Association, together with their brands, names of their foremen and owners. Appendix II is a folding map of the area, showing the brands of the various ranches in relation to the watercourses and range held by them at the time. By matching the Map of Appendix II with the Brand information of Appendix I it is possible to obtain a very complete picture of the Range Cattle operations of that era and in the Cimarron area.

It is the hope of the author that this volume of tales from the Cimarron country will serve as a bridge over which others may pass vicariously from the Present to the Past, now long ago when the cattleman was king. As a guide for those who may be interested in physically tracing the Old Trails, these little stories with their many facts may serve also to help locate the historical scenes where the actual events transpired. If the book helps more accurately to establish the identification of the men and women whose fragmented lives are the true Lost Trails of the Cimarron, then it shall, indeed, have served a good purpose.

HARRY E. CHRISMAN
Liberal, Kansas
April, 1961

Chapter I

"Of all the lives beneath the sun,
The buffalo hunters' is the jolliest one."
    —From an old plains song.

The first of the buffalo hunters to cross the region from the
Arkansas river in Kansas to the Canadian River in Texas found
it a great, high plain, sloping eastward from the mountains and
cut by the canyons and ravines of the watercourses that make up
the greater Arkansas river. This area they generally called
Cimarron country, named as it was by the earliest Mexican travelers for the many wild cattle, the *cimarrones*, which they found
grazing along the streams. But the Cimarron country embraced
a much greater area than that along the sandy banks of this
stream, for the lush region through old No Man's Land, along
the Beaver River as well as the vast expanse southward to the
Canadian River in the Texas panhandle was often referred to by
the same term. This grassy plain extended from the Rocky
Mountain foothills to the eastern edges of the Oklahoma and
Texas panhandle areas. And upon the broad and fertile tableland
lay a carpet of buffalo grass touched only by the hooves and
mouths of countless thousands of buffalo and other species of wild
game that inhabited the region.

For untold centuries the buffalo had made this land their home,
grazing on the lush grass and watering at the sweet, spring-fed
streams and rain-water lakes. Upward of five million buffalo
made this immediate region their summer and winter home,
grazing nothward as the grass greened in the spring, grazing back
to the Texas panhandle as the cold winds blew out of the frigid
northland.

In the middle 'seventies the High Plains area became the center
of the greatest buffalo hunt, the vast herds being destroyed for

their hides alone. The hides were purchased by eastern buyers who turned the tough skins of the big bulls into the broad and strong belts that began driving the industrial machines of an expanding nineteenth-century economy. As the beaver was systematically decimated in the previous decades to place a tall, beaver-fur hat on the head of every socially-conscious gentleman, so were the buffalo exterminated to place a lap-rob across the chilled limbs of a later society and to gird their new factories with strong belts. From 1872 to 1874 the Santa Fe railroad carried a half million hides. It has been estimated that from 1871 to 1887 approximately six million hides were shipped from the Dodge City gathering point alone!

By 1886 the last buffalo had been killed in southwest Kansas and by 1889 only a scattered few survivors of the former millions could be found, chiefly in the rough brakes of the Beaver river in No Man's Land, that *neutral strip* of Public Lands, as they called it, lying between Kansas and the Texas panhandle.

With the extinction of the great herds of buffalo, the nomadic hunting tribes of Plains Indians became the wards of the U. S. government and were confined on the new reservations. Now the entire area of the High Plains lay "fallow," devoid of the buffalo and free from great Indian interference—but not yet covered by the longhorn cattle from Texas which would soon replace the buffalo among the grassy swales and knolls on the prairies.

Tens of thousands of circular areas still dotted the plains, depressed areas of twenty to thirty feet in diameter and a foot to two feet in depth. In wet times the depressions would be water-filled, in dry years a pitfull of dust. These were the "buffalo wallows," left by the great herds. For many years they were still visible, long after the big beasts that made them had vanished. Though filled with blow-sand and tumbleweeds, they were set out on the prairie by a circle of dainty wild flowers in wet springs. The buffalo wallows were fashioned by the big fellows who rolled in them, hooking up the ground with their horns and dusting their hides to repel the bot flies, the itch, fleas, heel flies, lice and mosquitoes and other predators it was their lot to bear. In wet weather the buffalo wallowed in the mud in the pit, plastering his sides and belly with a thick layer of the clay and mud that encased the insects and pests in a poultice from which only death freed them. At a later date and place the buffalo would roll and work off the plaster cast, often leaving handsful of pulled hair with it on the prairie and frequently giving himself the appearance of nudity where the contrast between winter's long hair and the complete absence of it made the comparison odious. Today the old wallows where they can still be seen are only a circular indentation on the grassy surface. Occasionally a big skull will wash out of a river or creek bank during spring or summer storms. This is all that remains to remind us of the great herds that once dominated the High Plains of the Cimarron country.

Following the Civil War, Texas cattlemen looked north toward the railroads for transportation to market of the millions of head of longhorn cattle they were rounding up from the brushy thickets. Cattlemen who passed through the Indian Territory saw thousands of acres of rich buffalo grass prairie, ungrazed and unused by the Indians. In western Kansas and in No Man's Land they saw the same unused lands. Upon their return to Texas they told others of their discovery of this unused "sea of grass." When the buffalo hunts came to an end, between 1875 and 1880, many of the ex-hunters decided to enter into the cattle business along with the Texas drovers. Among such ex-buffalo hunters were men like J. H. Cator and his brother Bob. They had hunted since 1874. Early in 1875, with Sam Wilkerson and Mike McMahon, they camped south of present-day Guymon, Oklahoma, on the Beaver river. Another party of hunters composed of Jack Williams, "Little Hank" Williams, Ed Fletcher and Henry Worth camped nearby on Frisco Creek. Both parties hunted until April in that region. The Cators then moved to Horse Canyon where they killed 1,300 buffalo; later they moved to the Hackberry where they killed another 700 head of the doomed animals.

The Cator brothers had an opportunity to study fully the possibilities of ranching in that area and laid plans for the future. They stayed, though the other hunters moved to Dodge City (always called "Dodge" by the natives) for the winter. The Cators liked the region along Coldwater Creek, called "El Frio" by the

17

Mexicans. That summer they hauled their hides to Granada, Colorado, via Tepee Creek and Point of Rocks. There, they sold to Sells & Company and to Otero, hide buyers. The Cators eventually picked Hansford County, Texas, for their cattle operations, turning loose several hundred head along Palo Duro creek. Following many successful years as rancher, Bob Cator moved to Washington state in 1896. There, he met an untimely death when a gun, held by one of his sons, accidentally discharged. The brother, J. H. Cator, later judge, remained in the southwest for many more years, passing on at an advanced age.

Bob Cator once related a hair-raising experience he had when he was bringing a load of dried hides to Dodge. He had stopped at the springs at Sharp's Creek, at the Adobe Walls crossing of that stream, to water his team. While resting the oxen he noticed the dead body of a white man lying along the trail, only a few feet from his wagon. Cator sensed that the body had been dead only a short while and his caution paid off, for glancing into the brush that grew along the crest of the rocks on the south bank of the stream he spied an Indian, only partially concealed and apparently watching him.

Cator quietly moved his team away from the water, keeping the wagon between himself and the Indian. He drove the oxen down the stream a ways to where the trail turned up and onto the north bank. When he hit the "flats," north of the stream, he flogged his oxen on into the night to put as much distance as possible between himself and what might have been a war party of Indians. Reaching Dodge a day or so later, he reported the discovery of the dead body. Hoodoo Brown, the old frontiersman who operated a road ranch at Crooked Creek, returned with him to the spring and helped him bury the body. Cator remarked afterward that he never crossed the stream again at the Adobe Walls trail crossing but would always come back to the crossing from a bend in the creek, downstream, where he could make a survey of the bushes at the south side of the stream and determine whether an Indian was lying in ambush for him.

The stream here, at Sharp's Creek, was named after a young buffalo hunter, Charles Sharp. He was killed and scalped by

Indians on Frisco Creek in 1874. Sharp's pardner, Harry Lease, returning from Adobe Walls with provisions after the Indian fight at that place, found young Sharp's mutilated body at their camp and buried it.

Today, the old Adobe Walls Trail can be plainly seen here at the Smith Ranch, operated by a Mr. Nickeson. On a large rock where the spring formerly bubbled down from above, a staple had been driven in the stone. It held one end of a rawhide thong, the other end of which was attached to a drinking gourd. The staple remains there in the rock till this day. The stream at this point offers one of the most beautiful natural scenes in the Oklahoma panhandle.

Buffalo hunting had developed by 1874-75 into an all-year business. Hundreds of hunters swarmed the plains, made up into bands of five men and a wagon. They usually operated with a killer, two skinners, a wagon man and a cook. Larger outfits, consisting of sixteen men, would have two killers, a cook, a re-loader, a hide pegger, two wagon men who would haul out the hides to market, and nine skinners.

In an area for fifty miles in every direction, southwest of Dodge, one could scarcely find a spot on an average clear day where he could not hear the boom from the big Sharps buffalo rifles. In this area men like George Reighard, Hoodoo Brown, Hugh Henry, Wright Mooar and his brother Pat, Tom Nixon, Billy Dixon, John Goff, John R. Cook, Brick Bond, Jim Kelley, Bob Wright, Rufe Tarbox, Ham Bell, Charles Rath, Frank Collinson, Jim and Bob Cator, Tom Linton, Zack Light, Prairie Dog Dave Morrow, Joe McCombs, Mack Hart and scores of others scoured the plains for buffalo.

The killing was usually done in "stands," as the hunters called it, that is, where they could approach carefully and kill off the animals while they stood at one place. With this technique the hunter would approach within a hundred or hundred and fifty yards, carefully aim his Sharps, Henry or Spencer of .45 or .50 caliber and shoot one of the outside herd bulls "through the lights," that is through the lungs. This type of shot caused the bull to puff hard and blow blood for a few minutes while the others slowly milled around him as he lay dying. The hunter would then get in another clean shot without disturbing the herd. With this plan a killer could systematically kill off all the animals his skinners could handle. While he rested and cleaned up his weapons and made more bullets, the hides would be taken off, stretched on the ground to dry, fur down, and when dried, loaded on to the wagons.

In a single "stand" of this type of shooting, Tom Nixon was reported to have killed 204 buffalo; Frank Collinson killed 121; Vic Smith, 107. Jim Cator estimated that he killed 16,000 buffalo in the four years, 1872-75. Wright Mooar estimated his kill over a nine-year period at 20,500 head of buffalo. Tom Nixon told of killing 3,200 head of buffalo in 35 days on Rattlesnake Creek, 35 miles southeast of Dodge!

As most hunters stayed on the plains winter and summer, the belief among them grew that longhorn cattle could also weather the winters as their ox teams had been able to do, foraging a living on the natural grasses of the plains without added hay or grain. This belief grew among hunters and cattlemen from Montana to Texas. Red Cockrum, foreman for Beaty Brothers, told how the belief of wintering cattle came about in his region, southeastern Colorado.

The fall of 1876, said Cockrum, a number of freighters found themselves at Granada, Colorado, track's end for the Santa Fe at that time. Among the group was a man called Judge Moore. This was no doubt Judge R. M. Moore, an early pioneer of that region, who married Mary Bent on April 3, 1860, the daughter of William Bent of Bent's Fort. Mary's mother was Owl Woman, daughter of a Cheyenne chief. At any rate, Moore decided to find winter range where his ox teams could be useful and still sustain themselves until spring, saving him the trouble of re-hiring men in the spring. So Moore fitted five of the teamsters with a hundred head of oxen and dispatched them to the south to hunt buffalo that winter. The men took the Buffalo Hunter's Trail southeast to Bear Creek with instructions to return to Granada on May 1st, 1877. The men trailed most of the oxen behind empty wagons that held only their winter supplies and tents. No more was heard of the hunting expedition until the next spring.

By mid-May Moore became uneasy. He sent two scouts, John Donahue and Barney Gou, to search for the party. After a week's search the scouts came on to the hunting camp on Bear Creek. The five hunters were dead, two in their rough cabin and three of the bodies lying in a grove of trees a short distance from the cabin. The bodies appeared to have been dead at least two months, but they bore no wounds and were not mutilated as would have been the case had Indians killed them. There was plenty of substantial food left in the wagons and in a nearby cache. A pile of a hundred buffalo hides showed that they had worked successfully on the winter hunt.

The reason for their deaths remained a mystery, though the scouts reasoned that the hunters had either become poisoned or, what seemed more likely, had frozen to death. A cold and unseasonable "nawther" had probably swept down on their camp in March. They had probably let their wood and chip supply run low, since it was early spring. Unfortunately the names of the hunters were not recorded and their bodies were buried on Bear Creek where they died. But the astonishing thing, to the scouts, was that the oxen, grazing nearby and without any shelter of any kind, had wintered well without the loss of a single head. They were in good flesh when discovered and showed no signs of a hard or difficult winter.

Still later experiences proved that while big, mature and acclimated steers could survive a rigorous winter, poor cows, young stock and unseasoned stock of all types might well suffer and be lost without winter feeding on the part of the ranchers. But this lesson was not well-learned until the blizzards of 1885-86. And no one learned the lesson any clearer than Red Cockrum who saw one blizzard in 1889 sweep down through the Colorado cattle country, driving their JB cattle from their headquarters at Point of Rocks on the Cimarron clear down on to the Anchor D range on the Beaver river in a single night, a distance of forty miles. Six cowboys lost their lives in that storm in the vicinity of Clayton, New Mexico.

21

Neither blizzards nor Indians kept the hunters north of the Arkansas river, despite the terms of the Medicine Lodge Treaty in 1868. The fat prices paid for buffalo hides at Dodge and Granada sent the hunters farther and farther south of the Arkansas river, down into the Texas panhandle.

Among these hunters who struck off to the south when the herds grew thin north of the Arkansas river was George W. (Hoodoo) Brown. Brown was born in Newton County, Missouri, March 20, 1847. At the age of 18, he volunteered for service in the Union Army and served with the 3rd Regiment of Missouri Volunteers. Following several engagements he fell sick at Little Rock and later rejoined his outfit in Tennessee. When the war was over his unit drew horses for service on Dakota's northern plains. Here, he first fought Indians and learned the ways of the Plains Indians.

When he was discharged, Brown left Illinois, going west to Abilene that fall of 1868 and working at the shipping yards established by Joseph G. McCoy. Later he helped drive a herd of cattle to Colorado, at which time he first saw Dodge City. After cowboying, bullwhacking and freighting to Forts Harker, Dodge and Hays, Brown and a friend, the scout Charles (Jack) Stilwell, who had delivered the message to Fort Wallace of the plight of Colonel Forsythe's men on Beecher Island, were hired by General Carr to accompany elements of the 7th U. S. Cavalry to the Republican River in a scout against Indians. Brown was with the cavalry from the Republican to the Washita before being discharged from duty, and served with scouts "Buffalo Bill" Cody, Lt. Silas Pepoon, Wild Bill Hickock and others in the campaign. He was with the troops when they located the bodies of Major Elliott and his men, killed by Black Kettle's band. Elliott's body and that of Mrs. Cora Bland and her son Willie, also slain by the Indians, were returned in an army ambulance by Brown's group.

Following his discharge as a scout, Brown went west to Denver. Soon he took up buffalo hunting to supply the army posts with meat. This led to the killing for hides and he was engaged in hide-hunting in 1871-2 when he started his saloon business in Dodge, the second business in the new town. Brown hauled plank wood from Fort Hayes to construct his small building, a shack on the south side of the tracks and near the bank of the Arkansas where it was handy to get water to cut his whiskey with as well as for the Texas men to water their livestock.

By 1873 Brown was back at the buffalo hide business, one which he followed until the end of the buffalo herds. In 1885, on a hunt with friends, he killed his last animal near Point of Rocks (on the JB range) near the Cimarron in the southwest corner of Kansas.

When Dull Knife's band crossed Kansas, after fleeing from their Oklahoma Reservation, Brown was operating a road ranch on Crooked Creek, near Meade. When the Indians were reported heading for his location, Brown moved his family to Dodge. His neighbors, not practiced in Indian fighting like old Hoodoo Brown, called him "the biggest coward of all." Brown only smiled and looked out from his droopy eyes upon them with pity. For he had looked upon men, women and children who had been tortured and mutilated at the hands of the savages. He had killed Indians without remorse, lest he himself be killed by them. His had been a school that taught "Good Indian: Dead Indian." And it was too late for him to change his view.

East of the town of Meade, Kansas, is a high, rounded, wind-swept hill. Upon this hill lies Graceland Cemetery. The cemetery, on its west side, overlooks a lovely city park on the banks of Crooked Creek. It was in the winter of 1877 that Hoodoo Brown and another freighter spent a bitterly cold night on this spot, shivering beside their freight wagons in their buffalo robes. The other freighter pondered why no one had thought to build a road ranch at this spot on the Jones and Plummer Trail, the main trail into Dodge from the southwest. There was no other road ranch closer than Jim Lane's place on the river at Beaver City, to the south. Brown thought the matter over in the night. By morning he had decided to start up such a road ranch.

Hoodoo Brown erected a sod cabin to serve as his store. He built a second one to house his family, his wife Sarah and his three children, Nellie, Sonny and Grace. The soddies he located at "The Wells," as they were called, or artesian springs. A half mile downstream he erected strong corrals to hold the ox teams and mule teams of the freighters. In a nearby meadow he cut hay for winter feed. At this location Brown dispensed flour, meal, bacon, dried fruits, gunpowder and guns, rope, harness, saddles, ox yokes, canned foods, spices, tobacco, sugar, tea and the thousand and one items used by the people on the frontier. His customers were the freighters from Mobeetie and Fort Elliott, plying between there and Dodge, and the cattlemen who brought their herds for shipment to Dodge.

The death of his daughter, Grace, gave Graceland Cemetery its name. On December 10, 1885, a Land Office Receipt from the Garden City Land Office was issued to Brown. On December 28, 1889, a Patent from the U. S. Government, signed by President Benjamin Harrison, was issued to George W. Brown. On September 15, 1888, George W. Brown and his wife, Sarah E. Brown, deeded the east 30 acres of the NE¼ of the NW¼ of Section 12, Twp. 32S, Range 28 W of the 6th PM, to the Graceland Cemetery Association.

Hoodoo Brown has been given the dubious distinction of being a "gunman," at least by one western writer. There is little to support this statement, though Brown was a hard-bitten frontiersman, perfectly capable of taking care of himself in any given situation. He once told of an Indian coming to his camp and asking for food. The hunters shared their buffalo meat with the visitor. Questioning him, they found that his own camp was a couple of miles downstream on the creek where they were camped. While two of the hunters remained at the campfire, entertaining the Indian, the other three took their guns and crept down to the Indian camp. Though it was late for feasting they found the Indians, four of them, eating buffalo steaks and ribs, talking and laughing. The hunters quietly talked the matter over among themselves. They felt that the Indian lad who visited them had been a scout to see where their camp was located and that an attack was planned upon them for that night. The hunters silently took beads on the Indians and shot them down before they could escape.

Brown, recounting the massacre many years afterward, said

that they told no one about the matter, feeling that the Indians would have massacred them had they not beat them to it. As a sort of atonement, they let the Indian at their camp go free the following morning. It was a period of "kill or be killed" on the frontier, and they took no chances.

At a later time when he was operating the road ranch on Crooked Creek, Brown killed a man under somewhat unusual circumstances. Two men rode up to his soddy on a black night. As Brown heard the horses approach, one of the men called out "Hoodoo!" Opening the door a crack, Brown saw one of the men quickly rein his horse and turn it into some nearby trees and bushes where he sat waiting. Now suspicious, Brown stepped out the back door with his double barrel shotgun. He saw the man in the bushes drawing his rifle from the saddle scabbard. Brown instantly pulled up his shotgun and gave the rider a blast. He fired the other barrel at the man nearest the soddy as he leaped his horse from the ranch yard, dropping him into the yard, dead.

A stockman's group, among whom was Laben Lemert, according to Bernard Lemert, his son, found that the dead man had worked for Brown previously and that Brown owed him a considerable sum of money, some said $700. The shooting had its strange aspects. But when the evidence was all in, Brown was exonerated by the cattlemen. In that age, one never rode up close to a man's door without halooing from a distance first and being invited to ride in, either at a cow camp or a ranch. To announce your arrival was the friendly thing to do. But to draw a householder from the safety of his abode while a murderous companion lurked back in the shadows waiting to kill him was an old trick, too old to catch a wise old fox like Hoodoo Brown.

So the killing was regarded as an unfortunate accident, and the man who lurked in the shadows soon left the country. But because of the incident, a certain stigma did seem to attach itself to the name Hoodoo Brown, an otherwise excellent citizen, a good father and brave man.

Brown operated his road ranch for five years, making good money. But he held on to his land until the drouth years, then sold for a pittance. By 1886 Brown was nearly broke. In Janu-

25

ary, 1886, when a supply wagon arrived from Dodge at Meade, Hoodoo Brown and his partner Charles Edwards had given out their last pound of food to those who were trapped there by the storm. Brown and Charles Edwards were operating the Hotel at Meade at that time. Later, Brown made the rush into Oklahoma in 1889. Still later he was reported living on a good farm near a town, Henrietta, in Oklahoma. Little more is known about him by the author. Brown did leave one of the best accounts of the buffalo hunting days when he told of a trip into the Neutral Strip (No Man's Land) with a friend and fellow buffalo hunter, John Goff.

At the point where they hunted there is, today, a small stream called "Goff Creek." Hoodoo Brown named it after his friend. Goff Creek originates in northeastern Cimarron Country and takes a southeastern course down to its junction with the Beaver river north of Guymon. At that time, Brown and Goff had pooled their hunting outfits for protection against the Indians and decided to go south of the Arkansas to hunt. The time was in 1874-75. The battle of Adobe Walls was fresh on everyone's mind and it took nerve to enter the Indian's choice hunting grounds and attempt to purloin his life's victuals for the price of the hides that could be taken. Brown was at this time operating a saloon at Granada, Colorado, together with a pardner named Jack Williams. His word-picture of old No Man's Land when the white man first came makes an interesting story. Here it is, as he wrote it for the *Guymon Herald*, February 25, 1915:

THE NAMING OF GOFF CREEK,
AS TOLD BY GEORGE W. BROWN

The battle of Adobe Walls had been fought on June 27, 1874. The first we knew about the Indians being on the warpath was when a man rode into Granada, his horse lathered up, and he said that the Indians were after him and that they had killed a boy who had been with him. Soon after, when nine men came on into town, they were arrested on suspicion that they had killed the boy. But when on the next day Indians in the vicinity actually killed six more men, the suspects were liberated. A party of about 40 men was made up to go out and recover the boy's body. The Indians had scalped the boy. He

26

was only 18 years old, a shoemaker, but he had taken a notion that he wanted to go out on the range to herd cattle, and he was killed on his first trip out. * * * The band that made this raid was Bull Bear's outfit. He was a Southern Cheyenne and a bad one.

Granada was at that time the western terminal of the Santa Fe railroad and for about a year was quite lively. When the Indians got rambunctious the hunters began to rally at Granada so that before long none was out on the range. There were two commission houses in town—Chick and Brown and Otero & Sellers. They served as headquarters for the freighters who took goods from the end of the railroad and hauled overland to Mexico and all over the southwest. One day while I was taking a nap I heard someone say, "Brown, you seem to be very lazy today."

It was John Goff, an old hunter who spoke. He had a party of seven hunters and I had five, which would give us a dozen. He suggested by consolidating our forces we would have an outfit which, when well-armed, would be strong enough to stand off a large force of Indians. I thought it over carefully and concluded to go with him. I set my men to the preparations. I put my men to running bullets and making cartridges. We made about 2,000 rounds for our Sharps rifles.

For myself I had a big 50-caliber rifle, weighing 16 pounds with a 32-inch octagonal barrel. It used 120 grains of powder and bullets an inch and a quarter long. Sometimes when I was out in the main herd of buffalo with it, I would wear two belts of cartridges, each holding 42 of these big loads and I often carried a bottle of water to pour through the barrel when it got too dirty to shoot straight.

Railroad men coming into Granada from the east would tell us about seeing large herds of buffalo about 50 miles east of Lakin station. So we made our start on this hunt down the Arkansas river to Lakin. From there we went to the North Fork of the Cimarron river, where we camped. We killed 85 buffalo. But there were not enough of them to pay for the hunting, so I hauled those hides back to Lakin and sold them to old John O'Loughlin. He kept supplies for hunters and bought buffalo hides from them. When I got back to camp the next day we pulled out south and struck the Cimarron river again at Wagon Bed Springs. From there we moved up the river about 20 miles to a place called Sand Wells. As buffalo were scarce there we concluded to move from there south about 30 or 35 miles to Beaver Creek. But we were disappointed again in the number of

27

buffalo. All of the buffalo trails seemed to go west up Beaver Creek. This was my first trip up Beaver Creek, although not the first for Mr. Goff. We went up Beaver about 15 miles where we established a camp on a little creek which emptied into the Beaver from the north and which was afterward called Pony Creek. In this camp we killed about 200 buffalo. But the animals got scarce, so we moved about 15 miles farther west, where we found a nice little spring that also emptied into Beaver from the north. As there were many buffalo about, we camped for two or three days and hunted.

One night we got to talking in camp about being so far away from the railroad, and it seemed that along this little creek no white man had ever been before. We wondered whether the creek had ever been given a name, and we decided that it had not. You must bear in mind that in those days there were no wagon roads in that country, not even a wagon track. So I told the boys I proposed to give the creek a name. So I christened it Goff Creek, in honor of my hunting partner, and Goff Creek it has been ever since.

About a half mile from this creek was a high, rocky butte with some rocks piled on its top two or three feet high. I knew that Indians had piled those rocks up that way, so I went up there to investigate. I looked in between a couple of the rocks and saw 27 little sticks done up in a bundle. I took them down to camp and showed them to Mr. Goff. He told me that this was a message for the main band of Indians to pick up, and that it meant that 27 warriors had passed that way. We hunted on this creek for five days and killed about 400 buffalo. But the animals got scarce, so we again moved our camp, going this time about 15 miles farther west to another creek that was afterward called Tepee Creek.

We hunted for three days, but we observed that the trails still went westward, and that the grass was all beaten down by the big herd. I got on my horse one day and told John Goff that if the main herd was within 100 miles of us I was going to locate it before I came back.

I had not gone west more than 10 miles when I could begin to see more buffalo all the time, so I kept on for another ten miles until I came to a lake of water that covered about a quarter section of land. And all around the lake, as far as I could see, I could hardly see the ground for buffalo. This was a rainwater lake, and as my visit was in the fall of the year, this lake was covered with wild ducks and geese, and all kinds of water fowl. This scene out on the prairies, long before the white man had taken possession of this domain, long before the wagon trains or the railroads, was one of the prettiest scenes I ever saw in all my life. The lake and the wild water fowl, the buffalo, and also wild ponies running loose made it an unforgettable sight. Now and then among these wild horses, I made out horses and mules with saddle marks on them, signs of tame creatures that had broken away from their subjugation by man, and had drifted back for companionship with the wild creatures in the unmolested all outdoors.

It was at this lake that we made our good killing. We camped there for about ten days, and brought down 800 buffalo.

Shooting was so good that we found that we were running short of ammunition. Although all of the store provisions that we needed, since nature furnished us the rest, was flour and coffee, we were well-fixed but we were getting short even of flour and coffee. But it would not do for us to be caught in Indian country without plenty of ammunition for our rifles. So Mr. Goff and I decided that somebody had better go to Granada to stock us up again.

At this time I owned a half interest in a saloon at Granada, my partner in that being Jack Williams. I decided that I would make the trip back myself, so I loaded up my wagon with 100 buffalo hides, ready to start in the morning. So far as Indians entered the proposition, my trip alone seemed safe enough. We had seen no signs of hostile Indians since we left the Wagon Bed Springs on the Cimarron. My trip was to be about 125 miles from our camp on the lake up to Granada. But as I was short-cutting back, not over our route of the hunting camps, this journey put me into country which I had never been over. Mr. Goff had been as far south of Granada as Bear Creek, about 70 miles, and he told me as well as he could how I should lay out my bearings and my route. I was to set out almost due north, perhaps a little east of north.

I camped the second night at the Point of Rocks on the Cimarron. Mr. Goff had told me that I would find no water from the Cimarron to Bear Creek, so advised me to get an early start when I left the Cimarron so that I would make Bear Creek.

I saw no buffalo after leaving the Cimarron, so I figured that a hind quarter of an antelope would come in good. These animals were very plentiful in those days; they could be found almost everywhere. I had reached a big, high, level flat about ten miles beyond the Cimarron when three of these inquisitive animals started up, directly toward my wagon. I got down out of the wagon and flattened out on the ground until they come up within 50 yards of my rifle. I was feeling that my antelope was just about in my grasp, when my little plan was upset. I was just about to pull the trigger when my two dogs spied the antelope and made for them. The antelope turned tail and scampered off with the yelping dogs stretching themselves out and at every jump chasing my antelope steak farther away.

I watched them until they had reached about 300 yards, when I realized what the dogs were doing to me, so I had a sudden impulse to crack one of the dogs, giving the dogs the benefit of the doubt whether I could hit him at his speed and distance. Right here is one of the curious little episodes of the plains. I cut loose. I overshot the dog and broke an antelope's leg. This suddenly threw all the advantage to the dogs and they made short work of bringing down the antelope. Then my sentiments toward the dogs changed, because my antelope steak, once so near, then so far, was back again under my control. I went up to the dogs, patted them on the heads and told them what good dogs they were. It was a feast for the dogs and fresh meat for me.

My wagon journey took me over level prairie country with buffalo grass unmarred anywhere by any track of wagons except my own. I traveled through the afternoon and into the dusk and into the starlight and on and on until the gathering darkness brought fear to me. I don't know what it was I feared, but I kept feeling that something— I didn't know what—might happen to me in the dark. The fear of traveling alone in the dark over unknown country is the worst, for it's uncertainty of what danger might be. Perhaps somewhere in my thought might have been a lurking notion about Indians.

When one is all alone in such circumstances a curious sense comes over him which makes a difference whether you are moving or whether you are camped and standing still on the defensive. Perhaps this is the dread of moving into ambush, of moving yourself into trouble. But whatever this thing is, it got into me, and I stopped for a dry camp. The natural place to make a camp on the prairie is determined by finding water, since I had to have water for myself and my mules. But water or no water, this feeling that something might happen to me if I kept on moving got in its work on me and I stopped for the night. This decision took the brooding fear out of me by my acting. I was busy making camp. I was busy unhitching my mules, and unsnapping and unbuckling their harness, and in tying the mules to the wagon wheels. I tied up three of them, each to a different wheel, when I decided that the fourth mule needed all the grass he could get, and was too thin to spend the night tied tight. I figured that this thin mule was entitled to graze around for what he could pick up, but in order to keep him from wandering away, which would be a serious thing to me, I went to work to put hobbles on his front legs. This is what town people would recognize as a "handcuffing" stunt fastening the mules front legs together closely so that we would not "hobble" away very far.

To hobble the mule I got down on my knees in front of him and was working at the hobble when this position gave me a new vision into the darkness which closed around my little lonesome camp. The contrast between the black earth and the darkness of the sky makes a strip along the sky which is not light but which is lighter than anything else one can see at night. In this skyline I made out, very close to me, some kind of a white object, a white thing plainer and whiter the longer I looked at it. And which looked closer the longer I looked.

It didn't take me long to quit working at the hobbles for the mule. I just tied the fourth mule to the fourth wheel and let the thin mule line up with the rest! My whole thought was fully occupied with the white object. You see, nobody can camp well or rest easily with something white standing sentinel in the dark, not unless you know what the something is that is so white. When I would rise up it would be swallowed up into all the darkness of the night, but when I would stoop down, close to the ground, I could see a line on it again. So I was attracted toward the object, my whole business became one of investigation. I set out to see what the thing was, but then the thing would seem not so close. But I stuck to the trail of the white thing. I stalked it cautiously and took my time to figure it out. It was some rocks—some rocks outcropping at the head of a little draw. The head of the draw was a useful discovery, so I followed this little draw because I knew a draw should lead to a creek, and that was what I had been driving for all day, a camp on Bear Creek, which the coming of darkness had hindered.

I followed this draw down for half a mile until I began getting into tall grass, tall water grass which would be a sign of water close by. But fear came on again in tangible shape, a sense of *taking care,* of tramping too boldly up or down a creek because I might walk right into an Indian camp. Water was the thing I was hunting for and nothing else. So I slipped carefully along through the tall water grass. I expect to be believed when I state I was neither whistling nor singing.

Imagine my surprise when I slinked along so cautiously I came upon a mule on the north side of the creek. This mule, in that semi-star-light did not look good to me. I squatted down in the grass and tried to think what should be my next move. I tried to figure out whether I might be on the edge of an Indian camp or whether some white man might have camped there as myself had set out to do. I figured out that I would not find the answer by sitting there in the grass. But I also had in mind what is probably close to the fact that if I was close to Indians and the Indians saw me ducking around in the grass they would not hesitate to take a shot at me. It worried me to think they might see me first. I also figured that if the mule belonged to some camping white man he might not hesitate to cut loose if he saw me prowling about his mule. White or red, the spectator, would not have seen much in that light, as either one would probably shoot all the quicker on the trigger for it. I decided that the mule had to be investigated so that I might get an answer as to what the mule was doing standing there. So I was ducking along in the tall grass to get closer to the animal when all of a sudden my heart skipped a couple of beats and filled in then with double time as a shrill voice bellowed, "What are you doing there?"

I lack the means of telling how people can see the color of a *voice* in the dark, but I knew never-the-less that the voice was that of a white man. This was the first voice, outside of my own, that I had heard for three days and nights.

I know my voice must have been pretty deep and trembling, but I said, or tried to say into the dark, "I'm hunting for water."

He asked me my name and then told me his, which was Rush, and he asked me how I happened to be there. I explained how I had left my wagon up on the high land and was trying to find a way down to camp where there was water, and he went with me and helped me get my wagon down.

It turned out that Mr. Rush was out on Bear Creek poisoning wolves for their hides, and was using the mule I happened upon to carry his bedding and grub. At this time there were many wolves out on the prairies and this man was making good money just killing them for their hides. I saw him at Granada that following spring and he told me that he had made a thousand dollars that fall and winter killing wolves.

It took me three more days to drive on in to Granada with my buffalo hides, and it was a sight for sore eyes to see the hunters who had stuck around town gather around my wagon wanting to know where I had been hunting.

The profit from our enterprise was due largely to the fact that our outfit had been energetic enough to take the chance with the Indians, and to the fact that we had located a good hunting ground, so it is not likely that my answers gave these fellows at Granada much satisfaction. We wanted the game for ourselves. So after about two days in Granada I started back for the camp by the lake, with my wagon loaded with grub and ammunition. As near as I could make them out, I followed my own wagon tracks on my return trip.

As soon as the hunters in Granada found out that I had left town, they also followed my tracks and it was not more than two days after I joined our party at the lake before the hunters began to flock in. With all these hunters flocking over my tracks, we all combined made quite a trail through that country, which became known's as Brown's Trail, and afterward became a public road.

The boys had not killed many buffalo while I was away because they were fearful of running short of ammunition. The buffalo did not stay in the vicinity very long after the hunters began to flock around. Only for about five more days did our party stay there and we loaded up our hides and took them to Granada and sold them. We sold to Otero & Sellers. We hired a mule train to bring in the hides we could not haul in our own wagons. We paid 50c per hide for this hauling and sold the cow hides for $2.00 each and the bull hides for $3.00 each.

Brown's story ends there. It is a strikingly simple yet beautifully-drawn picture of the pristine land of the southwestern plains, covered with black herds of grazing buffalo, antelope and deer, with the shore of the fresh-water lake covered with an immense number of wild fowl which would rest there for a day or two in the course of their annual migration. This brief glimpse of the frontier of Hoodoo Brown's time shows a land rich with the natural game which provided the Indian with a sound, though primitive, economy. When that resource was destroyed by the rifles of Hoodoo Brown and his fellow hunters, the Indians, like the white hunters who had shot themselves out of a living, disappeared from the scene.

Now the land lay open and inviting the cattlemen.

Chapter II

The Santa Fe Railway reached Dodge City in September, 1872. That same summer, a trail herd from Texas reached the Arkansas River and were thrown along the river bottom west of Dodge that fall. With this herd came D. Welborn (Doc) Barton. Doc arrived in April, ahead of the railroad, bringing the herd up the Chisum Trail because of fear of trouble with the Indians who were bothering the drovers in the Indian Nations that spring. Doc's brother Alex and six other cowboys accompanied the herd of 2,300 head of two- and three-year-old steers.

Doc Barton was born in Bertram, Burnet County, Texas, December 22, 1853, one of a family of ten children. There were seven boys, Doc, Al, Clay, Henry, Dick, Bill, and Walter. There were three sisters who later became Mrs. John Bryson, Bertram, Texas; Mrs. Kate Willett, San Antonio; and Mrs. Wyatt Bailey, Austin. The Bartons came from old South Carolina stock, Doc's parents having reached Texas in 1848. Of tough pioneer stock, Doc Barton once remarked of his mother, "Never did we hear her make a complaint against her isolated ranch life in the new land of Texas."

When the herd, which they brought from Mason County, reached Rocky Ford, Colorado, they met up with the Beaty Brothers herd on the Apishapa River. Together the cattlemen turned their herds down the Arkansas, "drifting" them, that is, moving slowly and grazing as they moved, all the way to Dodge. There, they held them on the bottomland.

The following year, 1873, Doc selected range near the town of Pierceville and in this region he and his brothers operated for several years. When too many of the Cheyenne Indians came south from the Pawnee to the Arkansas in 1877, Doc moved his herds to Crooked Creek. He also ran cattle in Lipscomb county, north Texas.

Doc had married the former Belle Vandeveer in Texas in 1877. Now he brought her north with a trail herd, she driving a light spring wagon by herself. Once, in Colorado, when she was stuck on the muddy bank of a creek, a band of young Cheyenne braves swept down upon the helpless woman from a range of nearby hills. Belle was a girl with good nerves but she afterward confessed that she thought this to be her last day on earth. Her husband, from a distance at the point of the trail herd and much too far away to help her, looked back, heard his wife scream once. He realized what had happened but knew that he dared not show fear or concern lest Cheyenne bravado feed upon it and the Indians be tempted to murder his wife. So he rode boldly on ahead, trying to hold his head high and pay no concern, though he quietly loosened the Winchester in his saddle scabbard.

To the relief and amazement of all the cowboys who watched and waited for a signal from the trail boss, the Indians only whooped and hollered and rode around the team and wagon at breakneck speed. Finally, in a charitable moment, caused by what impulse no one would ever know, the leader dropped off his pony and gave the wagon a big heave, starting it up the muddy creek bank. Now all the Indians jumped off and pushed the wagon so hard that the team was in a trot when they reached the top of the creek bank. Mrs. Barton gave the team full rein, hurrying toward her husband. She never looked back after calling out "Thank you!" to the band. The Indians mounted and rode off, chattering and laughing. The trail boss turned, cut out a thin heifer that had been scouring, and signaled the Indians to come back and take the animal. They rode back, quickly killed and skinned the animal, and commenced eating the warm, fresh beef. Relieved, Doc Barton signaled his men to "bring up the herd."

Barton Brothers consisted of Doc, Alex, Al, Clay, and Henry Barton, but D. Eubank, Tom Connell and Bake Hungate were with them in business for many years. Many cowboys worked for the "Barton outfit" at different times. Bartons made many trips to Texas for both cattle and horses. Al, Clay, and Doc held range south of the Arkansas, receiving mail at both Cimarron and Pierceville. The brand book of 1883 lists only brands of the latter three—Cross H, TO Bar, and OS Bar—but brother Henry managed the ranches for them, listing no brand for his own. Like all ranchers who were constantly buying, selling and trading, they listed a sackful of other brands associated with their operations.

Doc Barton worked closely with the Western Kansas Cattle Growers Association from its start, serving on many committees. Once heading a committee, and asked to make a report on "the troubles arising over range between ourselves," Doc and his three committee members laconically noted, "There have been no difficulties among our cattlemen members. This committee has nothing to report." Privately, Doc and his committeemen had helped resolve the few disagreements among friendly neighbors, and they now sought, within their own ranks, to prevent any further talk about difficulties over range.

The Bartons were sagacious businessmen, luring many more Texas drovers to Dodge with their herds. The Barton herds once numbered 12,000 head. Doc, through a friend, C. C. Isely, who was a good writer, left some wonderfully descriptive tales of cowboy life on the High Plains. One story, "The Protector," told of a great buffalo bull that Doc had once seen that died in the defense of his herd against the terrible "loafer" wolves which frequented the high plains country, particularly after the great blizzards of 1885-86 struck the region and covered the plains with dead livestock for the wolves to devour. Doc had moved his herds on to the XY range, the range of Fred Harvey, later the "Harvey House" king, south of Deerfield. There the great herd of Barton Brothers, 12,000 cattle, died in the drifts as the cowman's paradise on the plains came to its icy end. Fewer than 500 head of the Barton cattle survived, and the other Barton brothers pulled out.

But Doc Barton was a cattleman first, last, and always. He served a term as Gray County sheriff, and when he had recovered financially he again entered the cattle business. He took no active part in the Gray County political war (one of the many "County Seat Wars" of that time). But he did not approve when the Dodge gunmen made the raid on Cimarron. They were representing the Soule interests of Ingalls, and one man, a Cimarron citizen named W. English, was killed in the encounter.

Of the fracas, Doc said: "It was done by Dodge toughs." The men he referred to were Bat Masterson, Neal Brown, Ed Brooks, Bill Tilghman, Jim Marshall, and some others. Some have recently become quite respectable through that mystery-medium for cleaning up old-time badmen, television.

Doc Barton died at the ripe age of 93 years, on January 11, 1946, at Dodge City. He was the first cowman to arrive, the last to leave.

The cattle trails that Barton and others cut out with the hooves of their longhorn herds on the way to Dodge frequently paralleled or fell directly upon the earlier trails left by the buffalo in their migrations and the ruts cut by the buffalo hunters' wagons. These trails usually passed between one watering spot and another. Still later the bone-haulers' wagons cut their own particular trail from the old shooting beds to the Dodge Trail, as the earliest settlers, in those hard years between the buffalo hunting prosperity and the full bloom of the range cattle industry, fought to exist on the arid plains. Most trails now led to Dodge. The virile young town on the north bank of the Arkansas, just four miles upstream from the Fort, drew trade from every direction, but chiefly from the southwest, that region still being without benefit of a railroad.

Leading in to Dodge from the south was the main trail, the Jones and Plummer Trail. It was a wide, straight thorofare, its ruts dug deeply into the prairie sod and sand by the wheels of ten thousand wagons. The remains of the old trail, today, show it to have been as wide then as a federal highway is today wtih a cut-into-the-sod depth of three and four feet! One place, near Beaver, Oklahoma, shows where the trail once made a sand cut nearly thirty feet in depth through a sandhill north of the Beaver River. This old trail, some say, was named after the buffalo hunters Ed Jones and Joe Plummer who operated a trading post at the head of Wolf Creek and sent their hides to Dodge. Others say that this trail was named after a "Jones & Plummer Cattle Company." There are still others who believe the trail may have been named after John Jones, a young Englishman who had been nicknamed "Cheyenne Jack" by the buffalo hunters and who was killed near this old trail by Indians, together with another hunter known only as "Blue Belly." These killings took place in the early spring of 1874, according to Billy Dixon, buffalo hunter, who was nearby in the region at the time. Joe Plummer, mentioned above, brought news of these men's deaths to Adobe Walls, just before the fight started there between the Indians and buffalo hunters. Plummer also told of losing his two partners, Dudley and Wallace, who were killed, scalped and the bodies mutilated by the band that attacked the hunters at Adobe Walls.

The Indians who attacked Adobe Walls that spring were marauding Cheyennes, Comanches, and Kiowas, among whom were Wild Horse, So-Ta-Do, Best-Son-In-Law, Wolf-Tongue, Slue-Foot, and Cheyenne of the Comanches and Chief Stone-Cay-Son, Serpent-Scales, Spotted-Feather, Horse-Chief, Coyote, Stone-Teeth, and Soft-Foot of the Cheyennes. All of these Indians were killed in the fight and their graves are now marked on that old battle site with a large marker erected by their tribesmen. The Indian's inscription on the marker states:

THEY DIED FOR THAT WHICH MAKES LIFE
WORTH LIVING — INDIAN'S LIBERTY — FREEDOM —
PEACE — ON THE PLAINS WHICH THEY ENJOYED
FOR GENERATIONS.

This band of Indians had been led—badly, the writer feels— by Chief Quanah Parker. The buffalo hunters beat off several attacks from the party of braves said to have numbered up in the hundreds. It is a fact that the Indians had greater legal justification for attacking the white hunters than did the white men for hunting and exterminating the Indians' food supply in the forbidden land, south of the Arkansas River, where the Medicine Lodge Treaty had set aside a hunting ground for the red man "as long as water runs and grass grows."

But nothing could stop the buffalo slaughter once the army's Phil Sheridan and W. T. Sherman had given the nod to killing off the buffalo as a means of breaking the Indian will to fight. Now the buffalo hunters' trail extended from Dodge past Beaver City, in the Neutral Strip, to Mobeetie and Fort Elliott and Rath City, the hide hunters' own town. Huge freight outfits of wagons and ox teams, later mules and horse-drawn wagons, now took bacon, sugar, beans, dried fruit, coffee, black powder, and bullets south and returned loaded with flint-dry buffalo hides up the Jones & Plummer Trail.

Another trail, the Chapman-Tuttle Trail, left the Jones and Plummer Trail at Beaver City, picked up the trade to the east on Wolf Creek and at the stage station on the Canadian River east of the present day town of Canadian. This trail bore the name of the famous Indian scout and hunter, Amos Chapman. However, the trail is said to have been named after the partners, Tuttle and Chapman, who ran the CT Ranch. They had bought the trading post from Jim Springer on Boggy Creek and made it their headquarters. After Tuttle bought out Chapman, about 1880, he sold the ranch to Aldridge and Rhodes. But the place was generally referred to as the Old Springer Ranch.

Jim Springer, the former owner, was killed in November, 1878, by a soldier, Sergeant Welsh, following a dispute in a card game at the ranch, 160 miles south of Dodge. An employee, Ledbetter, was also killed in the brawl between the two ranchers and three soldiers. A Private Brown, who was not involved in the fight, was wounded in the leg. Springer and Ledbetter were buried there on the ranch site, not far from the ranch house.

When the buffalo were gone and the cattlemen took over the country, a third trail, an auxiliary to the Jones and Plummer Trail, was laid out. This trail was also called the "Plummer Trail," after the Charley Plummer who laid it out, according to Boss Neff, an early cattleman who ranched in the Strip. This newer Plummer Trail made a junction with the main trail south of Beaver City, on the high ground, then struck off southwest to Fort Bascom, passing by the Zulu Stockade and Tascosa. The trail was used by cattlemen bringing herds to Dodge and also by freighters plying their trade from Dodge to the ranches of the southwest cattle range.

The main artery of the Jones and Plummer Trail leaving Dodge crossed Mulberry Creek, a few miles south of the Arkansas River, headed down to Hoodoo Brown's road ranch on Crooked Creek. There, the Fort Bascom Trail branched off while the Jones and

Plummer Trail continued down the east bank of Crooked Creek, cut across "The Flats," going south to O'dee Post Office where it crossed the stream southwest of Skunk Arroyo, and headed up over the hills toward Beaver City.

The O'dee post office was named after O. D. Lemert, a brother of Laben Lemert and uncle of Bernard Lemert, both of whom worked for the Crooked L ranch in the area. O. D. Lemert had submitted several names to the postal department before he conceived this one, formed from his initials, and which was finally accepted. The Jones and Plummer Trail crossed the Cimarron at a sandy crossing several miles on farther south where Charles Hines ran a road ranch and the Fringer Post Office. From there the trail headed directly in to Beaver City, in the Neutral Strip.

About ten miles south of Mulberry Creek, the Adobe Walls Trail, which had come out of Dodge on the same trunk as the Jones and Plummer Trail and the Fort Bascom Trail, branched off and turned southwest, crossed Crooked Creek high up on the stream, and then angled down to the Cimarron River to the southwest, crossing near the Price & Davies Ranch, on what is now called "the McClure property." Here, the old trail is plainly visible today.

Robert Davies and Thomas Price were the principals in the ranching venture mentioned above. This ranch continues in operation today under the direction of the Davies families. Robert Davies was born in Dembigshire, North Wales, May 7, 1848. After coming to the United States he was employed for ten years by Thomas Price at Emporia. In May of 1882, he accompanied Price and a man named S. R. Taylor to Seward County, Kansas. They found good range on the Cimarron and with Price's financial backing, Davies founded the ranch. The venture prospered until the blizzards of 1885-86 when the ranchers lost two-thirds of their livestock. Taylor returned to Lyons County and Davies then severed connections with both Price and Taylor and started up alone in the cattle business. By diligence and good management he prospered and found financial security for himself and family. Upon his death his sons took over and all, Price J., Rice, and Robert, became known as good cattlemen in their own right.

From the Cimarron crossing at the Price & Davies ranch, the Adobe Walls Trail continued southwest, crossing Sharp's Creek at the point where Bob Cator spied the Indian watching him through the bushes. On the south side of the creek, on a rocky ledge that overlooks the stream, Bartholomew Crawford, a pioneer, built a sod house for a road ranch and nearby erected a large stone corral where the freighter teams could be corraled and held for the night. A postoffice, called Tarbox, after the early cattlemen Rufe and Waldo Tarbox, was kept here in the early 1880's. It was maintained by a Frenchman named Machaud, and pronounced Mi-kawd. This was on the Dodge-Tascosa star route, and because the U.S. Government did not approve U.S. post offices in the Neutral Strip, the location was said to be listed as Tarbox, *Texas*. Another postoffice was established about this time at Zulu, Texas, where a stockade had been erected as protection against Indians.

About 1882 the XI 11 (called Eks I Eleven) ranch bought Crawford's holdings at Sharp's Creek. The XI 11 was a wealthy outfit, established by J. W. Summers of Keokuk, Iowa, and was first operated by McCoy Brothers and Summers. William Roberts, who married John Chisum's niece, Sally Chisum, was later taken in as a partner. The XI 11 built a large set of branding corrals on the north bank of the Beaver River, opposite the mouth of Willow Creek. It is today land held by the Blakemore T Bar T ranch. By 1902 H. G. Adams had acquired Summers' widow's interest, and Roberts and Adams conducted the XI operations for many years. It is today still the largest ranch operation in Meade County, Kansas, Helen Adams Smith recently selling her interest in the ranch, 18,309 acres with mineral rights, for $1,500,000.00 without greatly affecting the ranch operations. The purchaser was Raymond Adams of Topeka.

At the Sharp's Creek crossing of the Adobe Walls Trail the ruts show plainly today where the trail dipped down from the rocky ledge on the south bank and crossed the stream. The large spring at that point has dried up at the lower level, but fresh, pure water still seeps down from the rocky ledge above. At this point along the stream, Sharp's Creek is a photographer's paradise. From

41

here, the Adobe Walls Trail continues on southwest to the Adobe Walls in Texas, north of the Canadian River.

The original Adobe Walls, from which the place received its name by the buffalo hunters, was constructed by Mexicans, traders or Comancheros, probably in the late fifteenth or early sixteenth century. Billy Dixon told of a remark made by Brig. Gen. John P. Hatch, with whom Billy was a scout in the 1870's. Hatch, then a young officer, passed Adobe Walls on his way to or from Mexico in 1847-48 with a regiment of dragoons. The 'dobe walls, said Hatch, even at that time were only eroded butts with the old outlines showing where others had been nearby. Today, the Adobe Walls Trail is still visible near this point on the trail.

The Fort Bascom Trail came out of Dodge together with the other trails but left the Jones & Plummer Trail below present Meade, near Spring Creek. The trail swung down through Stump Arroyo, now the headwaters of Meade Lake at the State Park (Lake Larrabee). From there it headed southwest to the Sharp's Creek crossing, angled west along the Beaver River, where it crossed over at the town of Grand Valley, now a ghost site. From there the trail continued up Palo Duro Creek, passed by the Zulu Stockade, and went on west to Tascosa and Fort Bascom.

These, then, were the major trails leading into Dodge from the Cimarron and Beaver country. Later there were as many trails on the southwest cattle range as there were ranches, railroads, pioneer towns, and directions to get from one to the other. With no fences, the trails started out in all directions from every ranch and town—a pair of wagon ruts, sometimes six to eight ruts cut into the tough prairie sod to a depth of twelve inches before another trail was made with one of its ruts running directly between the two old ruts. In this fashion old trails got older, and the older they became the wider they grew, until some trails, like the aged Santa Fe Trail, in places became a quarter of a mile wide and were worn out, in some instances, to a depth of four or five feet!

Many cattle trails, where the thirsty animals walked unattended to their favorite watering places on streams and rivers or fresh water lakes, were a labyrinth of single trails, joining, crossing, coming together again, parting and weaving in and out until even the animals themselves must have wondered if they were on the right trail. Near a stream bank, where the banks were high above the water, the trails came together, and the cattle hooves and horns cut deep paths down into the clay banks to a depth of six feet or more, the passageway often being so narrow that a longhorn steer or cow had difficulty in making its way down to the water. On the north bank of Red River, Mr. John Estes, who has resided there since the days of the last trail herds, showed the writer where the old Chisholm Trail emerged from the river bottom onto the high ground along the north side of Red River. There, the cattle's hooves had carved out a wide and deep passageway from the hard sandstone, a cut that was at least fifteen feet in depth and twice that wide. Many millions of hooves took many years to carve out that niche!

A fourth trail out of Dodge, and the earliest man-made trail, after the Indians, was the Camp Supply Military Road. It was used first by the military, transporting supplies from the railroad to Camp Supply, and before that bringing down supplies from Fort Dodge to "Camp of Supply" on the Canadian.

There was a fifth trail, The Texas Cattle Trail from south Texas, called The Western Trail to distinguish it from the earlier Chisholm Trail, which came up through the Indian country to the east. This Western Trail made Dodge the Cowboy Capital. It came up from San Antonio by way of Bandera, Texas, to Doan's Store on Red River, in Wilbarger County, Texas. Heading north it came up through the leased lands of the Cheyennes and Arapahoes to Camp Supply, then missing the west edge of the Military Reservation it headed straight for Dodge. Up this trail came the longhorn herds that revived Dodge after the great buffalo hunts were over.

One old cowboy who rode on the roundup of 1884 described the Western Trail as a "chocolate brown and brick red ribbon that wound up over the hills and down to the rivers and creek bottoms and was fifty to a hundred feet in width, cut into the prairie sod a foot or more in depth by the hooves of the longhorn cattle." After leaving Dodge the Western Trail angled northwest through the Kansas flat land to the Republican River, then on to

43

Ogalalla, Nebraska. This was the cattle center in Nebraska in the late 1870's and early 1880's, the point from which the Indian Reservations were supplied with "woha," the Indian's beef.

By 1885 the cattle trails in Kansas had been pushed to the western border and finally clear out of the state of Kansas. The organization of new tiers of counties in western Kansas and the outcry against the "Texas tick" did the work. This brought plans on the part of Texas drovers for still another trail, this one to be six-miles wide, a strip of land extending from Texas to the Yellowstone, up which Texas cattle might freely walk to new northern markets. It would be called the National Cattle Trail and legislation was sought in Washington to insure its creation in a bill before Congress.

But time and tide wait on no man. This trail died a'bornin', though several thousands of head of cattle did make the trips north in 1885-86. But settlers were taking up claims, the region was being criss-crossed with barbed wire, and the tide of settlement was running high. Railroads were crossing the old cattle trails everywhere from south Texas to Montana. It was the end of an era.

The old trails were the arteries of commerce of that time, whether it was the XI Cut-off, a short trail running from Sharp's Creek to the Jones & Plummer Trail crossing on the Cimarron, or the main cattle trail from Texas to the Yellowstone. Now the old landmarks are plowed up, sand-filled, weed-grown, or washed out. At an occasional stream crossing or on tough, unplowed sod land the old trails may still be glimpsed. But like the animals and men who made them, their time has passed. In an age when people traveled with animal power—ox teams, mules or horses—all trails led to or paralleled the streams. For animals must be watered daily if required to do the strenuous work of pulling the heavily laden wagons. New trails were made where new cattle outfits moved on to a new range, and fast, horse-drawn stage coaches cut still newer, more direct routes as transportation progressed. The stage routes often paralleled old wagon train trails but sometimes left them entirely. The horse-drawn coaches were just as dependent on watering places, as they frequently made the same stream crossings at the old, well-known fords.

The stage routes from Dodge to Beaver, Beaver to Elliot, Elliott to Tascosa, or Garden City to Harwoodville were all pretty much the same. The flying wheels traversed the hard-packed buffalo sod and dipped up the sand in the river bottoms; they crossed the high, grassy plains and slipped down into the meadows and bottom lands where the blue stem sometimes stood wither-high on the stage horses. There were curves and high hills, and before the stage had gotten underway someone took sick, "stage sick," just as they take car-sick or air-sick today. The common treatment for this sickness was to stop and give a passenger back his land legs. If time was too valued to make such a stop, a vial of camphor was carried by the driver. A whiff from the bottle often helped the passenger to hang on to his breakfast or dinner a few more miles. But the nausea hung on every step of the way for those who have the weakness and such a trip was anything but pleasurable.

At the stage stations the Stage Jack (they were all called Jack, just as Pullman porters became George at a later time) helped passengers who suffered from heat or cold or the various illnesses that came from stage travel. Twin privies helped some; others found a good meal of buffalo ribs added to their comfort. After a few minutes of rest and a change of horses, they would try it again!

A set of rules, almost uniformly accepted on all stage lines, aided somewhat in setting the scene for travel. This set of rules was first published on the old Butterfield Stage Route. It governed, somewhat, the deportment of passengers while en route to their destinations. Among other items were the following rules, reprinted from a set published in the *Omaha World Herald*, Omaha, Nebraska, in 1877:

1. The best seat is the forward one, next the driver. If you have tendencies toward stage sickness when riding backwards, you'll get over it quicker in this seat and receive less jolts and jostlings.
2. If the stage teams run away or are pursued by Indians, stay in

the coach and take your chances. Don't jump out, for you will be either injured or scalped.

3. In cold weather abstain from liquor, for you are subject to freezing quicker if under its influence than as though you were cold sober.

4. But if you are drinking from a bottle, pass it around. It is the only polite thing to do. Be sure to procure all stimulants before leaving (Dodge City or Fort Elliott) for the ranch (stage station) whiskey is not nectar.

5. Don't smoke a strong cigar or pipe on the stage, especially when women or children are present. If chewing tobacco, spit to the leeward side.

6. Don't swear, snore or lop over on neighbors when sleeping. Let others share the buffalo robes provided in cold weather.

7. Don't shoot firearms for pleasure while en route as it scares the horses.

8. Don't discuss politics or religion. Don't point out sites where robberies or Indian attacks have taken place.

9. While at stations don't lag at wash basins or privies. Don't grease hair with bear grease or buffalo tallow as travel is very dusty.

10. Don't imagine you are going on a picnic, for stage travel is inconvenient. Expect annoyances, discomforts, hardships. Bear them with fortitude. Be friendly and helpful to other passengers and your trip will be a more pleasant one.

"No Man's Land," the Neutral Strip or Public Lands, as it was called variously, was a political and geographic paradox. It was an ungoverned rectangle of land bordered by Kansas on the north, Texas panhandle on the south, New Mexico on the west, and the Cherokee Strip on the east. The region was not an accepted part of any state bordering it, yet it had been formed by the time of the earliest survey of the Beaver River region, Wolf Creek, and the Edith Salt Plain in 1857. Its history is an interesting one.

Upon the conclusion of the Mexican War in 1848 the northern and western boundaries of Texas had not been settled yet with Mexico. Texas still claimed that her border extended west to the Rio Grande River. And she manifested a will to enforce her claims by arms. In the meanwhile, the newly acquired territory from Mexico gave rise to a renewed and angry agitation on the slavery question which was then before Congress. To insure a complete settlement of all questions growing out of the imperialist acquisition of territory that the United States had made from Mexico, Congress passed a bill proposing that Texas accept as her northern boundary a line on the 36th degree and 32nd degree of latitude west to the 103rd degree of longitude, and from there to the 32nd degree and west to the Rio Grande River. In consideration of this, the United States paid Texas the sum of ten million dollars.

Upon passage of the bill organizing the Territories of Kansas and Nebraska in 1853, the southern border of Kansas was fixed at the 37th parallel of latitude, being simply an extention of the southern boundary line of Missouri, westward to the mountains, thus allocating for the Neutral Strip the land that had formerly been Texas land at the extreme north edge of the Texas panhandle. The area was designated as simply Public Lands. Since it was claimed by no state, it became the "Neutral Strip," or "No Man's Land." The area involved in this rectangle is one-half degree (about 35 miles) in width and three degrees (about 210 miles) in length. It was to be a bone of contention for the next half century or longer by lawless men who desired to own and control it.

L. A. Allen, frontiersman and cattleman and lawman of the early times, comrade of Kit Carson, and the first sheriff of southeastern Colorado, made a name for himself in protecting old No Man's Land from outlaws. In one night's operation he, together with a possee of rangers, captured and hung eleven members of the infamous Coe gang who preyed on the Santa Fe caravans from 1855 to 1870. Allen also made something of a name for himself in his disagreement with the U.S. Government over the matter of ownership and land title to the Neutral Strip. An article by Allen in the *Kansas City Star*, April, 1913, set forth his views:

It was stipulated in the treaty with Mexico that this zone should be "neutral" forever. Mexico has never relinquished her rights under this treaty, so as a matter of fact Oklahoma has no right to this strip of ground because the United States of America had no legal right to cede it to the State of Oklahoma. It is today as much Mexican territory as it is United States territory and neither the United States nor the State of Oklahoma has any right to give title to the farms there.

Now you asked why Mexicans required a "road" 35 miles wide and I will explain that. In those days there were no roads. People traveled over the plains at will, following the watercourses or going from one water hole to another in a zig-zag way. And as they traveled they needed to graze their stock, to hunt or catch a wild horse or two. That "strip" was full of buffalo, antelope, deer, and wild horses. So the Mexicans insisted on a wide roadway that they could travel at leisure and live by the way. For many years the Mexicans used that strip to trade with the Indians in Indian Territory, used it without fear of molestation, for the United States Government had guaranteed them security from attack by the settlers on the north and the Texans on the south.

Those Mexican traders used carts made wholly of wood, wheels and all were wood. They were hauled, or rather pushed, by oxen, mules or burros. No yokes were used. Rawhide strips around the horns were connected with the front end of the cart tongue and the animals literally *pushed* the cart with their heads! The traders took with them from Mexico mainly silver and took back buffalo hides and dried buffalo meat. In those caravans of traders there were as many as 500 of those carts. The Mexicans were still using that "strip" as a trading route when I went out there fifty years ago (1863). And then it was gradually abandoned as a trading route as there was no government with jurisdiction over it and courts could not be established and it became a rendezvous for the worst outlaws of the southwest, who would run out of there and commit depredations and then drop back to the shelter of this "neutral strip."

One of the worst bands of outlaws that found refuge there was the Coe outlaw gang. Its headquarters were on the Cimarron River in the northwest corner of the Strip and the gang had a fort here, 100 miles from the settlement. I was at that time Captain of a company of Rangers in southeast Colorado. I was the first sheriff of southeastern Colorado when it was a Territory and May 8, 1868, we pulled off the first election ever held in Colorado.

We were in the cattle business and one time we got word that Coe and his band were coming to run off our cattle. I called my company together and we rode out, and by traveling at night we came to an

48

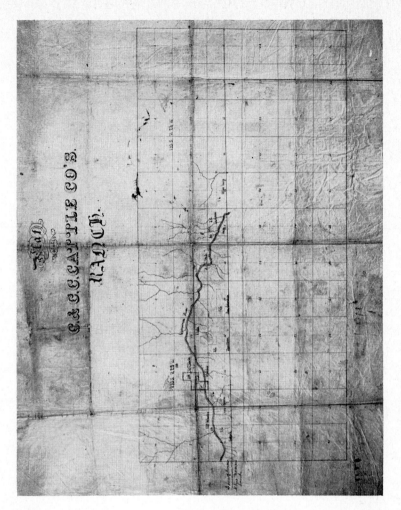

PLAT OF THE C & C C CATTLE COMPANY'S RANCH

The Cimarron and Crooked Creek Cattle Company was one of the earliest ranching ventures in this area, the original company forming about 1878 or 1879 when G. W. E. Griffith and others took range along the Cimarron river, upstream from where it dips down into old No Man's Land. They became known as the Chain C ranch. This photo is from an old Map on Linen, and shows the range occupied by this group among whom some of the names on the map appear to be R. E. Steele (later manager of the ranch), Crouch, McWhorter, Poehler, Fluke, Donaldson, John Johnston, Jamison, Hays, Oliver Hays. These latter names may have been claim holders in the area. *Photo courtesy E. W. McNaghten, Crooked L Ranch, Meade, Kansas.*

49

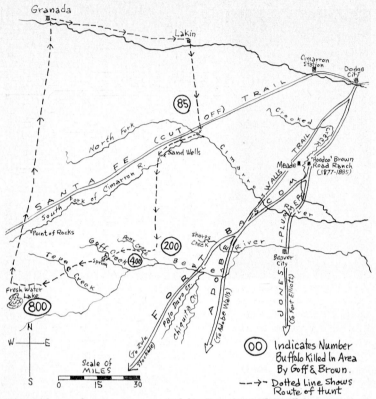

Map Above shows area covered by Brown and Goff hunt.

A recent picture of the old Jones and Plummer Trail that stretched from Dodge City to Mobeetie and Fort Elliott. This view was taken just north of Beaver, Oklahoma. *Photo by Author.*

50

William H. Jackson, famous pioneer photographer and artist, painted the above scene of the Chisholm Trail in 1941 from his early memory of that noted trail. The scene could be laid almost any place in the Indian Nations or in western Kansas where the new Western Cattle Trail (1876) came up through the Cheyenne and Arapahoe Nations and passed by Camp Supply, heading for Dodge, cattle center from 1876 to 1884.—*Published by permission of Clarence S. Jackson, son, Denver, Colo.*

Guymon, established in the Neutral Strip along the line of the Rock Island, soon became one of the centers of supply for the ranch country, such ranches as the Three C, Westmoreland-Hitch Cattle Co., the Anchor D. *Photo courtesy the late Burris Wright, Liberal, Kansas.*

From 1888 up to approximately 1900, Liberal had been end-of-tracks for the Rock Island, the tracks ending west of Liberal, just across the Oklahoma Panhandle (Neutral Strip) line. At the time this photo was taken, 1906, Liberal was making the transition from being a cattle town to that of becoming a broomcorn and wheat marketing center. The large Rock Island Railway Hotel and eating house is the big building at the top center of the picture. To the horizon extends the buffalo grass prairie, now all broken up and producing wheat, milo maize, oil and gas. *Photo courtesy the late Burris Wright, Liberal, Kansas.*

This 1893 view looks northwest from the south end of Beaver City's Main Street. Garrigue's Store, right front, was the site where Billy Olive was shot down by the saloonkeeper and the postmaster. Jim Lane's road ranch was at the end of the row of buildings at the right of the picture, where the Jones-Plummer Trail crossed the Beaver River. Up the main street, the wagons carrying the bodies of the gambler Thompson and the storekeeper, Bennett, pulled by oxen and accompanied by the members of the Vigilantes who "executed" the pair, headed south to the hilltop cemetery. *Oklahoma State Historical Society.*

When Liberal, Kansas, became the end of the line for the Chicago, Kansas and Nebraska Railroad (the present Rock Island) great stores of freight were received at that point, loaded on to big freight wagons and sent out in all directions to supply the big ranches of the region. Liberal gradually supplanted Dodge City as a supply point to the ranches of the Southwest Cattle Range. The above train heads south to Ochiltree, Texas. *Photo Courtesy of late Bernard Lemert.*

A Lee & Reynolds 8-mule jerkline freight wagon. Manny Leopold was wagon boss for this outfit which freighted into north Texas and the Panhandle of Oklahoma (No Man's Land), down the Jones & Plummer Trail. Eight mules were hooked to three wagons (one wagon and two "trails") and driven with a jerk line in the hands of the wagon driver who rode the near (left) wheel mule. The jerk line extended to the near lead mule. The off lead mule was controlled by a jockey stick, connected to the halter of the near lead mule. Freight was taken from Dodge to Mobeetie, Wichita Falls, Fort Elliott and Tascosa. *Photo courtesy the late Burris Wright.*

The Crooked L ranch had headquarters on Crooked Creek, southwest of Meade, Kansas. Shown above is Bernard Lemert, Crooked L foreman of the Sharp's Creek area, sitting with the pole at the right of the picture, in light-colored vest. He boarded at the Fulkerson ranch home. Mrs. Fulkerson is shown above him and Mr. Fulkerson, man with the mustache on the rock at the left. Beside Mr. Fulkerson is "Aunt Bettie" Smith, later Bernard Lemert's bride. *Photo by Steele, Beaver City, Okla.*

Adobe Walls Trail Crossing of Sharp's Creek. At this point on the trail a small Road Ranch and Ox Corral was run by Bartholomew Crawford in the late '70's. A postoffice, Tarbox, was established here later, on the Dodge-Tascosa Star Route. Here, Bob Cator found a dead man lying on the ground, then looked up among the bushes and rocks to spy an Indian watching him. *Photo by Author.*

Shade's Well, Neutral Strip, circa 1889 to 1902. This big water well (later using steam pumps) was erected by the railroad to water Texas cattle shipped from Old Tyrone. Cattle from the XIT, Turkey Track, Backward LX and the LS and other ranches watered here. When the Rock Island Railway built on to Tucumcari, New Mexico, the well was closed down. Mr. and Mrs. Zack Cain, who ran the place, are in the buggy at right. The second girl from the left is Carrie Cain, later Mrs. George Ellison of Guymon, Oklahoma. Small boy on horse at left is Homer Cain; the two men on horseback are trail men. Girl at left was Mattie Horn. The postoffice kept here was called "Shade." The location is two miles south of present Tyrone, Oklahoma. *Photo courtesy of Mrs. George Ellison.*

This stage line operated between Dodge City, Kansas and Camp Supply in the Indian Territory (Cherokee Strip), about 1882. It was well-suited for trips down the old Military Trail, light, sturdy and was pulled by two teams. The stage line also carried the U.S. Mail between these two points, passing by way of Deep Hole postoffice on the Cimarron river, near the Kansas line. *From Original Robert E. Eagan Collection, Dodge City.*

This was the sod home of Jim Lane who ran the Road Ranch on the Beaver River crossing at the point on the Jones & Plummer Trail called "Beaver City." Lane kept both wet and dry goods and freighters' supplies. When the Vigilantes took over Beaver City, Lane played a lone hand, continued his business and kept out of the mischief. The building stands today and is used by Mrs. Pearl Sharp and her daughter Louise as the Beaver, Oklahoma, Museum. *Photo courtesy Beaver City, Okla., Museum.*

DODGE CITY IN 1879
The tracks of the Santa Fe can be seen in the foreground. The old Santa Fe Trail comes in from the right hand (on Trail Street). Boot Hill School is the large building on the hill at the left of the picture. Front Street, famous in story, is the cluster of frame buildings in the right center of the photo.—*Photo from the Original Robert E. Eagan Collection, Dodge City.*

56

abandoned 'dobe where the gang was resting for the night. We tied our horses a distance away, and with a revolver in one hand and a rifle in the other we crept up to the cabin, burst in the door and took the whole eleven outlaws and hanged them to the cottonwood trees along the river bank. But Coe was not in the 'dobe hut. He was at another place, some 15 miles away, and we rode there and captured him and as there was a big reward for him we strapped him to a horse and rode with him 100 miles to Pueblo and surrendered him to the sheriff who put him in jail. But that night a mob took him out and lynched him.

An old freighter, Charles Raber, told of accompanying a cavalry group under the command of a Lt. Campbell on a raid to Coe's camp, "Bummer's Retreat," near the upper springs of the Cimarron in July-August, 1867, at which time a Cyrus Coe, "who had served with an Ohio Regiment" during the Civil War, was taken prisoner to Fort Union. According to Raber, this was the Coe who was the leader of the outlaw band whom L. A. Allen mentioned in his story. Coe apparently escaped or was turned loose by the Army, for Allen's raid ended his activities along the Cimarron for all time.

L. A. Allen lived with Kit Carson in New Mexico when he was a boy. Allen's brother married Carson's only daughter, and the pair lived at Trinidad, Colorado, for many years. Kit's wife died at Allen's ranch at Boggsville, which the historian C. W. Hurd has characterized as "the cradle of the Colorado cattle industry." Mrs. Carson was buried in Allen's garden. Only a month later, Kit Carson died and was laid beside his wife. In October of that year 1868, Allen and a friend W. K. Irwin moved the bodies to Taos, New Mexico, where they rest today. Allen described the death of Carson's wife as a scene of great pathos:

Kit's wife's death at my ranch was the most pathetic scene I ever witnessed. They had seven children, the youngest being a baby of two weeks. Mrs. Carson was very sick and two Mexican women were nursing her. Carson was suffering with heart trouble and he and I were lying on a bed in another room, and he was telling me some adventure of his. We did not expect Mrs. Carson to die when suddenly—it was April 27, 1868—the Mexican woman ran in crying out, "She is dead!"

57

The six children ran in and all of them piled on the bed on top of Kit and he wept with them. I buried his wife in my garden. Three weeks later he died, and I buried him, too.

Allen himself passed on after a long and interesting career. In his later years he was a commission merchant at Kansas City. He had, at various times, several businesses, known as White Allen & Company, then Irwin, Allen and Company, and still later the Kansas City Livestock Commission Company. He was in the livestock commission business forty-four years. Allen had been but a mere boy when he crossed the plains with his first herd of cattle from Kansas City. He drove herds through the deserts and mountains to California and the Pacific coast states. He came to southeastern Colorado and followed the old buffalo and Indian trails down into No Man's Land, at this time meeting Kit Carson. Allen helped lay the base for the peaceful development of the range cattle industry of the area, following the many old trails and making a few new ones for the late-comers to follow. He died in 1917.

Among contemporaries and friends of L. A. Allen who helped bring civilization to the foothills of the Rockies were such men as Thomas O. Boggs. Boggs was born in Indian Territory, August 22, 1824. He came to the Arkansas valley in 1840. Boggs had served as a courier between Fort Leavenworth and California posts during the Mexican War. He was associated with William Bent at Bent's Fort on the Arkansas River for seven years. He built the town called Boggsville, on the Purgatoire River, in 1866, coming over from Cimarron, New Mexico, and bringing along with him a youngster named L. A. Allen, noted above, as partner. Their partnership and friendship endured many years.

Boggs dealt in cattle and horses but was principally a sheepman, having in 1875 some 17,000 head on his range. Boggs was a man of fine character and with a fine wife, and when Kit Carson's seven children were orphaned the good couple took the children into their home and raised them. Boggs was the first sheriff of Bent County and served a term in the State Legislature in 1871. In

1877 the family moved to New Mexico and Boggs served as Territorial Governor. They lived at Springer, but Boggs died at Clayton, September 29, 1894. Mrs. Boggs survived her husband until January 13, 1906.

A second pioneer of the area, John W. Prowers, was born at Westport, Missouri, January 29, 1838. Prowers came west in 1856 and was employed at Bent's Fort as a clerk. He married Amache, a Cheyenne girl, and thereby cemented a life-time friendship with the Northern Cheyennes. When Col. Chivington started his march to Sand Creek, where his Colorado guard troops massacred the camp of the Cheyenne men, women, and children under Chief Black Kettle, Chivington had Prowers held under arrest lest he send warning to the Indians of their doom. His wife's father, Chief O-Kinee, was at the Sand Creek camp of the Cheyennes. Chief O-Kinee led his family to safety when the attack came, then returned and was slain while standing under the United States flag which was flying over the tepee of Chief Black Kettle.

John Prowers became the leading businessman at Boggsville with a large general store which served a wide area. When the Kansas-Pacific Railway built out to Las Animas, Prowers was one of the first to help build the new town. He experimented to find the cattle best suited to the plains country, bringing cattle from Ireland (the Kurry breed) and others from Canada. At last he turned to the Hereford as the best North American beef animal, calling it the "American type."

Prowers died in Kansas City February 14, 1884, at the age of 46. He left ten children and an estate estimated to be upwards of a million dollars. He is regarded as the man who established the Colorado range cattle industry, though men such as John Iliff and others were holders of greater herds.

Others from this region who helped build the range cattle industry and pioneer the frontier towns were R. L. Lambert, Rufe and Waldo Tarbox, Robert Bent, John S. Hough, Charles Rite, and P. G. Scott, to mention but a few. These men with their families fought Indians and blizzards, made the long trail drives to Dodge and to Trinidad. They fought drought, lack of sleep, blizzards, shortages of food and water, and poor shelter. Yet they married, had families, built ranches and towns, and brought the first wave of civilization to southeastern Colorado and northwestern No Man's Land.

In the latter part of the 1860's, two Texas men, Jim and Peyton Jones, brought a herd of longhorns from Texas and threw them along the Nine Mile Bottom on the Purgatoire—or "Picketwire," as they called it. The new range was excellent and the Jones Brothers commenced branding their cattle with a JJ Up and a JJ Down, that is, inverted. This helped the brothers identify each brother's cattle. The Jones brothers soon brought in shorthorn grade bulls to cross with the longhorn cows, then bought some good pure bred Durhams. From this breeding, by 1881, they had 30,000 head of good stock on about 16,000 acres of good range land. Their cattle spread south to the headwaters of the Cimarron and east to the Kansas line. One fall shipment alone, to Granada, on August 23, 1878, filled 98 cattle cars—a total of 3,000 head of top-condition, grassed-out, fat beef steers!

The Bent County Cattle and Horse Growers Association, of which the Jones Brothers were members, once ruled that all mavericks (unbranded cattle) found on the roundup would be branded B-4-J and held for a special disposition by the officers of the Association. One day Peyton Jones came to P. G. Scott at the bank and told Scott that they had branded 500 head of mavericks along with their own cattle and now wanted to make restitution by paying the Association for the cattle they had branded. Scott, the treasurer of the Association, answered Jones, "Why Peyton, you know the rules. We couldn't *sell* these cattle to you and issue a *bona fide* bill of sale to Jones Brothers for them. Now, could we?"

Peyton Jones pushed his big felt hat back on his head, tugged at a lock of hair, then grinned at the treasurer of the Association.

"Yep, Scotty, that's sure right," he said. "But we'd be dam fools to buy cattle *without* gettin' a leegitimate bill of sale for them." And Peyton Jones dropped the matter right there. Everyone agreed afterward that Jones had found the cheapest way for enlargement of the JJ herds without going to the expense of *buying* more cattle!

In 1882 Jones Brothers sold to a British group, the price being given at the time as $625,000.00. Jones Brothers later agreed they had sold too cheap; in fact, they attempted to stop the sale. But the money was paid according to the terms they had agreed upon, so the JJ was no more. The buyer was Prairie Cattle Company, soon to be the largest company on that part of the plains.

Jones Brothers kept back some land and a few horses on the Picketwire. Peyton lived at La Junta for many years. Jim Jones, after residing at Las Animas a few years, returned to his beloved Texas.

The above are but a sampling of the men who created the range cattle industry along the headwaters of the Cimarron. There were many others, equally capable and energetic and good men, but for the most part their names as well as good deeds have been lost to posterity; the trails they followed and which they created at times, now are grassed over or filled with the plowman's dust of a later age.

Chapter III

With the organization of the western tiers of counties in Kansas came the influx of settlers that pushed the Texas cattle trails westward. As new counties grew, first from Abilene and Ellsworth, then west from Hays and Dodge, the need for a western cattle trail from Texas to take the heavy cattle traffic off the old Chisholm Trail also grew apace. By the time Doc Barton and others had established ranches along the Arkansas, from 1872 to 1880, eleven new counties had been added on Kansas' frontier. As a result land values skyrocketed, increasing 400 percent from 1881 to 1887. Soon, three millions of acres of land would be filed on by the settlers. Development came so fast, even by 1872, that the upstart *Hutchinson News* revealed in its first issue how the town of Hutchinson had missed the cattle drives and their subsequent riches for local businessmen. Now sulking in his offices the editor, in volume I, number 1, gave out with this sour grapes editorial:

THE TEXAS CATTLE TRADE

Hutchinson could undoubtedly secured a large part of the Texas cattle trade had she made a decided effort with that end in view. Being situated on a popular trail and well off in the way of grass, water and shipping facilities, it is a natural point for the drovers to aim at—so natural in fact that we have some difficulty in keeping them away.

In addition, the AT&SF railway offered to put up a cattle yard here, which alone would have determined many thousands of head to this point. Although there is much ready money in the trade, we congratulate ourselves upon being without it. For according to our observation it is deleterious in the long run to the towns which have it. It collects a transient, a vicious and often murderous population which terrifies the better class of immigrants away and leaves so soon as the cattle trade shifts to another point. It introduces "Texas fever" . . . it makes crop raising insecure . . . it keeps out settlers and strangles agriculture. When it leaves the town, the place collapses.

It was to avoid these objections we refused the Texas cattle trade. . . . We say to others: You take the Texas cattle trade and we'll take the settlers.

So Hutchinson whistled by the graveyard of its previous hopes. By this time the cards of the Texas cattle trade had fallen against all of the towns east of Dodge City, and while Hutchinson called the grapes sour, foxy Dodge merchants and editors were well aware that with the buffalo gone for good, the sweet fruits of the Texas cattle trade would be welcomed by the palates of all Dodge citizens.

Cattle-conscious Dodge newspapers had promoted the Texas cattle trade from the beginnning. The *Dodge City Globe,* Christmas Day, 1877, had some two seasons of the Texas cattle business to look back upon when it pledged itself to the cattlemen to keep Dodge "their town." The *Globe* had witnessed the mistreatment of the Texas cowboys and pledged them its support against the gamblers, cheats, card sharks, and dead-beats "south of the deadline," that is, across the Santa Fe tracks where many of the Dodge businessmen ran their saloons, dance halls, and sporting houses ever since Hoodoo Brown and earlier pioneer businessmen and hunters had opened their tent and sod saloons in '72. But all infamy in Dodge was not just south of the Santa Fe tracks, this the *Globe* editor knew. For as late as 1885, when two blocks of Front Street's business section was destroyed by fire (the *Globe* office included), seven saloons and sporting houses were burned out just west of the Santa Fe passenger depot, *north* of the tracks.

The *Globe* editor had appealed to the laxity of police control within Dodge which forced visiting cattlemen to park their hardware when entering town only to be imposed upon and robbed by the armed thugs, gamblers, outlaws, and pimps which the town had spawned. And too, too often, crooked Dodge police officials who worked "for bounty" became the target for caustic *Globe* editorials, as in the issue of March 15, 1878:

We think there is something rotten with a man's conscience when he parades the streets with an exposed six-shooter, knowing he is violating the law with impunity simply because he is a friend of the Marshal or Policeman.

63

On January 15 of the same year the *Globe* begged of the mayor and the city council:

Again we appeal to our City Authorities to prevent all "sure thing" men from running their games in Dodge this summer. *We know that nine-tenths of all the bad blood that has ever cropped out in Kansas cattle towns, has been engendered by those robbing concerns.* (Italics are the author's).

The Dodge City law apparatus in May, 1876, acquired the services of one Wyatt Earp, an ex-Wichita officer who, after a desultory career in that town as a policeman, had been more or less dismissed from the force for conduct unbecoming an officer of the law, that is, withholding city funds which he had collected and fighting and quarreling with candidate William Smith who sought to become marshal of Wichita in a contest with the incumbent marshal, Mike Meagher. In Dodge, Earp was deputy city marshal, serving under Lawrence E. Deger, a burly bully-boy who later served under Charles E. Bassett. Marshal Deger drew a salary of $75.00 per month and Earp received even less. So it was natural that such officers participated in other extralegal activities—Deger being a partner with a McGinty in a saloon and dance hall, Earp and other under-officers taking such pay-offs as could be arranged. And it is not surprising to note that one old document unearthed in the Dodge police files reveals the names of twenty-two ladies of the night with a notation following each name of "$5.00." This was not the usual, formal police booking, with the charges shown and bearing the name of the police judge and arresting officers. It appears to be more the "kick-back" sheet which unwittingly was left in the police files and was preserved permanently. Only the Dodge officers and the ladies of the *demi monde* would know its specific purpose. But May The Innocent, Mattie Prince, Sadie Burr, Bedelia McKinney, Emma Vaughn, Mabel Gorman, Grace Roy, Emma Brace, Abbie Green, and the thirteen others who paid out $110 in that one transaction to Dodge police officials and town officers understood its purpose, no doubt considered it in the nature of a Work Permit and paid it willingly.

One old southwest cowboy, Pink Simms, who later moved to

Montana, once said of the redoubtable Dodge policeman, Wyatt Earp:

I knew Wyatt Earp and have seen him shoot a revolver and he was not a peerless performer with one by a long shot—and I never knew a man I was less afraid of, though he hated cowboys in general and Texans in particular.***

They (Dodge officials) would get a law passed prohibiting a cowboy from packing a pistol and then proceed to take his money; they couldn't lose. An old timer told me they controlled the liquor, gambling and everything else. If the cowboy gets boisterous and objects to the manner in which he lost his money, he is pistol-whipped and if he returns armed, is cut down with shotguns. The badges they wore were the variety that today's (1935) honkey-tonk operators get to protect their places so they can keep a pistol under the counter.***

Truly, old Dodge was as Hoodoo Brown put it: "Men shot out their difficulties in Dodge; the city officials were controlled by the saloon keepers and gamblers."

The *Globe* carried one story, on August 6. 1878, which told of the extent Dodge officers went to in subduing helpless and drunken cowboys, oftimes as a prelude to robbing them:

The policeman who pounded the Mexican over the head with a six-shooter last Thursday night did not display either much manhood or bravery. When we consider the fact that the poor "greaser" was sitting on a bench almost helpless from the effects of a previous beating, we don't think that even a Dodge City policeman (who is nearly the greatest man in the world?) has any right to walk deliberately up to him without any provocation, and knock out one or two of his eyes.

The *Globe's* defense of the drovers and their cowboys brought forth some threats that the editor might wind up one evening picking up pied type from off the printing house floor. This brought forth from the tough *Globe* editor the caustic comment:

Some of the boys in town having an antipathy to the *Globe* are constantly blowing about what they will do if the *Globe* says anything about them. Now we want to inform them that our space is too valuable to spare any of it to them or their private doings; but boys, if you do anything that comes within the province of journalism, we'll say what we want to about you, and will takes chances on your "pieing" our type.

That's why all the southwest cattlemen loved the *Globe*. It was their champion as the *West Central Kansas Cowboy* became for the ranchers of the Western Central Kansas Stock Association around Sidney, north of Dodge, in the 1880's. The old *Globe* carried their livestock estray notices and their brand advertisements and the news of their individual and corporate lives. D. M. Frost was the editor, assisted by W. N. Morphy. It went all out, plugging for the Texas cattle business, as its story of April 28, 1877, shows:

Dodge City is bracing herself for the (seasonal) cattle trade. Places of refreshment are being gorgeously arrayed in new coats of paint and other ornaments to beguile the festive cowboy. Masterson's and Springer's place can scarcely be recognized since the bar has been moved and operated upon by Mr. Weaver's brush. The graining is finely executed. Charley Lawson's orchestra is mounted on a platform enclosed by and tastefully ornamented with bunting. . . . The grass is remarkably fine, the water plentiful, drinks for a quarter and no grangers to bother around. The facts make Dodge *the* cattle point!

Editor Frost later took a squatter's claim on the Fort Dodge Military Reservation in what is now the corporate limits of the town, just east of the Lora Locke Hotel, where a plaque on the sidewalk today marks the exact northwest corner of the old military reservation.

Morphy, Frost's assistant, later editor of the *Kansas Cowboy*, once entered into a feud with Robert M. Wright, the merchant prince of Dodge who later operated the Cresent W ranch, south of the town. Wright had to thresh the newspaperman on the street, but not without a struggle. This act brought a $50,000 lawsuit against Wright which was settled in the true spirit of the times with a fine of $5.54 being levied against the businessman.

When Judge Frost was made an honorary member of the cattleman's association, he changed the name of his paper to *The Globe-Livestock Journal*. Its last issue was published on July 3, 1888. There was a break of more than a year, then on October 23, 1889, the *Globe* was consolidated with the *Ford County Republican* and the new creation named *The Ford County Globe-Republican*. This newspaper still championed the cattlemen, though the range cattle industry for all purposes had since reached its end.

But back in 1876, with the arrival of the big herds of Ellison and Dewees, Olive Brothers, the Barton Brothers, and other Texas drovers, Dodge took on its first tremendous boom. Its successes— and excesses!—drew the envy of all the towns up and down the river. It was the first flush of youth for Dodge, and everyone from priest to pauper saw her. Though in 1874 Dodge had shipped only 318 cars of cattle, by 1875 she loaded 5,826 cars of the long-horns. In 1876 she shipped immense trainloads, and many herds passed through Dodge for the railroads to the north and to the Indian reservations.

In 1877, though suffering from the Texas drought, the government estimated that Texas drovers pushed 201,159 head up the Western Cattle Trail. Now many cattle were also coming to Dodge from the ranches to the southwest, the Texas panhandle, New Mexico, and No Man's Land, as well as from the far reaches of the Cimarron and the Picketwire and from the red hill country of the Cherokee Strip. By 1880, though her position was now disputed by Ogallala, Nebraska, as largest shipping point, Dodge saw 287,000 head of Texans and 'Meskins' walk into town, cross the Arkansas, and graze on the river bottoms. In 1884, as the business expanded, 106 herds totaling 300,000 head moved into Dodge from the rounded hill to the south. This was the full bloom of the range cattle industry, for by 1884 mature beef steers who had Texas mothers, but had never tasted Texas grass, were now in the shipping yards at Dodge and the ranches of the southwest were at their productive and well-managed best. And the development of this mighty industry on the plains called for better controls than the ranging of beef cattle had ever needed before. So meetings were called, cowmen talked together, and the cattlemen's associations were born.

Two major cattlemen's associations served the ranchers of the southwest region which was supplied by Dodge City in the 1880's. First was the Western Central Kansas Growers Association, organized in the spring of 1883 by forty-five livestock men in and near Dodge, most of them north of the Arkansas River. They adopted a constitution of 21 articles, establishing the association's authority, offered a $500 reward for the arrest and conviction of rustlers who had bothered them and also a $200 reward for an arsonist who had burned off the range in 1882. The *West Central Kansas Cowboy,* a newspaper published at Sidney, Kansas (later at Dodge City), was named their official newspaper and thereafter served the interests of the cattlemen and their cattle pools in that area.

The second major organization was named The Western Kansas Cattle Growers Association, and it was also organized that spring of 1883, holding the organizational meeting at Dodge City. The hope of its organizers was that it could serve the needs of the cattlemen south of the Arkansas, those in the Neutral Strip, the ranchers in the Comanche Pool (or in the Cherokee Strip), and a few of the ranchers in the Texas panhandle who marketed cattle at Dodge and depended on Dodge City to some extent for supplies. This latter group of cattlemen had, by a wide margin, the stronger organization, since it had double the membership and occupied the range area three to five times as great as the northern cattleman's association, above the Arkansas. It claimed practically everything from the Medicine River in Kiowa and Barber counties in Kansas to the Purgatoire (Picketwire) River and Blanco Creek in the west, and everything from the Arkansas on the north to the Canadian on the south.

Still a third cattleman's organization came into being, but this one much later than the other two majors. This third group was The Beaver River Cattleman's Association, and it served principally only the ranchers along the Beaver in the Neutral Strip. It was organized late in the 1880's or the early 1890's. At a meeting at Old Hardesty, May 7-8, 1901, the chairman was listed as J. C. Denison, who owned the Little Bar V. R. B. (Dick) Quinn, former cowboy, roundup cook, and later editor of the *Hardesty Herald,* was the secretary. Though no roster of membership or published Brand Book for this group has ever reached the attention of the author, the membership no doubt included such well-known Beaver River cattlemen as Tom and Bake Hungate, John George, Hooker Threlkeld, Al Buchanan, Bob McFarland, the Westmoreland-Hitch company, Boss Neff, the Cator brothers, Judge S. C. Tyler, Frank Longnecker, Jim Williamson, the Kramers, George and Frank Healy, George Ray, Herb Craig, Fred Taintor, McCoy Brothers, McKenney-Over & Co., Jim Herron, Bob Maple, and probably others not known to the writer. Some, who might possibly have been members, include T. S. Bugby, A. J. Bolton, Hullitt Brothers, C. E. Dudley & Son, Arnold Brothers, George Overrocker, D. S. Johns, T. C. Schumaker, Weeks Brothers, Thomas J. Martz, Jim Beasly, Tobe Taylor, Jim Sawtell, Leonard Crow, Stonebreaker & Zea, John Sconce, and others, for there were many cattlemen at one time or another in No Man's Land. But this is sheer speculation. Suffice it to say that many who survived the Great Die-Up of 1885-86 found it expedient to join with friends along the Beaver in the interests common to all engaged in the growing of beef cattle.

And this association was still not the last, for as late as June, 1915, we read in *The Liberal News* of the organization of the final cattleman's association, the remaining ranchers selecting doughty old John E. George of the T Bar T as their president and John L. Boles, secretary—which brings us so close to the present we are hardly dealing with history and must return to older times.

At no time in history did Dodge City serve a wider-flung empire than the range cattle days of the Eighties. For all trails turned toward Dodge at that time, even as they had turned there when the old town was the hand-maiden of the buffalo hunting interests.

One of the interesting, and one might say typical, characters of that era whose broken trails may be picked up as far apart as Texas, Dodge City, and New Mexico was Sim Holstein. Sim ranched in the early Eighties on Wolf Creek, running the Cross-H 7 brand. He was a neighbor and friend of Clay Allison, who ranched on the Washita. Sim Holstein was a Texas man. By 1880 his name was known from the Mexican Gulf to the Yellowstone. He was rated one of the top trail bosses of the time, often was captain of the roundup wherever he was working on the range. In that huge volume of cowboy lore, *The Trail Drivers of*

Texas, its stories all written by actual trail drivers who drove the herds north to market, Sim Holstein is mentioned along with such trail greats as Ab Blocker, Fayette Butler, Pleas Butler, Gus Black, and others who could be depended on to take a great herd north 1,000 or 1,500 miles and reach the railhead without loss in numbers and with a reasonably fat herd. That was a hard test for any cowman to pass.

In Texas, Holstein had trouble as many others before him who had come up the trail. He had somehow been drawn into the biggest of Texas' feuds, that between the Taylors and the Suttons. When in Kerrville, in September, 1871, Doboy (Phillip) Taylor, son of old Creed Taylor, made a bid for the same boss-job that Sim Holstein bid on—trail boss for the KH, the New York Cattle Company. As qualified as any man who ever straddled a mustang, Sim got the job. This infuriated Doboy Taylor, and he went to Sim's hotel, called him out for a talk.

The *San Antonio Express*, at that time, reported the results of that discussion between the tough Sim Holstein and the ready-for-trouble Doboy Taylor:

The men had discussed the matter only a few moments when . . . suddenly Taylor drew his pistol and fired at Holstein but overshot him. Holstein sprang over the gate, and before Taylor could shoot again, wrested the pistol from him and felled him to the ground with it. Taylor regained his feet but was immediately shot down a first, second and third time. Then Taylor ran toward his house, calling for his friends for assistance. Another shot from Holstein brought him to the ground. His friends were prevented from doing anything (to Holstein) by the determined attitude of Holstein.

Taylor survived six hours and died at eleven o'clock the same night. He was sensible to the last, and spent his last hours imprecating and cursing the man he had attempted to murder.

That Holstein was an able man, and a determined fellow, is evidenced from a story concerning him told the author by Bernard Lemert who rode in the roundup under Holstein's captainship in 1884. They were working west up the north bank of the Beaver River and had gathered about five thousand head of cattle in the Sharp's Creek region and bunched them in three herds to work. As the work of cutting out, branding, and throwing back the cattle proceeded, Bernard heard the cowboys talking of an OX steer with a confusing road brand on him. When the OX (Towers & Gudgell) rider cut the animal out from the herd, the roundup captain, Holstein, called the animal an R Bar S steer and ran him back into the herd. It seemed that Word & Byler, whose brand was R Bar S, had brought up a trail herd the previous summer whose road brand curiously resembled the OX range brand. The OX rider, not knowing this, again called for the steer and brought him out of the herd. Again Holstein ordered the steer put back. Now another rider backed the OX rider, telling him, "Take out your steer; don't let Holstein run it over you just because he's captain of this work." So once more the OX rider went up against the steel of Sim Holstein's nature. And Holstein acted.

Holstein had been sleeping and eating with the XY wagon which was now standing down the creek about a quarter of a mile. Sim rode down to the wagon on a lope, soon re-appeared with two six-shooters buckled on his belt, a Winchester rifle in his saddle boot, and a Bowie knife in his belt. He rode directly over to the OX rider, looked him in the eyes and said, "You cain't take that steer as long as I'm boss of this work. What you can do is this: Choose two men familiar with these brands we're working. I'll pick two men who are familiar with them. They can decide who the steer belongs to. If they cain't decide, I will. While you decide this, ride into your cut and get that steer back out of there! Now, ride!"

The OX man rode slowly toward the cut, then he touched up his horse with the spurs and quickly brought out the disputed animal. Later, when joked by the others about Holstein's order, the OX man laughed and gave them McGinty's answer: "That man's *mind* was *stronger* than mine!" But most of the men agreed later, after the brand was inspected, that Holstein was right.

"He appeared to me like a man who meant business," Bernard Lemert remarked later. "Sim was a very *determined* man." •

Young Lemert once riled Holstein when he was riding through a herd, looking for his father's Crutch L cows. Sim saw the fifteen-year-old boy and thought he was just wandering around for the ride. "Get out of there, boy, and stop chousing up them cattle," he called. Bernard came out meekly. One of the older cowmen said to Bernard, "If you want to look for your pappy's cows, go right in that herd and look. Pay no 'tention to that damned Holstein." But Bernard was satisfied to obey the roundup captain.

Sim Holstein operated his own ranch on Wolf Creek for several years. Later he moved to a ranch near Deming, New Mexico, where he died suddenly about 1900. Joe Davis, an old cowboy who had worked for the Star Grocery in Liberal at one time, brought back the story of Sim's death.

Holstein, Davis said, had been staying indoors at the ranch where he was employed as foreman, since he had not been feeling well. That afternoon, at a nearby trail crossing of a small, sandy-bottomed stream, a wagon became stuck. The driver came to ask Sim's help, and Holstein, a rugged man physically, left the house to help him. Placing his back against the endgate of the wagon, Holstein gave the signal and the driver urged the team up the creek bank. Sim managed to lift the wagon enough to free the rear wheels from the sand and the team pulled the load up the bank.

At home a few hours later, Holstein told his wife that he felt very ill. He walked to the bedroom, lay down on the bed. His wife came in and removed his boots and in a few minutes Sim Holstein was dead.

So passed a typical cowman of the Southwest—and a *determined* man—in his own bed, with his boots off.

Another ranch foreman who comes to mind when speaking of typical cowmen of that age is Richard Joyce, foreman for John O'Loughlin's Pigpen 7 ranch, a brand that would be exactly like that of Sim Holstein's had it one less cross bar. O'Loughlin ranched near Wagonbed Springs, on the old Santa Fe "Cut-off Route." And his foreman, Joyce, also had a mind of his own.

An amusing story is told of an encounter between Richard Joyce and a neighbor, George Kell. Kell was a straight-laced churchman while Joyce, though a good Christian man, fell somewhat short of being a strong church-goer. One cold Sunday in mid-winter, Joyce and several of his cowboys worked like roping horses at branding time to build a sod house for ice storage on the stream near Wagonbed Springs. They then cut ice on the river, packed it in straw in the sod building. It took two or three Sundays to erect the soddy and fill it with ice. But they were pleased with the thought that their women-folk and children could enjoy home-made ice cream the summer days ahead.

A few days after filling the soddy, Joyce was astounded in a chance meeting with George Kell to be bitterly criticized for working his men on the Sabbath. Joyce said nothing, took the criticism with studied grace.

On a hot Sunday in the middle of the following summer, Kell and some friends were having an ice cream social at the church. They needed ice to make ice cream, but the Pigpen foreman, Joyce, and his men were absent at the time. Knowing Joyce would raise no objection, Kell and his friends visited the icehouse and took enough ice to make the ice cream for themselves and the children, leaving Joyce a note on the soddy door.

Joyce later met up with Kell. "Now who in hell is the most religious, George," he asked Kell, "us boys who worked several cold Sundays so the women and children could have ice cream in the summertime or a son-of-a-bitch that comes around when a man's away and steals ice out of his ice house without asking his permission?"

Joyce wasn't angry and Kell realized why he was so cruel in his questioning. So Kell offered Joyce no answer, but afterward understood him much better.

Chapter IV

On the headwaters of the Cimarron, and westward on the Purgatoire, cattle ranching had begun as early as 1861, when Joaquin Young and his family settled in the valley of El Rio de los Animas Perdidas en Purgatorio, as the Spaniards called it, or the River of Lost Souls in Purgatory. The river was known by the cowboys as the Picketwire, and had been referred to in a letter from F. E. Cavanaugh at Fort Union to Kit Carson, May 1, 1855, as The Pickett-ware. So it had probably drawn its nick-name from army troops, as have so many streams, towns, and objects both before and since.

In that region south of Pueblo were also the ranches of Francisco and Daigrie at La Veta, on the head of the Cucharas; Bobais' Ranch at Huerfano (The Orphan); Hicklin's Ranch on the Greenhorn; George Babcock on the St. Charles; Isaac Boss on the St. Charles; the Charles Autobees; and others. The post office at Gray's Ranch was later, 1863-64-65, moved, to Trinidad. Bent's Fort was now 65 miles distant—Maxwell's Ranch 75 miles away. The traders, Felipe Baca and Pedro Valdez, were using the trail from the south to move much-needed flour to the Denver mining region, and Baca soon decided to settle in the valley at what is now called Trinidad. The place soon became a mecca for cattlemen in the later 60's and 70's. The town was said to have been named Trinidad by Gabriel Gutierrez, after a sweetheart he had once loved in New Mexico. And to the festive cowboys who trailed herds to old Trinidad for shipment on the railway, the town itself became their sweetheart for many years.

In the western portions of No Man's Land, served equally by Trinidad and Dodge City, several cattle outfits had appeared in the early 1870's. The longhorns and the 'Meskin' cattle ranged back from six to a dozen miles from water, and a cattleman who controlled a length of stream also controlled the government range

74

back of that water as far as his cattle could forage and still make it to water. The fresh-water lakes of the area made the problem of long-ranging a simple one in the wet years, but in dry years even the "live water" streams would not provide a really adequate supply of water for the livestock. So the early ranchers picked the best streams first, and among the finest streams in the region was the Beaver and its tributaries, running as it did the length of the Neutral Strip.

The 101 ranch appeared in the early Seventies, with ranch headquarters on the Texaquite Creek; their earlier headquarters was four miles southwest of Kenton. It was an English syndicate, the principals being Doss, Taylor & Horn. Sam Doss and his partners had earlier bought out Jose and Benito Baca, Bernal Brothers, and Juan Lujan to make their start in the 101. By 1882 the Western Land and Cattle Company had been promoted in London to run the 101 and the V1 ranches on the Cimarron. T. H. Burnett at one time managed the ranches, living for a time at Hymer, in Butler county, Kansas. The 101 at that time had extensive feeding operations in the Flint Hills and at El Dorado where they grew grain and put up hay to pen-feed the big grassout steers before shipping them.

The 101 selected the Kenton canyon area on Diamond Creek, where the stream flows into the Cimarron from a protected valley. There the first ranch buildings were erected from sod and stone and the cedar wood from the canons. About 1904 the headquarters were moved to the Rio Blanco, near Dalhart, Texas. The 101 employed such riders as John Dacy, who ranched later on Texaquite Creek; Fred Hollister; Henry Jones, foreman under Follis; Labrier brothers; Lynn Mansker; "Nigger George," a most competent bronc-stomper; Hiram Porter; Jinks Sayre; Charlie Zuric; and many others.

In the later Eighties the 101 ranged cattle in Nebraska and Wyoming, sending the two's and coming three's to the northern short grass country to mature. From there they were shipped to their big fattening yards at Ames, Nebraska, where they were fed out and shipped to market under the direction of R. M. Allen, general manager of the Standard Cattle Company.

The OX ranch, operated by Towers, Gudgell and Simpson, located downstream from the 101 about 1877. Major "Hi" Towers was its manager. The OX continued in the cattle business both in the Cimarron country and in the northern maturing grounds until 1892. Downstream from the OX was the Box H, operated by a Mr. Burnett. Burnett sold to the Muscatine Cattle Company, a Scot and English syndicate, about 1881. Their offices were at Catalpa, New Mexico, and they established the Z Lazy H brand, building their headquarters about 20 miles northwest of present Boise City, Oklahoma. They also received mail at Trinidad.

In the early Eighties there was a rush of Scot and English money to the plains of the southwest and west of the United States. The long profits made in the Texas cattle business, in the trail business, and on a few of the ranches convinced the usually canny Scots that there were immense profits to be taken in the American beef cattle business. As a result many new cattle ranches were organized throughout the west and southwest during these years, such as the Prairie Cattle Company, The Texas Land and Cattle Company, the Matador, the Hansford Land and Cattle Company (which included the Turkey Track, the Bugbee properties, and other ranch lands), the Cattle Ranche and Land Company (on Kiowa Creek, in the Indian Territory and northern Texas panhandle), the Arkansas Valley Land and Cattle Company, The Maxwell Cattle Company, Ltd., and others as far west as the Pacific coast and north to Canada. These Scot and English synicates, while in most cases being honest business enterprises, were in some instances mere stock floating ventures and, as such, came to the usual end. Buying livestock "range count" on the western and southwestern plains, employing managers who were not competent to wrestle with the range problems of the day, floating huge capital stocks out of which they first paid high dividends in lieu of honest earned profits, all these and many more, if not "shady" then unwise practices, finally brought the end of the syndicate in disaster. Aided by the hard winters of 1884-5-6 on the southwestern plains, few of these enterprises lasted more than a few years and by 1888 had sold out and left the region.

One of these companies, The Prairie Cattle Company, the larg-

est of them all, established offices at Trinidad, then the cattle
center before the Santa Fe reached Dodge. This company started
with the purchase of Hall Brothers' Cross L brand, an old brand
of Mexican origin. Hall brothers, Nathan, Jim, and William Hall,
made their start in cattle early in 1871 by purchasing land from
Felipe Baca for an amount said to be in excess of $20,000, a most
considerable sum in those days. The Halls were Texans from the
San Saba region, and they ranged their cattle 30 miles northeast
of the Malpais cone of Capulin, in the upper Cimarron valley in
New Mexico. Following Hall brothers' purchase, the sheepmen
left that country, never to return. In 1881 the Cross L was reorganized into the new Prairie Cattle Company, and by 1885
listed 124,000 head of beef cattle. But the company had never
paid an honest dividend from earned profits until W. J. Tod was
appointed general manager and Murdo McKenzie became secretary and cashier. Under their management William Withers was
superintendent of the Arkansas river division, with a ranch post
office west of Las Animas; W. J. Cartwright was superintendent
of the Cimarron River division, with post office at Catalpa, Colfax
County, New Mexico; A. F. Mitchell was superintendent of the
Canadian River division, with ranch post office at Tascosa, Old-
ham County, Texas. By 1903 the better management had pulled
the company out of the red ink and Prairie Cattle Company quit
the southern range and retreated to the Dakotas.

In its earlier days, R. G. Head had been superintendent and a
Mr. Grubb was the general manager. Bob Robinson managed the
Canadian River division at that time. In the brand book of New
Mexico for 1885, Prairie Cattle Company listed seventeen brands,
among which were the old Jones brands, JJ and JJ inverted; LIT,
the George Littlefield brand; 77, TXT, J, JL, XT, TF Connected,
H Bar Connected, AT Connected, HL Bar Connected, Roman
Three, Cross L, and others such as 14 and J Bar. Many of these
brands became most complicated in structure in the urge to make
a different mark from all other cattlemen, one which could not be
re-done with a "running iron," that is, altered and changed by
rustlers.

The oral calling off of a brand of an animal, cut out at roundup time, fell to the regular cowboys. Unaffected men, as they were, they learned to simplify the most complicated work of the iron so that the brand name could be understood by all. For example, a Snyder brand from north Texas had the numerals and figures 7 J H P L all tied together (connected) into a weird graph that rivaled an Egyptian hieroglyph. "The boys soon solved it though," said an old brand inspector. "They dubbed it the 'Peter L,' and that's what is was from then on."

Prairie Cattle Company, later sold to Lee Bivens, employed such capable cowboys as Frank Forrest, one-time foreman of the Cross L and 7 ranches; Charlie Hedrick, who later owned the LIV brand; Henry Jones, once foreman for the 101 under Follis; Bob Lane; brothers Kit and Johnny Nelson; Jimmie and Johnny Stinson, the latter of whom once ranged sheep and cattle in Baca County, Colorado; Bruce and Ed Sayre and Sam Collins, among others. It is ironical that the name of a one-time Prairie Cattle Company rider, Sam Smith, is best-remembered of all these good men.

Sam Smith was a flamboyant character who captured the imagination of some writers of police and detective stories through which his name has been preserved while others are forgotten. No one knew where Smith came from, but he was polished in manner if not urbane when he came to Prairie Cattle Company for a job. He gave the impression he was from a good family of wealth and refinement. But it may have been just a good act. He worked with Mexican Joe Bush; Cal Clellan; Kid Doss, the Regulator for the JJ who was shot by Ubank; Lon Ford, later Clark County, Kansas, sheriff; Milt Hightower; John Labrier; Lynn Mansker; Chet Malcolm, the wrangler for the JJ and the JJ wagon boss; Hiram Parmer—all of whom remembered Sam Smith as a capable cowboy and a good fellow to rub stirrups with on the roundups.

Sam spent a year or two on the Cimarron range but soon he was building too big a loop and his own brand was being burned on other mens' cattle. He was arrested and taken to Woodward, Oklahoma Territory, to the jail. Sam broke out of the flimsy structure, delivering several other prisoners with himself. He went to Colorado and found work but was soon caught and again.

back, this time in the Beaver City jail. Though Beaver City had since replaced the stretched steer hide jail, under which they confined prisoners, Sam proposed to break out of the weak frame jail that substituted for it. The Beaver sheriff, a tough nut, encouraged Sam to go ahead, break out—then he could shoot him and save watching the jail nights, as he told Sam. So Sam stayed, never poked his head out the window!

From Beaver City they took Sam to Alva, a supposedly unbreakable jail. A day later Sam was out, delivering two more prisoners with himself. Sam fled to Kansas, married the daughter of a respectable cattleman. But he rested there only briefly. Soon he was robbing a Missouri-Pacific train. The officers that fell on Sam's trail killed one of his accomplices, but Sam and another got away. Shortly afterward, Sam was accused of a bank robbery, was captured and sentenced to Leavenworth Federal Prison.

In a coal mine, Sam met the notorious Ben Cravens of Oklahoma. Bold, nervy, intelligent in their nefarious schemes, the pair carved wooden pistols and with these held their guards at bay and escaped to the open area outside the mine entrance. As they scaled a high rock wall within range of the Guard Tower, Sam was shot through the head and killed. Cravens escaped, was later apprehended and sentenced to life for murder of a guard.

So ended the career of one of the old "hands" of Prairie Cattle Company, leaving only a broken, wind-scoured trail behind him.

Another extensive cattle spread in the central-western portion of the Neutral Strip was that of the Anchor D, the property of E. C. Dudley and Son. Dudley was a Boston capitalist with a marine background. He established the Anchor D in 1878, and it was managed for a good many years by C. H. Bagbee. The ranch was first known as the Double X, but the brand was too easily mis-read as the "Double Cross" and the sensitive Bostonian soon changed it. After Dudley's reign, the ranch passed into the hands of T. C. Schumaker and still later became the Anchor D ranch of Stonebreaker and Zea.

In its best years the Anchor D ran upwards of 30,000 head of cattle. The ranch headquarters was 20 miles west of present Guymon, Oklahoma. The range extended from where Hooker,

Oklahoma, stands today to a point southwest of Elkhart, Kansas, and from the Kansas line on the north to the Texas panhandle. This huge pastureland comprised some 1,500 sections of excellent buffalo grass, well-watered by the Beaver River and its tributaries, many fresh-water lakes in wet years and 47 hand-dug wells with windmills and large metal tanks and earthen reservoirs. A maintenance crew of three men constantly attended these big U.S. windmills. Such riders as Tom Stephens; Josh Thomas, the ranch manager; Kirk Richards—sometimes called Curt Rickard; "Scandless" John McCandless; John Luce, later drowned in a North Platte River crossing with a trail herd; Arthur Armstrong; and scores of other top men worked for the Anchor D.

Boss Neff, who had been in No Man's Land for many years, stopped one day with a small herd of range bulls to water at an Anchor D windmill on the prairie. As he and the other two cowboys approached with the thirsty animals, they were surprised to see a newly erected sod house near the mill. A settler stood in its doorway, a double-barreled shotgun resting in the crook of his arm. Neff rode up to the soddy.

"Howdy," he greeted the stranger. "What's going on here?"

"Jest this," the granger replied, patting the weapon. "You bring them cows any closer to my mill and I'll blow you offen the hoss."

"Now see here," the unarmed cowman expostulated, "this mill's the property of the Anchor D people and we're welcome to water here any time!"

The settler pointed the gun barrel up to the windmill fan, upon which was painted in large letters U.S. WINDMILL with the manufacturer's name in smaller letters below.

"These here wells was dug by the U.S. Guv'ment for us settlers, so we could hev water here," the man explained to the flustered cowman. "We don't puppose to hev you people mussin' up our nice yards an' fields and breakin' up these nice tanks. Now jest take them cows o' yourn an' drift!"

Neff looked again at the shotgun. There was nothing to gain in staying, unarmed as he was. So pounding the bulls with their lariat ropes and hollering themselves hoarse, they managed to push the thirsty bulls on another nine miles to the next mill.

"I never failed to carry a Winchester in my saddle boot after that day," Neff laughed as he retold the story many years later to a friend.

Among the earlier ranch hands of the Anchor D who came over to work on the range when it became the Schumaker ranch was an old horse-breaker named Marvel Brown, called "All" by the other cowboys. Brown was second to none in his profession. Once he received a shipment of young, unbroke mules at Liberal, the "end of tracks." He yoked the mules by pairs and headed for the ranch. Eight days later, "All" Brown pulled into Liberal with a 10-mule, jerkline hitch, pulling three empty wagons and ready to pick up freight for the ranch. A young editor of the Liberal paper talked with Brown, inquiring if he hadn't set some kind of a record for breaking and taming young mules.

"Nope," said Brown. "I'd a made a record three days ago if I could a got that nigh leader taught to straddle the chain, but the iron-head never caught on what I wanted until yistiddy when a rattlesnake lyin' in the trail did it for me. Since then he's crossed over puffictly ever time I shake these rattles and holler!"

Among early settlers who came to western No Man's Land as squatters on cattle range were some who remained to work on ranches after "drying out" on their claims. A few were such as Pap Keyes, W. E. Davis, Smith Allen, Steve Penny, Pap Fletcher, Record brothers, Charles Wagner, the Thorps, Labriers. Cochrans' Hugheses, Rowans, Joneses, Cal Cleland, and A. C. Easely. The last ranched near Kenton. Easely was rawhide tough as a range man but was an affable, gentle family man when the work was done on the range. Because of the soft inflection of his voice, he was often accused of being a Texan, but he would laugh softly and say, "No, I'm from the Show Me State!"

Easely was born near Kansas City in 1859. He lived in a hot-bed of guerillas during the Civil War. Coming west as a young man, he found ranch life to his liking. "I worked with not less than a hundred outlaws—lined up with them at the chuckwagon for fifteen years without changing base. I worked for the Al

81

Peacock and Cross L ranges where thousands of cattle ranged. Al Peacock bought too many Meskins and they broke him. Ranchers in later years tried to hold their ranches by 'squatters rights' but it was no good. The range cattle industry was dead."

The big XIT threw up such a long string of the new "ribbon wire' with the sharp points attached to it that Easely, then working on the range, decided that "if you caint whip em, jine 'em," and went to work for the XIT. Later, when buying beef for the railway gang working into Clayton, New Mexico, Easely had an unusual experience. One night a cowboy rode up to his tent, weaving on his horse, and said, "Albert, c'mon out heah, I'm in sore trouble. I jes shot a man—killed him I reckon. He was drunkern a skunk 'n so'm I. I caint get away fum here, for I done tried three times and every time old Jake, my hoss, brings me back when I fall asleep. If you'all will take me to Texline, Albert, an' I get out of this scrape I vow I'll never touch a drop of redeye the rest of my life—so help me!"

Easely looked at the cowboy to see if he was joking, but saw he was completely sincere. So he saddled his own horse and led the drunken cowboy's horse behind him. Out ten miles toward Texline he saw the cowboy was gradually sobering up, so he pointed out the direction to him and returned to his tent. "I knew one of two things would happen," Easely said: "Either the first saloon he hit at Texline would get him and he would end up in jail, maybe prison for life, or if he kept his word he might become a genuine abstainer and lead a good and free life in the future despite his fall from grace. But I never learned which happened."

Albert Easely and his brother Lee went into the cattle business together and bought and shipped trainloads of Meskins from the old Company M ranch south of Boise City. Easely married a Missouri girl, Mollie Clements, and the couple had six children. They lived a happy life together, and when Easely died he was buried under the towering cliffs of Black Mesa, in the lovely Cimarron valley which he loved in life and which would enfold him forever in death.

Another old landmark ranch, near Point of Rocks at the old Santa Fe Stage Station, was that of Beaty Brothers. They branded a JO and a JB. The principals were Missouri-born men, Alvin R., Jasper N., James W., and John W. Beaty. Coming to Colorado in 1866, they had by 1898 built up ranch holding of great value which they sold to H. S. Boyce Cattle Company, the sale comprising 18,000 acres of land and 12,000 head of cattle and horses. Alvin Beaty later owned the big TO ranch in Grant County, Kansas. The Beaty brothers pioneered Otero County, Colorado, founded the town of Manzanola and later entered into many phases of business and banking in the region. Red Cockrum was their foreman for many years.

One of the most popular ranches in No Man's Land was Hardesty Brothers Half Circle S ranch. Colonel A. J. (Jack) Hardesty was the front man for the enterprise and a better one could never be found, for he was a man with dignity and aplomb, yet one who won and held the esteem of every cowboy who rode for him. "Col. Jack don't expect a man to do anything he cain't do from the back of a hoss," they explained, when asked to submit a reason for their loyalty to Hardesty. John Durfee was Hardesty's foreman and had been with him since he held land on the Colorado border in 1871. Both Hardesty and Durfee knew such stalwarts of the Colorado range cattle business as the Beaty Brothers, John W. Prowers, Thomas O. Boggs, L. A. Allen, and John Lee, some of whom have been previously mentioned. Durfee was an Iowa boy, born in 1850. His father died when he was a boy and his mother and the children joined an emigrant train to California.

Durfee came to Colorado with a trail herd from California in 1871. Together with four men who accompanied him, they launched the California Ranch, later a portion of the big Holly Ranch spread near Holly, Colorado. Durfee lived in the saddle for forty years. He married a niece of E. P. Barber, president of the New York-Syracuse company which founded Syracuse, Kansas. When old and gray, Durfee said wistfully to a friend one day. "I sure miss the life in the saddle; but I don't miss the chuckwagon, for we always had the lousiest cooks on the range!"

Col. Hardesty's name is preserved today in a Dodge street named after him as well as in the town of Hardesty, Oklahoma, in the panhandle, where he ran his cattle in the old days. Another

Dodge man, Dr. T. L. McCarty, ran his SIS brand with Hardesty on the range. The original town of Hardesty, at the confluence of Coldwater Creek and the Beaver River, is now but a ghost site. But four miles southwest, on a busy highway, is thriving new Hardesty, Oklahoma.

There was a time when many of these promising towns were building in this part of the Neutral Strip. Rothwell, west of Beaver City, had a two-story hotel and other buildings. Boyd was a village of importance. Paladora, north of the Beaver and a few miles west of Sharp's Creek, was of growing importance. Eagle City, a brave attempt to make a town on the hill on the west bank of Fulton Creek, a short distance east of Grand Valley, interested many town boomers, and Grand Valley itself, under the guiding hand of the land shark and promoter, George Scranage, was assuming considerable importance in the area where Palo Duro Creek flowed into the Beaver River.

Up Coldwater Creek (El Frio) from Old Hardesty about seven miles was Lavrock, which "budded, blossomed and died," as Dick Quinn so aptly expressed it. Old Optima lay on the north bank of the Beaver, northeast of present Guymon, Oklahoma, on a beautiful grassy area. Eastward, up the Rock Island tracks, was Buffalo, now marked only by an Oklahoma Highway Historical Marker. Old Buffalo was once the site of the U.S. Land Office and a town whose prospects were bright and cheery and where cattlemen and their women-folk came from miles around to dance and entertain themselves. The Land Office was moved from Buffalo to Beaver City when a complaint was made, and Colonel Newsham, special U.S. land agent, came out for an inspection and recommended the change. So old Buffalo died.

Most, in fact, all of the towns generally regarded as "ghost towns," can better be described as "ghost sites." For the wheat growers' plows have spared no trace of the old towns and settlements where they interfered with their profits from the golden grain, so highly subsidized by a paternalistic government. Such former towns as Springfield, Fargo Springs, Oak City, Lafayette, Vorhees, and Woodsdale, in Kansas, and Rothwell, Palodora, Grand Valley, Old Hardesty, Old Optima, Sodtown, and others in the Oklahoma panhandle are but vacant areas on the prairie and in the wheat and maize fields today, where no new town has sprung up to carry on a once-proud name given them by optimistic town boomers in the Seventies and Eighties.

It was near where the Hardesty and Kramer ranges overlapped that the decision to turn back the Texas trail herds was decided. The tick-infected stock from Texas was causing great anxiety to Strip ranchers in the Eighties. Col. Hardesty and Ludwig Kramer met and organized a fighting group of ranchers to stop Texas herds from passing over their range unless the Texas men agreed to follow a pre-arranged route established by ranchmen of the Neutral Strip. Cowboys guards were posted at the eastern end of No Man's Land with orders to stop all Texas herds coming up from the Camp Supply area, up the Western Cattle Trail.

Soon drovers, such as John R. Blocker, from Texas took the matter up with Washington, D.C. It was apparent that U.S. Cavalry troops would soon enter the picture, so the Hardesty-Kramer forces withdrew to their range within the Neutral Strip. Before long a Texas herd under a foreman named Moore, from Tom Greene County, Texas, was given the choice of following the Beaver River trail established by the Strip ranchers on the south bank of the Beaver or using the north bank trail as some had been doing as a passage for the cattle traffic along what they were calling the new "National Cattle Trail." Moore took the south route and established the final National Cattle Trail across No Man's Land.

About this time, Ab Blocker, then with a title of "king of the trail drivers," came along with a herd of 2,700 big steers. He got in a mix-up with Hardesty and Kramer men for not following the pre-arranged route. At that time cowboy "guides" were used to show the Texas men the proper route up the Beaver River to the Kansas-Colorado line where the trail headed due north. When the rep met Blocker at the mouth of Fulton Creek, Blocker was making his speed and hoping to establish another record for taking his herd through in fast time and in neat condition, a feat for which he was famous on the trail. And the Blockers were tough Texas men, not inclined to be told where to drive across the free range country. When he found the guide taking him much farther west than he calculated by his compass to go, Ab Blocker was mad clean through.

"I'll take this herd just where I goddam please from now on, and without your aid," he told the guide. Blocker ordered the herd thrown off the trail for a quick noon lunch at the chuckwagon, and the guide hurried to tell his boss what had happened.

The Hardesty men soon gathered and with a few Kramer cowboys who were working cattle nearby the group rode over to Blocker's chuckwagon for a talk. Tom Hungate, now Hardesty's foreman, and one of the top cowmen of the southwest in his time, was head of the delegation. All the men were well-armed.

Ab Blocker was lying under the wagon, taking a short *siesta* when Hungate and the men arrived. Blocker told of the experience later in these words:

The cow outfits up there in the Neutral Strip had organized to fight rustlers and to keep their stock from mixing with trail herds. We heard of this down the trail, even before we got to Fort Worth, and we found that these men meant business. It looked like every man had a Winchester rifle in his saddle boot and a six-shooter or two strapped on him. And even the *boys* were dressed that way! The way I remember it was that it looked like a place where the kids teethed on forty-five caliber cartridges!

Ab Blocker showed his usual restraint and good judgment when faced with a crisis on the trail. Tom Hungate, another wise head about cattle and men, talked quietly with the trail boss for a few minutes. Blocker invited all the Hardesty and Kramer men to a dinner of "choice Blocker trail beef." The two groups intermingled during the lunch that followed. Blocker agreed to follow the trail guide wherever he led them and afterward made light of the incident, though he knew what a deadly serious business it would have been had he not showed good judgment in respecting the rights of the Strip ranchers.

The old town of Hardesty, named after Colonel A. J. (Jack) Hardesty and his brother, was abandoned in the spring of 1901. There is nothing there today to mark the site except an indenta-

86

tion in the tough prairie sod that was Hardesty's main street, its southern end pointed to the lowland of Coldwater creek. A few pieces of the old Hardesty schoolhouse stove remain scattered on the prairie. Boss Neff II, son of Jake Neff and grandson of the early pioneer cattleman, Boss Neff, pointed out to the author, when he visited the location, that the old townsite would be under water if the plan to build the "Optima dam" ever went through.

Old Hardesty was originally settled by Dodge City men among whom were Hardesty brothers, Captain Furley, Charley Briggs, Wiley Byram, Capt. A. J. Howenstein, Henry Frank, W. A. Sullivan, and Billy Bailey, the latter of whom for years operated the Hardesty saloon. Jack Hardesty was a great favorite of the cowboys, even though he would not "go soft," as he expressed it on matters pertaining to supplying adequate cooking utensils or supplying sugar for the men's coffee. Once, when a supply wagon of Allen Walker's was in Dodge, Walker had a barrel of sugar thrown on and marked it "sow belly," and so had the merchant charge it to the Hardesty account. Now it seemed that Hardesty enjoyed bringing a friend, Walter Hart, down to the ranch to fish in the fine, deep water holes of Palo Duro Creek and the Coldwater. On this particular occasion they made a fine catch, using a seine as well as lines. They decided to "salt down" a barrel of the fish to take back to Dodge with them. Inadvertently, they got Allen Walker's barrel of sugar and promptly "salted down" the barrel of fish with his purloined sugar!

Walker and the cook, watching the boss and his friend at work, were afraid to mention their duplicity. So it was not until Tom Hungate, Jim Mahoney, Hal Darling, and Bob Campbell rode in that evening that Colonel Hardesty was informed that his fish were salted down in sugar.

Hardesty took the joke in his stride and permitted Walker and the cook to clean the sugar from the fish and get real salt to preserve them in the barrel. Hardesty later told his men the fish were excellent, "nice, sweet meat," he expressed it. But Hal Darling complained later that every cup of coffee he drank with sugar tasted like fish to him, so he was obliged to break himself of the practice of using sugar in his coffee.

Allan Walker once shot a skunk near the flour barrel in the Hardesty camp, causing himself to make an extra trip to Dodge for more supplies. The Colonel laughed and sent a gallon of good bourbon whiskey back on the freight wagon for his men.

On a cattle shipping trip at Kansas City one time, the Hardesty men had been whooping it up for two nights and two days at one of the hotel saloons where they stayed. Colonel Hardesty, looking out the window that night, saw two huge brewery wagons loaded with beer back up to the rear doors of the saloon in which his men were comporting. He turned sadly to his men, held up his hands and said:

"All right, boys—let's knock it off." He pointed out the window to the two wagons of beer. "Let's get out of here. They're running in two more loads of beer on us and I'm sure we cain't drink it all!"

It was the Colonel's manner and way of ending festivities and getting his men back to their jobs again.

Billy Bailey ran the Hardesty saloon in a soddy. He had cooked on the roundups, rode with the cattle drives to Dodge, and knew all the cowboys. Even the hardiest punchers were said to have cried out loud when they drank Billy's tiger milk. So Billy commenced the practice of handing out a small glass of blackberry wine to chase each drink of his red-eye. The effect was like that of throwing a rock into a pool of still water, the ripples began spreading farther and farther. This was the way that Dick Quinn, the *Hardesty Herald* editor, described Billy and his bug juice:

Billy had drifted about all over the country. He was a former companion of Buffalo Bill Cody and knew him like a book. He roamed all over the western country for years and after a trip down into Old Mexico drifted back into this region with a companion, Joe Cruse, who was afterward frozen to death with his wife on Home Creek, near Beaver City.

In those days there was no liquor license to pay, no officers to collect, and the courts had no domination. This was a land with a total absence of government, except that every man was a law unto himself. Billy's place filled a "long-felt want," an oasis in the desert, where at times the cowpunchers assembled and "tightened their hoops" loosened by many weeks of abstinence. But no matter how bad the boys wanted to act, Billy never permitted a tragedy to occur in his place, in fact not one killing occurred in the old town of Hardesty, largely due to the cool head and iron nerve of Billy Bailey in a crisis. Long experience on the plains had trained him in handling such emergencies. His only employment in this country was the saloon business and he left these parts when business got dull, going from this country to Nebraska, where he died ten or twelve years ago at the home of his early youth.

Billy was not bad; he was not good; just mediocre, and took life along the lines of least resistance and filled a niche that some other fellow would have filled had not Billy come along. He handled a fiddle in a way that delighted his customers, let them ride in through his building on their horses when they pleased, but abruptly ended the revelry when anger gave advanced notice of gun play.

Billy was broken in health when he reached this country; had "fought the fight" as an active plainsman and his business was the only occupation at hand for him, and he seemed to be the right man in the right place. Billy Bailey is remembered with a kindly feeling and many an old timer will recall long rides to get to Billy's Thirst Emporium—and the headaches that followed these visits!

Few men, if any, living today will remember Billy Bailey. The author has met only one man who knew Bailey, Bernard Lemert, and he died two years ago at the age of 89 years. To paraphrase a verse of old Badger Clark:

> The settlers and the cowboys,
>   Who drank at Billy's store,
> Have gone to their Last Roundup,
>   Over on the Other Shore.

The first burial in the Old Hardesty cemetery was that of Joe Cruse and his wife, on the last day of December, 1887. Cruse, as mentioned above in Quinn's story, was the man who came to Hardesty with Billy Bailey and started the saloon. Both men had worked for the land shark, George Scranage, in booming the town of Grand Valley but had fallen out with Scranage when the town boomer hired gunmen to dominate the settlers and the new town governments in the Neutral Strip.

Joe Cruse and his wife started to Beaver City on December 22nd, spreading the word of a dance to be held at Hardesty on Christmas Eve. A great blizzard rolled in from the north that afternoon and evening and the first knowledge of the couple's deaths was when their team, with the neckyoke and doubletrees still fastened on and the lines dragging, drifted in to the Kramer cow camp west of Beaver City. A search was immediately launched by the cowmen and the bodies found nearby between Six Mile and Home Creeks. Joe lay on his back, his wife on her side with her head pillowed on his breast. The bodies were nearly drifted over and were frozen stiff.

At Hardesty, the thawing of the bodies so the limbs might be straightened in death was an ordeal. Finally the two bodies were placed in a single crude, home made pineboard coffin, padded inside and lined with black muslin.

A group of townsmen and cowboys, laboring under the direction of Billy Bailey and the Hardesty foreman, Tom Hungate, selected the high hill northwest of town as a proper place to start a cemetery. Tom Hungate took the detail of cowboys up the hill with picks and shovels and selected a proper burial site. He marked out a rectangular pattern for the double grave and said, "We'll bury them here. Now dig until I stop you." With that, Tom returned to Hardesty—and promptly became engaged in a poker game at Billy's Saloon.

Time passed, in fact a considerable length of it. On the hill the cowboys kept digging, in town Tom Hungate kept playing. Once the grave diggers broke through the frozen top layer of sod, the digging became easier in the sandy earth below. When Tom Hungate returned to the burial ground, he found one puncher standing in the bottom of the hole which was now deeper than he was tall. The cowboy in the hole was passing up the dug earth a shovelful at a time to another cowboy who lay on his belly at the graveside, reaching down into the hole to take the shovelful of earth. The chilled punchers told their foreman they were planning to get lariat ropes and a windlass to assist them in raising earth if he hadn't shown up.

"Jesus Christ," Tom said, not reverently, "that's deep enough!"

Joe Cruse and his woman were lowered into what is probably the deepest hand-dug grave in Oklahoma. The parson said a few and kindly words over the bodies. All agreed that the couple had been two of old No Man's Land's best-liked and finest citizens.

Sometime later Billy Bailey and other Hardesty citizens received letters from a "Mrs. Joe Cruse" in Illinois. She was writing the Hardesty folks seeking confirmation of an "estate" left by her husband, Joe Cruse, and intimating that anything Joe left her in No Man's Land would be more than he had left her and their several children in Illinois.

Dick Quinn, the *Herald* editor, commenting on the matter a quarter of a century later, wrote:

Their bodies are buried so deep in the old Hardesty graveyard on the hill, that Gabriel will have to toot his horn good and loud on the final day or they won't hear in time to get in the Great Roundup, when the last Great Herd is worked by the Riders of Judgment.

In the eyes of some, Cruse and his common-law wife had sinned a plenty. But most folks who knew them well reserved judgment, allowing the others to cast the stones. For the Cruses had been friendly people, helpful in times of sickness to others and always the first to organize the community for dances and other entertainments. Their good qualities covered up their multitude of unknown sins, Old Hardesty folks thought, so they carved on the wooden cross this inscription:

Rest In Peace
Mr. and Mrs. Joe Cruse
Died 1887
December 22nd.

Then the Hardesty folks returned to the peace of their homes and the cowboys back to the ranches. But it was a sad Christmas, that of 1887, to many folks in No Man's Land who had learned to know and respect the man and woman who called themselves "Mr. and Mrs. Joe Cruse."

The blizzards, especially those of the winter of 1884-5 and the winter of 1885-6, found Colonel Hardesty with cattle in New Mexico, in the Neutral Strip, and some in Montana. Though he didn't go broke, Hardesty took great losses. But his men were loyal and fought blizzard after blizzard, to turn back the cattle that drifted and keep their boss solvent.

One of Hardesty's top men was George F. Ray. His name has appeared, the author believes, as "John" Ray in some stories. Ray was one of the southwest's first frontiersmen in the period of settlement. He arrived shortly after the Civil War from Maine, and most of his adult life was spent between the Arkansas and the Canadian.

George Ray had hunted buffalo; he had been in Indian fights; he was on the Palo Duro when the Rifle Pits were dug (in what was later the Irv Steele pasture); he had hunted for gold in Colorado. When Colonel Hardesty established his ranch on the old "Thompson place" in 1879, George Ray came down from Dodge on a freight wagon and helped construct the house and outbuildings. Later, when Hardesty moved to the Chiquita, Ray again helped build new buildings. He was a skilled man with rifle, revolver, hatchet, or tomahawk; with saw, broadaxe, and hammer. He was a good stonemason, as well. Ray stayed with Hardesty until the ranch was abandoned in 1885-6.

George Ray did the ranch freighting for a while, later became its cook, and was one of the famous roundup cooks of that area. When Hardesty withdrew from the range, Ray took a claim on Hackberry Creek. He lived to a ripe old age in Texas County, Oklahoma, passing over the divide March 23, 1913.

Probably the best-known foreman for Hardesty Brothers, after Durfee, was W. T. (Tom) Hungate, mentioned above as captain of the burial squad. Tom had two brothers, Cap and Bake, and the Hungates ran the Quarter Circle 7HL Connected, south of the Arkansas River and west of Cimarron station. Tom was selected Beaver River Roundup captain several years, and that was a great favor and acknowledgment of respect among the cattlemen of the day. Tom Hungate was said to have handled a hundred roundup cowboys as easily as some men handled five. Men who knew him best and have spoken highly of him were such as Hal Darling, Harry Reas, Herb Craig, Oliver M. Nelson, Bill Jay, George Ray, Arthur Daugherty, Jim Mahoney, Lew and Frank Kramer, Rube and Perry Chilcott, John George, Al Buchanan, Jim Denison, Bernard Lemert, Burris Wright, Boss Neff, Jim Herron, R. E. Steele, and others. After Hardesty withdrew, Hungate moved to Indian Territory in eastern Oklahoma. In a few years he moved to California, where he died of blood poison March 31, 1913, at his home in Moneta. He was only 57 years of age at death.

Jack Hardesty had preceded his foreman in death, passing on and having been tucked in at Maple Grove Cemetery in Dodge City in 1910, aged 77 years. Now the memories of the Half Circle S are only a bare image in the minds of our very oldest pioneer citizens. Their day has come and gone; they played out their parts with distinction and Colonel Jack Hardesty and the cowboys of the old Half Circle S served an important part in opening up the High Plains area of the Southwest.

Chapter V

The cattlemen at the eastern end of the Neutral Strip and in the Cherokee Strip began establishing their hegemony early in the Seventies. The Cimarron & Crooked Creek Cattle Company (Chain C Brand) was organized by G. W. E. Griffith, a Mr. Cockins, "and others," the records state, in 1878. C. T. Herring was later manager of the firm. The Chain C's held range on Crooked Creek, both in Kansas and the Neutral Strip. Following the disastrous Die Up in the Eighties the firm showed an indebtedness of $50,000.00 and only dead cattle to meet it.

The firm then reorganized, taking in a Mr. Harbach, an Omaha financier, and they changed the brand to Crooked L. The old ranch today, though only a portion of the original lands, still retains the name, Crooked L, under ownership of McNaghtens and Dutton. At the time of the reorganization in the mid-Eighties, R. E. Steele was hired as manager. He proved to be a most competent manager. Mr. and Mrs. E. W. McNaghten, son-in-law and daughter of Mr. Steele, and Mrs. Anna Dutton, another daughter of Steele are the principals today. A Mr. Batman is half owner of the cattle and Resident Manager.

R. E. Steele was born in 1850 and reared in Prince William County, Virginia. In 1876 Steele moved to Barber County, Kansas, and in 1882 to Meade County. There he married Jennie W. Mills, and the couple had two daughters, later Mrs. Eustace Smith and Mrs. E. W. McNaghten. Steele's first wife died in 1907 and he later married Miss Curtis Harsha of Pittsburgh, Pennsylvania. Steele organized other cattle companies such as the Meade Land and Cattle Company, Steele and Cockins, and the Cimarron Land and Cattle Company. Under the Crooked L brand, the firm in the Eighties and Nineties operated ranches on both Crooked Creek and on Sharp's Creek in the Neutral Strip. This arrangement, said a one-time competitor of Steele's, per-

mitted the Crooked L to usually have most of the taxable assets
of the firm in No Man's Land at assessment time. But this appears
a rather harsh judgment against a highly respected man as Steele
was always considered by contemporaries. A Mr. Holloway was
manager of the Crooked Creek operation and Bernard Lemert
was for several years the foreman at Sharp's Creek.

Other cowboys listed on the Crooked L payroll for 1884 were
Dave Mackey, then foreman; J. Marts, Howard Wright, M.
Gaines, Frank Campbell, Charley Sealey, George Campbell, Bill
Foltz (or Folks), R. E. Dill, Allen McCandless, the cowboy poet,
Lee Davenport, William Price, John Maledon, and William
Brown. The men drew from $30 to $40 per month "and found."

Two brands closely associated with the Crooked L operation
were the brands WAT and RAT. The former was purchased
from an eastern man named Watt after he and his wife and young
son had spent a lonely and unhappy period on the Cimarron,
trying to establish themselves "in cattle." They sold to Crooked
L and returned east. The other brand, RAT, was the brand of a
herd of several hunderd head of good roan and shorthorn cattle
the Crooked L bought for breeding purposes. Laben Lemert was
with the Crooked L at this time and cared for these cattle on
Stump Arroyo, near where he later made a claim.

About this time a Mr. Deerdorf from Kansas City became interested in the Crooked L. Though the early operations of the
ranch made little money its land sales were said to have kept the
company solvent and relieved their indebtedness.

Among Crooked L cowboys was a top hand, Bill Foltz, mentioned above. One day another cowboy named Arnold admired
Bill's ivory-handled six-shooter. He asked Foltz to let him handle
it. Foltz handed him the gun, Arnold immediately started twirling and holstering the gun. While engaged in this practice Arnold
caught his thumb on the hammer, pulling it back and accidentally releasing it. The big gun fired, the 44.-40 slug going completely
through Arnold's body.

The cowboy had a bad time, and when he thought he was
going to die he called for Laben Lemert and asked the older man
to pray for him. "Pray for yourself," Lemert advised him. Arnold

confessed he did not know how to pray, had never been taught as a child.

"Well, it's a mighty good time to learn—though awfully late," Lemert told him. After cleaning up the bad wound and stopping the flow of blood, Lemert advised the wounded man how to clasp his hands, bow his head in humility, and beg forgiveness for his sins.

The two men prayed together for the redemption of Arnold's soul. And the young puncher pulled through all right.

Dave Mackey, another Crooked L puncher, married Arabelle Sewell in 1884. She was the foster child of John Marts, also mentioned on the payroll, and her folks came out to the Cimarron country in 1879. The Sewells, so the author was told, left for New Mexico, looking for better land, then again returned down the Cimarron valley. The party had two covered wagons, horse drawn, as well as a small herd of cows with them. Near Black Mesa, outlaws disguised as Indians raided them and took their horses. The family managed to get back down the valley, to where the Kneeland ranch was later, by hooking their milk cows on the wagons. The family was nearly destitute, Arabelle having walked barefoot all the way back. They took a claim in that area and later sold it to Kneeland and Edmunds.

John Marts, Mackey's father-in-law, then bought out a Nebraska man by the name of Baker who had a claim on Crooked Creek. The Mackeys came over to the flats west of Stump Arroyo creek for water and while there inquired of Laben Lemert about a good place for them to locate. He recommended a spot on the Jones & Plummer Trail, about where Odee post office was later located, at the crossing of Crooked Creek. The Mackeys settled there in 1882, prospered and lived exemplary lives.

That region down Crooked Creek to the Cimarron was a wild country infested with loafer wolves, "catamounts," coyotes, and other predators that gave cattlemen much trouble. The coyotes were capable of dragging down small calves and the 'cats could destroy larger cattle weakened by storms. But the big *lobos*, the wolves, would pull down full-grown and healthy cows and leave a range bull so cut up that it might have to be put out of its misery. Boss Neff once told of a work mule that had a piece of meat hanging from its buttox as big as a beef liver, torn out by wolves. So it was the big, grey wolves—the lobos—that the ranchmen most feared and hated.

One particularly vicious wolf was a depredator known as "Old Two Toes." A trap had clipped off part of one front paw, making him easy to track. But he always got away. He ranged in the southern part of Meade County and along Crooked Creek in the Neutral Strip. A huge, grey fellow, he ruled the range along the bluffs and sand hills where Taintor's cattle fed. He was so destructive that the cattlemen's association offered a large reward for his head and two-toed foot. But he was cunning and bold, and continued leaving in his pathway steers whose stomachs had been so deeply torn that their intestines dragged along behind them until they fell in a spasm of death.

About this time Old Two Toes took a large, black, and fierce bitch wolf to mate. The two, now working together, tripled the destruction. The pair seemed more bent upon mutilating and destroying cattle than upon simply satisfying their hunger. The cattlemen raised their reward offer and Meade County now set up a liberal reward. Still the destruction continued, a score of Crooked L cows being found over a few month's period with their udders ripped and long strips of hide hanging from sides and backs. Even the tough range bulls now had to fight for their lives against such a pair. Some of the cattlemen hired "wolfers" to trap or shoot the varmits, and though they did kill off several other wolves on the range, Old Two Toes and his rough mate continued their depredations.

At this time there was a colored man, Willis Peoples, who had taken a small ranch in the neighborhood south of Meade. One day Peoples was in town and talked with several ranchers and county officials about Two Toes.

"If you'all will promise to leave the wolves alone for a month and he'p me in a campaign against them, I promise to end their destruction of our cattle," he said. The proposition seemed náive to veteran cattlemen.

"How do you propose to get them, Willis?" they asked.

97

"I'll camp on de trail; I'll live wid 'em; one day dey'll come in wid paws in de air beggin' fo'giveness fo' dey sins," Peoples answered humorously, but without smiling.

Some town folks laughed at the idea, but ranchers who knew Willis Peoples backed him to "bring in the wolves."

Peoples took up the wolf trail, followed by a colored boy he engaged to keep him supplied with food and water and fresh horses daily, which were supplied him from the closest ranch. For two weeks Peoples remained glued to the two-toed track of the old wolf, through sage and sand, up sandy streams and down slopes heavily covered with buffalo and Indian grass, across rough bluff country in the breaks of the Cimarron, and down on to the flats. By staying doggedly on the trail of the killers, Peoples prevented all but a few fresh beef kills.

At the end of his second week, Peoples found only the trail of Old Two Toes. The bitch wolf, finding no rest and little food to eat, had quit the range. Ten days after the bitch had departed, Peoples came suddenly upon old Two Toes at a calf kill. The famished wolf was given no time to enjoy his feast, but unfortunately the horse Peoples was riding had gone lame that day. So the wolf escaped into the dusk of the evening while Peoples waited for a fresh mount to be brought up.

Early the following morning Peoples, mounted now on a fast, fresh horse, took up the trail. He followed the wolf's tracks across the flats, down to the waters of Crooked Creek, where the animal drank, then up Skunk Arroyo. He noted the lack of guile, the old wolf no longer doubling back, attempting at times to walk along the rock ledges and on the matted grass of the hilltops. The tracks were now open, obvious, easily seen and followed like the old wolf had finally determined on a destination. At dusk Peoples had a fresh horse brought up and loped up through the arroyo, fully expecting the wolf to make a hard run before he would overtake him. But in a ravine, well up in the arroyo, he suddenly caught a glimpse of the evening sun across the glistening hair on the old fellow's back. It was the killer.

Under a clay bank the wolf lay clearly in sight, apparently resting, the last rays of the evening sun playing across his gray and dusty coat, bringing it to life against the green of a clump of yucca which stood slightly behind him, its dry pods rustling in the evening breeze. Peoples pulled his fresh mount up to a walk, slipped the Winchester rifle from the saddle scabbard, and levered a .45-90 cartridge into the breech. Then he studied Old Two Toes, lying so quietly on the narrow ledge as he drew him into his rifle sights.

Two Toes lay with his tongue lolling out one corner of his mouth, his long yellow fangs showing plainly. As the colored Nemesis measured his distance between himself and the beast, he found the old wolf's eyes looking directly into his own. Could it be possible the old wolf had actually given up the fight, Peoples asked. He lowered the rifle, carefully dismounted, keeping in readiness for a quick shot should Two Toes change his position. But the old wolf only watched, his ears twitching, as the hunter walked slowly toward him.

At fifty feet distance, the nervous horse which had now smelled and seen the wolf paced wildly back and forth at the end of the reins which Peoples had wrapped around his right arm. Fearing for both his own safety and losing the wolf, Peoples drew a careful bead on the wolf's head.

"Youh my fair game," he whispered as he pressed the trigger. Old Two Toes' head nodded gentle agreement. The bullet smashed directly into Two Toes' brain, stretching him out on the narrow ledge of earth in silent death.

At Meade the following evening, Willis Peoples dropped the carcass of the beast out the tail-gate of his wagon in the presence of half the town's population. A young cowboy from the Crooked L ranch stepped into a dry goods store, borrowed a tape measure, and with it they measured old Two Toes, nose tip to tip of tail. He measured exactly seven feet.

The ranchers who were present that day showered their thanks on Willis Peoples and county officials congratulated him for his energetic pursuit of the killer wolf. Asked one, "How come, Willis, that you knew from the first you could get him?"

"Dat wolf," said Peoples, "represent *Bad*. He *bad* fo' dis community. I know dat only *Good* can kill dat wolf. I was not sho

99

dat *I* rep'sent Good, but I know dat any man wid his mind made
up is a majority. My mind was made up to get dat wolf. Dat's
how it was." Peoples bowed modestly.

One of the cattlemen who supported Willis Peoples' campaign
against Old Two Toes was Joe Mason, a partner in the firm of
McKenney, Over & Company. Mason was a Civil War vet. He
came down to Skull Springs from Dodge and entered the cattle
business with John E. (Toot) Over and J. E. McKenney. The
firm, originally A. E. Reynolds Land & Cattle Company, accumulated about 7,000 head of cattle, branding with a Running M Bar
iron. They ranged near Round Timbers, thirty miles west of
Camp Supply. Mason had been an Indian scout, soldier, lawman
at Dodge and buffalo hunter. He had "killed his man," one Ed
Ryan, at Fort Elliot, and had been exonerated before a Board of
Officers convened by Brig. Gen. Hatch, Jan. 5, 1875.

John Over, a principal, was a Pennsylvanian who came west in
1868. He married Bernadine Huerte at Camp Supply in 1883.
Once, during one of the frequent Indian scares of the Eighties,
Toot Over rode from Dodge to the ranch, nearly seventy miles,
in approximately seven hours. He expected to find everyone dead
and scalped by the Redskins, the buildings in ashes. Fortunately
the rumor was unfounded, there were no Indians on the prowl.

A half-brother of Over's, Jake Miles, settled just north of the
McKenney & Over range, east of Otto Barby's ranch. The great
blizzards nearly wiped out all the cattlemen of that area, but
Barby, Mason, Over, and McKenney all found financial success
as individuals later in life. Joe Mason died in 1889, Over and
McKenney a few years later.

Philip Scanlon was one of McKenney & Over's cowboys. Phil
was a young, rash, wrong-headed fellow but with the usual good
qualities of loyalty to his boss and sincerity with the other punchers. At a ball in Englewood one night in the summer of 1885,
Phil clashed with another young fellow over a girl. Phil died
from the other young man's bullets. The coroner's jury consisted
of Chalkey Beeson and C. J. Garvin, of Dodge, both of whom
ranged cattle in the Strip and south of Dodge City; M. L. Munn

and T. P. Kendall of Englewood; Smith Ruble and J. E. Over of the Neutral Strip. Phil's body occupied the first grave in the Englewood cemetery.

At about this same time Tobe Taylor, the Ashland killer who broke jail at Dodge ("there were no jails south of Dodge," they said), was caught at Deep Hole, on the Cimarron, by lawman Jim Sawtell.

Northeast of the McKenney & Over range were several ranches in the Cherokee Strip, some of which, like the Day, lopped over into Kansas. Day brothers branded with a Bar Running M in the Cherokee Strip but a D and a D Cross on the Day range. J. M. (Doc) Day was the principal. Below the Day range was that of Word, Byler & Co., the R Bar S. Dawson Word managed the ranch; Red Odem (real name Bill Meadows) was the foreman. Odem was a top hand, a Texas man who was said to have left three men sleeping the long sleep in Texas. In 1889, Odem is said to have run the U. S. Marshal back to Gutherie. Later, Odem went back to Texas and there died in jail. In the Brand Book of 1885, Word, Byler & Company is listed as the Buffalo Ranch Company, J. H. Mussett, manager.

One of the Word & Byler cowboys was Wylie Bell, a man who rose to range fame with a fiddle, entertaining the men and lending his talents to make a success of each neighborhood dance. A fiddler was a valued person on the frontier, and it is said that wherever Wylie Bell pulled his saddle from his sweating horse, gloom fled. One old waddie recalled an evening spent under the leaking roof of a soddy during a heavy downpour on the roundup of '84. The roundup had reached D. S. John's ranch on Sand Creek. All the riders in the group, about a dozen men, trooped into the little ranch soddy to get out of the rain. This night Bell was along, but had left his fiddle with the Running M wagon. As luck would have it, Johns had a battered, but useable, fiddle hanging on a peg on the soddy wall. Wylie Bell tuned it, soon was bringing forth sweet melodies into the dark room.

Soon some one found a lantern and they had light. The room was crowded, there were only two chairs, so the men sat in a circle on the floor, their hats and some pans arranged to catch the trickles of water that came through the soddy roof. Now the evening, from one of discomfort and loneliness for the men, became one of music and merriment. Songs, the clapping of hands and the tapping of a boot heel, wherever the hard ground could be found to send back an echo, were soon filling the air of the soddy. Wylie Bell gave forth *Fisher's Hornpipe, Arkansas Traveler, Old Folks at Home, Peek-a-Boo Waltz, White Wings,* and other favorites of the day. Many years later, one of the old cowboys who then, as a lad of fifteen, heard Wylie Bell's concert, recalled the memory in the following words:

By the time the rain had stopped and we left the house, the night had cleared with all the stars out in a big show of nature's brilliance. As we bedded down and pulled the tarps over our heads on the wet ground, all agreed it had been a wonderful evening. It was, at least to me, since I have fondly remembered the music provided by Bell of the R Bar S and the warm companionship of the cowboys around me for more than seventy-two years.

South of Word, Byler & Company's range was the Camp Supply Military Reservation, called *Fort Supply,* and originally called The Camp *of* Supply. By 1884 it had a good fence running all the way around the reservation. Wagon trails came in from all directions: From the west, down the Beaver river (which incidentally becomes the *North Canadian* when it reaches Camp Supply), came freight wagons and cattle herds for the army post garrison; from the east came salt wagons down the wagon trail from the salt beds on Moosasi and Sand Creeks, both of which flow into the Cimarron from the north; from the southeast came army freight up the Fort Sill-Camp Supply Trail. From the south, up the Western Cattle Trail, came the big Texas herds, passing by west of the post and plodding on to Dodge City, Ogallala, and the Yellowstone.

A main trail from the southwest was the old buffalo wagon trail, up which later came beef herds for army use. Another older trail, both for army freight wagons and for a later cattle trail, was the deep-rutted trail that paralleled the Western Cattle Trail between Camp Supply and Fort Dodge, by way of Deep Hole. They called it the Military Road. A military telegraph line ran along this old trail. This was one of the earliest trails in the area made by the white man, U. S. Cavalry troops, when Fort Dodge and Camp Supply were important to protection of the frontier.

South and east of the Camp Supply Military Reservation was the range of J. V. Andrews, and north of him the Arthur Gorham, Half Circle Box range. Gregory, Eldred and Company held range southeast of Camp Supply and Day Brothers occupied land southwest of them. The Eagle Chief Pool lay to their east and on this range also lay the Walnut Grove Cattle Pool. South of there was Geever and Houghton's 21 Ranch with Dickey Brothers on farther south, adjoining the Cheyenne and Arapahoe Leased Lands.

The Texas Land and Cattle Company, the T5, held a wide range east of there, almost at the center of the Cherokee Strip. There were at least 30 or 40 more cattle outfits with their ranges specifically mapped east of the T5, and running over into the Ponca and Pawnee Lands.

Back north, across the Kansas border at the western end of the Cherokee Strip, the flat prairie landscape is broken by high, rolling hills, some with sharp declivities and with deep canyons. The cured buffalo grass on the hilltops here was nearly always swept clean of snow by the sharp winter winds, and cattle could eat and stay fat in this region in the coldest winters and go to the broken hill lands and the canyons and ravines when bad storms blew in from the north. Westward a few miles is the great sinkhole called the Big Basin, and to the east of it the smaller sink hole and the all-year spring called Jacob's Well. Here, thousands of range cattle watered throughout the years, their hooves carving lace-like patterns on the valley floor below that can be seen to this day. The towering rock walls that enclose these basins are of a sedementary deposition laid down millions of years ago in an old sea bed. Subterranean washing away of the gypsum and salt beds that underlie this limestone crust has permitted these huge circles of earth to collapse, dropping the earth a hundred feet or more into the ground in spaces that are as much as a mile in width.

Many of the early cattlemen and settlers who first saw these yawning holes believed them to be extinct volcano craters. One folk tale tells of chilled cowboys on the winter range who "warmed themselves" at the crevices and crannies where warm air currents arose from the "hot lavas" below through the rocky conduits. The author knows of no one who has ever warmed a toe at such a crevice. But the Edith Salt Plain on the Cimarron River, fifty miles to the southeast of this area, and the Great Salt Plain on the Salt Fork of the Arkansas, between Alva and Pond Creek, Oklahoma, testify to the millions of tons of salt and gypsum washed from under the earth's surface in the region of the Big Basin and Jacob's Well. That a great new oil strike, to match or beat those of the Texas and Oklahoma strikes of the past, is possible in this region is worth mentioning. Westward from this area producing oil wells are already being brought in at the rate of a half dozen wells each week. Drilling operations appear to be moving eastward, to the point where mighty salt domes may stand beneath the earth's surface, beckoning the oil discoverer to come ahead, make his strike.

Today, the massive hills of this Clark County region are covered with a labyrinth of cattle trails, old and new, and jeep trails made by ranchers today as they go whizzing around the precipices and canyons in jeeps where once the longhorn held dominion. The Open Anchor ranch of Bob Hood, Liberal businessman, today encompasses most of this area.

In 1869, George W. Reighard, following his service in the Union Army as a teamster, came to this section of the country. He fought Indians, freighted to the Black Hills and hunted buffalo. On the spot where Ashland, Kansas, stands today, Reighard killed 2,000 buffalo. He killed another 3,000 of the big animals on Sand Creek, nearby. Once, at a single "stand," within less than a quarter of a mile in extent, he killed 68 head of the dumb beasts.

Reighard knew Wild Bill Hickock and other plains personalities. On January 27, 1873, together with four other hunters, he encountered a blizzard on the Cimarron River, not far from where the Texas Cattle Trail later crossed the stream. The other hunters were away from camp at the time and all froze to death in the storm. But Reighard lived through that day, night, and a second day, by walking and exercising for a period of many hours in a narrow area between their wagon and the hide stack.

George Reighard was once a passenger on the Fowler stage when three drunken horsemen attacked the stage. Grant Wells of Dodge was shot through the hand but managed to kill the outlaw who wounded him. Reighard, unarmed, "sat within the stage as a spectator and played no part in the festivities," the story goes. Later in life he established a road ranch on Bluff Creek, on the Camp Supply Trail and Western Cattle Trail, where he sold to freighters and cattlemen. He hauled freight for Lee & Reynolds, Indian traders at Camp Supply, and he hauled buffalo bones to Dodge following the big kill of the Seventies. In 1878 he sold his mule teams and his wagons and entered the cattle business south of Dodge, near the old COD range. In the blizzards of 1885-6 he saved but 66 head out of one herd of 1,608. From another herd of 600 head of young stuff, he saved 30 head.

The settlers were closing in on that region in 1886 and Reighard quit the range, bought a farm one and a half miles east of Dodge where he farmed until his death, in 1896.

South of the old Driskill range in Clark County, Kansas, on Kiowa Creek, was the YL range. The YL was a popular stop on the trail for all going to or leaving Camp Supply. The YL was established by Webster, Hoare & Co., Ltd., an English syndicate, with Scot stockholders. Later the company name was changed to Cattle Ranche & Land Co. They held range in common with the 777's.

Cattle ranges in the Cherokee Strip in the Eighties were fairly well defined since the companies leased land of the Cherokee Nation, which had received a patent to the lands and held them in fee simple. The Cherokee Strip Livestock Association was organized at Caldwell in the spring of 1880. The boundaries of each firm's range were loosely defined by the physical characteristics of the land—rivers, creeks, low hill ranges usually being the accepted boundary lines, since there were no mountain ranges or heavily wooded areas to shut one range off from another.

To the west of the Cherokee Strip were the ranches of the Beaver River, Kiowa and Wolf Creeks. Southwest of the Cherokee Strip was the leased lands of the Cheyennes and Arapahoes. They ranged the Apple Outfit, claiming 40,000 head "range count," and with four wildly flung line camps. The AV and the 7K Connected brands also ranged the leased lands, the latter company being that of the Washita Cattle Company, a St. Louis group headed by F. B. York as general manager and Frank Biggers, another top cowhand, their foreman.

In the western portion of the Cherokee Strip, west of the big cattle trail, were ranches of Hi Kollar and his brother, Henry Kollar, using CY brand. South of their range was the YL (the YL previously mentioned). Farther south, south of the Clear Fork of the Beaver River, was the Dominion Cattle Company, branding a Box T. East of the Box T was range of the New York Cattle Company, the KH. The KH was centrally located on the trails and was a great stopping-over place for travelers, largely because of the fame of its cook, Bill Buttons.

The foreman of the KH was Al Thurman, a hard-bitten cattleman of the Old Texas type. The Box T foreman was G. C. Smith, equally hard-bitten but a genial man, considerate of his riders and fellow cattlemen. Thurman, though a driver, also maintained the respect of his cowboys. But between the two men there was ill-feeling; the smouldering fires of dislike, kindled by range problems, were fanned into a blaze whenever the two met.

The range between the two ranches was rather poorly defined. There was no stream of importance, nor a ridge of hills to mark clearly that imaginary line running south from the crossing of Wolf Creek by the Texas Cattle Trail and the other line running northwest and southeast, marking the boundary between them.

The KH had a poorly watered range in dry times and there was a tendency for their cattle to drift northward, down on to the Box T range, toward Buzzard's Roost Creek and the stage station at the mouth of Little Wolf Creek. This awkward situation eventually brought tragedy. One day the two foremen met, quarreled violently about range rights and drifting cattle. Thurman drew his six-shooter and killed Smith. Some say he out-drew Smith; others contended that Smith never drew at all. Both men had loyal followers who would fight, so after that Thurman never rode without a well-armed bodyguard along.

In 1884, on New Year's Eve, Thurman again made news when at a dance at the Bond & Nixon Hall in Dodge, Thurman stabbed

George Miller, a Santa Fe Railroad employee, twice—once near the heart and in the shoulder. Thurman was arrested and Miller lived. On June 24, 1884, Thurman's case was "discontinued for want of evidence." The KH foreman was free to shoot and stab again.

One of Thurman's bodyguards thereafter was Joe Sparrow, a big, handsome, ne'er-do-well Texas cowboy, about twenty-two years of age. Sparrow had come north with an Olive herd from Goliad, Texas, his old home. Like many other young cowboys, Sparrow was eager to "make a rep," by killing some other young cowpuncher. He was proud to associate himself with a man like Thurman who had killed. So it was good training—and within two years Sparrow made his brief and notorious appearance in history when he shot down the aging Print Olive, who was in his shirt sleeves, unarmed. This killing happened at Trail City, Colorado, a boom town on the National Cattle Trail, just across the line west of Coolidge, Kansas. Olive was slain in his own place of business as Sparrow and an accomplice, John Stansfield, laid in wait for him to return to the business the morning on which Olive planned to leave Trail to take care of his ranching enterprises near Dodge on the Sawlog and on the Smoky Hill river. It was over within a matter of seconds, Sparrow firing three shots into Olive, the last one when he lay on the floor helpless.

The act nearly cost Sparrow his freedom for life. He was immediately tried and found guilty at Las Animas. But his lawyer won a change of venue to Pueblo. There he was tried and the jury hung. At a second trial, three years after Olive's murder and with the state willing to call it all off to save the trial money which was increasing furiously, Sparrow was found "not guilty." He returned to Texas, died at Tampico, Mexico, in 1924.

Print Olive was a Confederate veteran, a *tough hombre* as he was called by those who knew him best in Texas. He killed several rustlers in Texas and left after they had succeeded in killing his brother. In Nebraska, where he took his immense herds, he again ran against rustlers, two of whom shot his younger brother when he was deputized to arrest one of them. When the pair of murdering rustlers fell into Print's hands, he promptly hung them. In a macabre scene in which two of the accompanying men at the lynching burned the bodies, Print was forever blamed for the act, though the jury found him not guilty of that act, only guilty of the hanging. The pyro-maniacs were Plum Creek, Nebraska, businessmen. But Print Olive's spotted background served to win Sparrow's freedom for him.

Print Olive had four sons, Billy, Harvey, Tom and Al. Billy was a chip off the old block, knew no fear and like the other young men hankered for a "rep." In a drunken moment at WaKeeney, Kansas, Billy made the grade, for he killed his best friend when the young man, Dave Harrison, attempted to intervene in a fight in which Billy sought to shoot another boy, named Beam. Billy fled to No Man's Land, lived at Beaver City, then a booming sod town with miscellaneous card sharks and land sharks, making about equal progress in building a town, giving it the appearance if not the substance of economic and social good health.

At Beaver, Billy ran around with another footloose young man, John (Lengthy) Halford, and the boys kept a couple of loose-living girls with them. They supplied the townsfolk with low-cost beef, anyone's beef and Joe Sparrow's beef in particular. For Billy was awaiting the day the Bird (Sparrow) returned from his trials to claim his loot. In September, 1887, Billy and Lengthy refused to use their guns to aid the land shark, Scranage. Billy was thereafter marked by Scranage. One day shortly afterward Billy became embroiled in an argument with a bartender named Henderson who had a picture of Billy's trollop, taken among a group of Dodge dance hall gals. Henderson refused to give Billy the photograph. Billy and Lengthy therewith shot up the saloon and put a bullet or two in Henderson' coattails. Then the two retired to the hills to skin beef.

When Billy and Lengthy rode in to Beaver City's main street, Henderson and Hodge, two Scranage backers, ambushed them from behind beer kegs across the street. Lengthy escaped, but Billy was shot to death on the Main Street of the little sod town.

Billy's body was returned to his mother at Dodge on an LUK freight wagon. She laid Billy beside Print Olive at the Maple

Grove Cemetery, and on the tall obelisk upon which his father's name appears his mother had inscribed:

WILLIE P. OLIVE
"Gone But Not Forgotten"

Lengthy never came back to Beaver City until Scranage left. Then he returned, hopeful that some of his would-be assassins would take up their guns again. But Lengthy was mature and hard now. No one wanted any part of him. Lengthy worked for the XI and Bernard Lemert rode with him on the roundups and heard the facts of Billy Olive's tragic death. Lengthy became a respected cattleman in the Strip and in Texas.

East of Beaver City was the town of Gate. Near there, two outlaws had holed up. One was Bill Williams, the other was known only as "Big Jim." Bill Williams was "pure worthless," as they said. "Big Jim," some say his real name was Fred Ailward, was six foot two inches and in the prime of life, really no one to run with such as Williams.

Returning one night from a spree in Neutral City, the pair passed by Ira Norton's claim shack. In high, though drunken, spirits they blasted away at his soddy walls with six-shooters, all the while riding around the soddy and yip-yipping like a pair of lonesome coyotes.

Ira Norton sat inside the claim shack with his big old muzzle loading double barrel shotgun, but without a pellet of shot with which to load it, though he had a horn full of black powder. Norton had waited sometime for their departure but when the ruckus continued for a half hour he decided he must make a fight for his life. So he looked around the cabin for material to use for lead shot in his gun. Spying the old cast-iron lime-caked teakettle on the stove, he grabbed it and reduced it to small pieces with his hammer. Ramming the pieces of cast iron into the barrels of his weapon, Norton then stood near a window and watched the pair of drunken outlaws in his yard. They had just stopped for a moment and were taking a swig from the jug Big Jim carried on his saddle.

Quickly slipping percussion caps over the nipples of the shotgun,

Norton took careful aim and discharged the iron from the tea-kettle at them. The blast knocked Bill Williams from his horse, killing him instantly. A part of the second barrel caught Big Jim in the shoulder and neck, putting him out of action for the night. When he had recovered he pulled his freight from that section.

Several years after this shooting episode, Lyman Savage, who related the incident, was in England visiting an old friend of No Man's Land days, a Dr. Vardan who had lived in the lawless old place for several years and who had patched up Big Jim after he was shot.

"Would you care to meet an old friend?" Dr. Vardan asked Savage, taking him into the next room where he opened the lid on a long pine box.

Within the box was the reclining skeleton of a man. "Do you recognize him?" Dr. Vardan asked. Lyman Savage studied the skeletel bones, noted that they were filled with small bits and pieces of lime-encrusted cast iron.

"By Jove," Savage exclaimed, "It's Bill Williams!"

"Right you are," Vardan assured him. "As a young doctor in that wild and lawless land, I badly needed a specimen but was unable to pay for one. So the boys agreed to exhume Williams' bones. You can see it is him." Dr. Vardan pointed to the bits of cast iron.

"Yes," Savage agreed. "It's Bill Williams for certain. And this is once he is serving *a useful purpose* on earth!"

Chapter VI

George Scranage, the land shark, mentioned in the previous chapter, put the finger on Billy Olive and Lengthy Halford and brought about Billy's death. And Billy was not the only man killed or run out of No Man's Land by the little schemer. Scranage was a cold-blooded and ruthless killer. But he was exceedingly clever, maintaining his power through his Vigilante organization. So he was never personally charged with a murder. He had others for that task.

Two of the Scranage faction, "Judge" O. G. Chase and Rev. O. M. Overstreet, varied in their beliefs, but both were joined in a grab for land in Beaver City. They lent an aura of respectability to Scranage's nefarious schemes. Chase came from Pueblo, Colorado, to No Man's Land and gained "possession" of many town lots along with Scranage. Scranage was operating not alone in Beaver City but was booming towns and grabbing land all up and down the Neutral Strip. To this region Rev. Overstreet came a little later.

Chase became "governor" and his son-in-law, W. B. Ogden, became secretary of the "Cimarron idea," a clever scheme to obtain Federal recognition for their land theft by gaining status as a "territory," Cimarron Territory, in the United States.

All this subterfuge was made very "legal," on paper, and this appears to be the reason that historians have failed to denote the Beaver City vigilante organization and the Cimarron idea for what it was—a land grab by a pack of thieves. This is not to imply that honest settlers were not pulled into the enterprise, for they were, a good many of them. Some knew better than to oppose the Scranage faction; some enjoyed the thought of bettering their own hard lot. These are not to be excused, but they are to be better understood, for many, like Billy Olive, had no other place to go and they hoped to build a new life in the Neutral Strip.

111

Chase it was who took charge of the Great Seal and the election machinery which consisted, according to Elmer E. Brown, publisher of *The Territorial Advocate* in 1886, "mostly of announcement of the votes—cast or otherwise obtained." For it was a fact that Chase once brought in a tally of 300 favorable votes majority for himself and blandly announced they were from "Carizzo Precinct," a precinct no one had heard of up until that time!

Scranage's organization became so vicious that men like Billy Bailey, the Hardesty saloonkeeper, and his friend Joe Cruse, sometime bigamist, rough as they were, could not tolerate the practices advocated by the Beaver City vigilantes and quit the organization, though they had been members in good standing. The vigilantes, said A. N. Howe, a pioneer cattleman who came to the Neutral Strip in 1883 as a boy of sixteen, once held a young man accused of horse theft. When the prisoner promised to give them a check for $125.00 on his Kansas Bank, he was promised his freedom. As soon as the check was drawn the committee put the noose around his neck and hung him to his own wagon tongue. Two of the committeemen were held in Federal Court in Dallas, Howe said, but were later released. "The Vigilance Committee got worse then than the criminals who were giving them their trouble," Howe concluded in his Memoirs, written in 1938.

When Billy Olive failed to cast his lot with the Scranage gang, his goose was cooked. Billy was an individualist and preferred to exercise his own hates according to his own best tastes. Once he was brought before "Judge" Chase's court to answer for taking a laprobe out of a buggy and putting it in Charley Tracy's privy. Billy disliked Tracy, as did the committee. He told the court he hoped by doing this mean act that he would get Tracy in trouble. Billy was ordered to leave Beaver City or stop stealing—and the court knew that Billy and Lengthy lived by their beef thefts, for the committee members bought their beef from the boys!

Billy had a bellyful of the "Committee" by this time and was ready to break someone's head. He pulled out his two six-shooters, took the judge off the bench and walked him to Jack Garvey's saloon where he ordered two drinks. The judge said he didn't drink, so Billy promptly made him drink *both* servings. The fat

112

judge, who wore white chinwhiskers like the fleece of an Angora goat, was white with rage. Billy then told the judge and the rest that whenever they needed him again, he would be "right at home in my soddy." When Chase made his final call for Billy, it was through the barrel of another man's gun.

Two men had previously been slain by the committee, acting as always "in the interest of peace and good order." They were O. P. Bennett, a businessman, and Frank Thompson, another land chisler and gambler, but a man who operated free of the Scranage committee. Oliver M. Nelson in his book manuscript, *A Little Bit of the West and No Man's Land*, a transcription of which is in the author's library, tells of this event and other sordid affairs while he lived in No Man's Land and bucked up against the Scranage committee.

Nelson was then about 25 years of age, thin, wiry, rawhide-tough. He had been a cowboy and range cook on the T5 ranch, had freighted and made his way on the frontier since he was sixteen. He possessed a calm, good sense that made him a leader in any group with which he associated. His strongest characteristic, one of which he retained to his death, at age 96, was his absolute independence. Nelson had a rule to be beholden to no man, and his own strong and calm self-assurance was the fruit of this self-discipline. He was a non-drinker and avoided the dance hall women of his time, yet he was always amused and sympathetic to the antics and follies of the cowboys around him. He never preached to them, but counseled moderation where they would listen. Nelson never married. He attributed his failure to marry to the fact that he cared for his parents until his father was past 50 years of age, a strong man and quite able, had he so desired, to provide for himself and Oliver's mother. But the father preferred to let the son bear his burden.

Oliver Nelson, his brother Harry and a friend, Jim Staton, took claims on Palo Duro Creek, southwest of Grand Valley, George Scranage's town. To the northwest of Oliver's claim was the Hardesty Brothers ranch and the sod town of Old Hardesty, on the Coldwater and Beaver confluence. Billy Bailey and Joe Cruse, former Scranage men, now ran the saloon at Hardesty.

113

Oliver cut hay for Hardesty, earning enough cash money to keep himself in grub on his claim. He found other odd jobs, cutting posts, shooting wolves, and quarrying a magnesia type stone which the settlers used for building. He and his brothers and friend dug wells, planted a few acres of crops and garden vegetables, but mostly "just waited to sell their claims." Since no government existed in No Man's Land, the young men held their claims simply by "living on them." There were few buyers for that land, and it was not long until Oliver Nelson's trail crossed that of George Scranage, the land shark, and his "Committeemen."

George Scranage had a clouded past. He was said to be from "Idaho." But his deals with an Ohio riverboat captain by the name of A. J. McAllister seem to point out Ohio as a former stomping ground. The two men engaged in exploiting other men's ignorance by "selling" them town lots and farm lands in the Neutral Strip. Scranage had come to the area from Dodge City on the Dodge-Fort Elliott stage. He set himself up at Beaver City as a man of means and entered the real estate business. It was not long until he had gathered around himself an assortment of men anxious to do anything to make a living without working.

Scranage plowed furrows here and there in rectangular patterns and set these plots aside as "town lots." Chase, Overstreet and others followed suit, claiming these to be town lots "owned" by themselves. These lines, of course, proved nothing and their "ownership" of lots was backed up by only the jawbone and jackass nerve of the men who claimed them.

Among those who supported Scranage's nonsense about "property ownership" were such men as Addison Mundell, a rough and uncouth fellow about whom little was known but whom they soon made "marshal" of Beaver City. Another was Mundell's partner, L. N. (Big Mack) McIntosh, who weighed 250 pounds and threw his gross weight on the side of Scranage. W. J. Klein, Scranage's brother-in-law, was a dependable supporter of the vigilante committee. Joe Hodge, a store owner and postmaster, served Scranage, as did Herbert Wright, Oliver McClung, W. M. Dow, Dr. J. A. Overstreet (no relation to the preacher), and others.

A semblance of respectability was given Scranage's organization

114

by inveigling Jim Lane, who ran the road ranch at the river crossing at Beaver City, to smile upon them. But Lane had had earlier experience in "town booming" and remained apart from Scranage and his men, though offering them no open opposition. So the *de facto,* though pure kangaroo, government of Beaver City lay in the hands of George Scranage.

So subtle was Scranage's operation in seizing power that lone wolf Billy Olive was led to sign a list of thirty-five petitioners who met at the new sod schoolhouse on October 26, 1886, and petitioned for a February 22, 1887, meeting at which time a Territorial Council would be elected and a Claim Board set up, to commence work immediately in clearing up claims and arranging for quit claim deeds and other property settlements. When it became apparent "whose" government it was to be, Billy, as well as others, got out. But this quasi-legal instrument to introduce the Cimarron Territory plan drew and held many honest settlers to it, despite its origin in greed and selfishness. And this body of honest citizens was able to direct, after a fashion, the plan to more wholesome ends than its originators had intended.

George Scranage was not interested in Beaver City alone. And down on the Palo Duro Scranage's "Committeemen" soon called on Oliver Nelson and explained to the fresh young settler just how he was expected to vote and to act while in the Strip. The independent Nelson was bristling when they left. Later, Nelson was present when the townsmen, O. P. Bennett, a merchant, and Frank Thompson, another land shark and gambler, were "executed" by Scranage's committeemen.

The actual bullets that killed Bennett and Thompson were fired by Mundell, Hodge, McIntosh, Wright, and a fifth committeeman upon whom writers disagree. Some claimed he was Klein, Scranage's son-in-law; some say he was Lee Harlan, a former Dodge law man; Mundell, when giving his account of the murders nearly two years later to the *New York Sun* reporter, J. R. Spears, fastened the guilt on the dead Billy Olive—who the committeemen themselves had killed six months earlier! Billy was not alive to speak for himself, and as the French proverb says, *"The Absent and the Dead are always in the wrong."*

Every committeeman present was required to fire into the bodies of Bennett and Thompson to seal lips forever about the matter, thus twenty-three holes were counted in the crippled gambler's body and half again as many in Bennett's.

A whitewash in the form of a coroner's inquest followed. It was signed by a picked group (Chase, Wright, Dr. J. A. Overstreet, etc.) among whom were some who played a part in the affair. The bodies were interred upon the crest of the high hill southwest of Beaver, marked only by plain limestone slabs. The Rev. R. M. Overstreet preached the funeral sermon to the handful of Scranage men who, alone, were allowed to accompany the corpses on the wagon to the graveyard. Using the passages from the Eighth and Twenty-third verses of the Ninety-fourth Psalm he warned:

> Understand, ye brutish among the people; and ye fools, when will ye be wise?
>
> And He shall bring upon them their own iniquity and shall cut them off in their own wickedness; yea, the Lord our God shall cut them off.

After the funeral, Overstreet confided to Judge Chase, "We will mold public opinion, Judge, and let the young men do the work."

Oliver Nelson, in Beaver City the day of the funeral, was told by Mundell to stay out of the funeral cortege, which consisted of a pair of oxen with five-foot horns pulling the wagon upon which were stacked the two pine coffins, and five guards with rifles, walking, leading a handful of Scranage supporters. "We'll bury you on top of the boxes," Mundell warned the young man. A deep disgust at the whole shameful performance filled Nelson.

A cowboy friend, "Red" Norton, told Nelson that day, "It's the coldest-blooded murder I ever saw, Ollie, an' I've been in Hays, in Dodge and in Caldwell. But I never saw anything worse than the killing of these two men by this mob."

Oliver made his own quiet investigation of the affair. He found it had been the plan of the committee to kill several more men, including Charley Tracy who ran the feed yard; Pat Tracy, Charley's younger brother; Norton, the livery man; a young man

116

staying at the widow King's sod hotel—and possibly Billy Olive, who was now high on their list.

Nelson, now realizing the danger in holding a claim that lay under the eyes of the greedy Scranage, worried about his vulnerable position. Scranage was exacting tribute from all the squatters in the Beaver valley, and fealty to him was one method of payment in a land that was practically without means of cash income. Nelson soon found, to his relief, that the Hardesty cowboys despised the Scranage committeemen, but Colonel Hardesty was having enough trouble of his own holding range to take sides in the land war. The settlers, for the most part, were a weak lot, unaccustomed to the sort of gun-fighting to be expected from such bully-boys as McIntosh, Mundell, Klein, and the rest.

One night when Oliver and his brother Harry returned from a trip to Dodge where they had taken two wagonloads of buffalo bones and horns, they found two visitors at Oliver's shack. One was a neighbor, Sol Bigham, friend of the Nelsons, the other was a strapping big man, middle-aged, by the name of Warren Park.

"This place was abandoned and I've taken official possession, backed by The Committee," Park told them, his attitude very officious. Oliver meditated but refused to be buffaloed by the older man.

"I don't believe it," Oliver countered. "Get your Committee." Park left at once for Grand Valley, where Scranage was staying. He was riled and mean when he left. Oliver's friend Bigham now spoke to him.

"There's a woman with a child camped in your cabin, Ollie. She's no kin to Park, and the Committeemen ordered her to get out so Park could move in." Oliver investigated. The woman and child were there, all right. She told how her husband had gone to Beaver for supplies. They were looking for land to locate on. Park arrived after her husband left, she said, and claimed the shack she was finding refuge in. He said it belonged to Scranage, the woman told Oliver.

"Lady," Oliver told her. "I own this cabin. We built it last year. I've never abandoned it. If you want to stay here, you're welcome. You can stay here until your husband fixes you a place to go to.

Don't worry, all we ask is that we may come in if a bad storm comes up." The woman readily agreed to Oliver's offer.

In a day or two, Park returned. He was brusk. Scranage had sent word for Oliver to vacate at once, Park said. Then Park explained why he though Oliver should vacate and relinquish the claim to him. Park said he had met Scranage on the train when he came in to Dodge from the east. Scranage soon learned that Park had $250 on him in cash money with which to buy land. Scranage warned Park not to enter No Man's Land with so much cash on his person. He told Park he would give him title to a fine claim "with a good house and well on it and some land broken up for farming." It was Oliver's claim Scranage had in mind, never thinking for a moment but what Oliver Nelson would run from his "Committeemen" when they called. So Park paid Scranage the $250 he carried.

Nelson whistled at Park's proposition and at the effrontery of the land shark. But he only made Park a counter proposal at the time, knowing that the elder man had been bamboozled by Scranage and wanting no trouble.

"Dad," he said to Park, "there is some good land just west of here. Now George Scranage has foxed you, no matter how highly you may regard him. But if you'll let me, I'll show you this good land that no one has yet claimed. And I'll help you fix yourself a house and there's creek water close by. What do you say?"

Park agreed, somewhat reluctantly. He still could not believe Scranage was a crook. So Oliver helped Park get settled on his claim and hoped that the big fellow would become neighborly. But it was no use.

Nelson then started a campaign to get more settlers on nearby land, hoping that by winning greater numbers to his cause than Scranage could muster, he might keep the committee at bay. Another brother, Delos Nelson, took a claim near Oliver's shanty. Within a few days the committeemen posted a notice on his door:

LEAVE IN 24 HOURS OR SUFFER THE CONSEQUENCES.
THE COMMITTEE.

Delos stayed. The three brothers, Oliver, Harry, and Delos Nelson, dug rifle pits fifty yards away from Oliver's shack and spent their nights there, awaiting an attack by Scranage's vigilantes which they knew would come at night if at all. Strangely enough, notification soon came from Beaver City headquarters that the three brothers could stay for a while. The Nelson boys breathed easier.

Another settler, Daum, lived nearby. Park stole some property from Daum. In the settlement, Park got his hip filled with buckshot from Daum's double barreled shotgun. As a result of this fracas, Daum was called on by the committeemen and ordered to Grand Valley to attend a "hearing." Daum consulted with Oliver and his brothers and they advised him to go without causing trouble. But when the committeemen called to get him and Oliver examined their wagon, he found it loaded with seventeen rifles and shotguns and a hanging rope, with the noose already tied. So he advised Daum not to go.

"This is a mob of murderers," he said, "a lynch mob—not a group of law enforcement officers."

So Daum stayed away, but Oliver went along to represent Daum, taking Harry and Delos, both well-armed, and Jim Staton and a couple of other friendly settlers with them to back their play. At the Sutton soddy in Grand Valley the two groups met.

Scranage was not there but Davis, the head committeeman, described by Nelson as "a tall, red-muzzled puke," started to take charge. He was backed by two other hard cases known locally as Johnson and Buck.

The two groups came to no agreement about handing Daum over for trial, for Oliver knew the settler would get a death sentence. The meeting broke up and Oliver and Staton rode on over to the Hardesty cow camp where Tom Hungate, a good friend of the Nelsons, was boss. Daum was there ahead of them, anxious to hear the verdict.

They told Daum what had happened, then ate a late supper with the cowboys. As dark fell, Hungate was called out of the ranch house and handed a note from the committee. It was for Daum and read:

LEAVE THE COUNTRY IN 24 HOURS OR SUFFER THE CONSEQUENCES.

THE COMMITTEE.

Daum was now really scared, ready to leave, but afraid he would be bushwhacked while returning to his shack. There were just twelve Hardesty cowboys at the camp that night, including Hungate, the foreman, and the cook. One tall Texas cowboy canvassed the opinion of the group, then came over to Oliver and Daum with an expression from the Hardesty men.

"Every gun in this camp is fo' youh defense," he told the settlers. His voice was soft, but his demeanor was that of a man who meant business. The other cowboys nodded and Tom Hungate, though non-committal, gave them a broad wink.

About an hour later Oliver and a settler Barnett, accompanied by Staton, left for their claims. A mile southeast of the Hardesty camp they came upon Scranage's committeemen lying in the tall bluestem grass in a hollow along the trail, cocking and uncocking their rifles.

"Which one of you men is Daum?" the leader asked.

"Daum is not along with us," Oliver quickly replied, identifying his companions.

The committeemen let them pass, largely, Nelson thought, because of the presence of Barnett who was paying tribute to the vigilantes every time he was asked for something, though he didn't like it a bit.

The following morning Tom Hungate came over and offered to mediate the dispute for Daum. They agreed to let him act for Daum and all rode over to see the red-bearded committee leader—Davis they had learned was his name. After a short meeting in the yard, during which at one point, Davis' wife handed a six-shooter to their son who placed it in his father's belt, the two groups came to an uneasy truce. Daum, Hungate pointed out, had been a trouble maker. So was Park. Hungate promised to purchase some feed for the Hardesty cattle from Davis and offered him an

120

WRIGHT, BEVERLEY & CO.,

DEALERS IN

GENERAL MERCHANDISE.

Sold to *C & C. C. Co.*   Dodge City, Kansas   *Aug, 27th*   188*3*

100	OK. Flour		4	00
100	B Bacon	15	15	00
20	Arb Coffee	17	3	40
1 - 5 Gal Pickells			3	25
50	Potatoes			85
1/2 Bu Onions			1	00
1 Gal Oil				25
1 Case Corn			3	50
1 " Tomatoes			3	50
25 Currants			2	50
25 Prunes			2	75
2 Sk Salt				20
5 Soap				30
1/4 Gal Oil Castor				50
12 Rope	15		1	80	$42 80

STATEMENT OF CHARGES FROM
WRIGHT, BEVERLEY & CO

DODGE CITY, KANS.
TO
CIMARRON AND CROOKED CREEK CATTLE COMPANY
August 27, 1883

This old Statement, reproduced above by photo-stat (slightly retouched to bring out letters and numerals) shows the value of food items as sold to the original Crooked L ranch, headquarters on Crooked Creek, southwest of Dodge City. Dodge was at its peak as supply point for the southwest cattle range at this time.—*Document courtesy E. W. McNaghten, Crooked L Ranch.*

BENJAMIN F. HODGES ? - 1929

Ben Hodges was a notorious deadbeat, cattle thief and general high-binder in his days at Dodge City. Still, he was generally liked and put up with in a community that enjoyed roistering and needed men like Ben to give them some action and entertainment. *Photos from R. E. Eagan, Dodge City.*

EXHIBIT OF DEMAND

The "flush" days of the late 1870's and early 1880's were over for Ben Hodges by 1899 when he made this modest claim against the estate of the deceased widow of the cattleman, Hi Collar, for $2.00 for "one day's work driving Mrs. Jennie Collar down to Ford City on or about the month of December, 1898."

Men of the West

Ham Bell-Pioneer—

He came to Dodge City with the railroad in 74. Started his own business at 91 is in his store every day. For 70 years a business and Civic leader. During the 80's his White Elephant stable was the club room of the ranchers and starting point for the Homesteaders. A peace officer 36 years 12 of them as U.S. Marshall and one of Dodge City's most popular Mayors.

HAMILTON B. (HAM) BELL

A U.S. Marshal and peace officer for 36 years at Dodge City, Ham Bell was one of Dodge City's best-known citizens. For 70 years he was a respected Dodge citizen and merchant, his White Elephant Stable the club room for scores of Texas drovers and cowboys who brought trail herds into Dodge. The stable is shown in the picture. *Photo courtesy of Boot Hill Museum, Dodge City.*

Left to Right: Col. Jack Hardesty, cowman; his dog, Tick, who always accompanied Hardesty on the streets of Dodge City; Frank Chapman, cowman, buffalo hunter, Indian trader.

Chapman and his partner John F. Tuttle, a Co. I, 2nd Michigan Cavalryman of the Civil War, ranched south of Dodge and had the Chapman-Tuttle Trail named after their Road Ranch on the buffalo hide trail.—*Photo from the Original Robert E. Eagan Collection, Dodge City.*

123

R. W. Day, pioneer photographer, titled this picture "A Son of the Plains." It was well-captioned, for the young man in the photo has been identified as Jimmy Daicy, son of John Daicy who ranched about ten miles west of the Custer T Circle Ranch on the Cimarron River, northwest of Liberal, Kansas. Daicy, Sr. once ranched on Texaquite Creek, north of the 101 ranch. *Photo by R. W. Day, Doby, Kansas.*

THE MILLS AND GARVEY SALOON, BEAVER CITY, NO MAN'S LAND, CIRCA 1887.

Billy Olive and his friend Lengthy Halford frequented the Mills-Garvey saloon during Billy's stay in Beaver City in 1887. The late Ban Kinder, Beaver pioneer is the bartender in the photo. *Photo courtesy the late Ban Kinder, Beaver, Okla.*

Beaver City Residents about 1887. Joe Hodge, the postmaster and general store operator, is shown before his place of business with Big Mack McIntosh and other members of the Beaver City Vigilantes. Hodge, O. G. Chase, "Big Mack," Herb Wright, W. J. Klein and others "executed" the storekeeper, O. M. Bennett and Frank Thompson, a gambler and townlot speculator and later arranged for the bushwhacking of Billy Olive, by the saloonkeeper, Henderson and another man whom some say was Joe Hodge. *Photo courtesy the late Ban Kinder, Beaver, Oklahoma.*

Group at Rock Island Hotel, Liberal, Kansas, circa 1889-90. L to R: J. U. Shade, founder of Shade's Well, and Livestock Agent for the Rock Island R.R.; Myra McDermott, daughter of hotel proprietor; Will Lipscomb; Olive Lipscomb (seated); Mamie Roarke (small girl); Mrs. Billy Newhouse, nee Florence Fouts; Mrs. Webb, hotel guest (seated); Dave Jones, Rock Island Clerk; Mamie Hood; Belle Holloway; Mrs. B. L. Lemert, nee Betty Smith, seated; Tom McDermott, hotel proprietor; Lee Latty, Rock Island Clerk. It was at McDermott's Dining Room, in this hotel, where the "coats on" policy was brought to an end by Fishtail-slicker-wearing cowboys. *Photo courtesy Maurine Tate, Liberal, Kansas.*

Union soldier, Indian fighter and scout, buffalo hunter, freighter, road ranch operator, participant in the "run into Oklahoma," 1889, George W. Brown left some of the best written accounts of the pioneer days in southwest Kansas, the Neutral Strip and eastern Colorado. *Photo courtesy The Kansas State Historical Society.*

D. M. Frost was editor of the *Dodge City Times*, Oct. 14, 1876. Later edited the *Dodge City Globe* in 1878. He was a friend of the cattlemen and was one of the enumerators of the Dodge City census of 1880, W. C. Shinn being the other enumerator. *Photo from the original Robert E. Eagan Collection.*

COL. RICHARD J. (JACK) HARDESTY, Dodge City cattleman, 1833-1910. Col. Hardesty and a brother owned and operated ranches in southeast Colorado, the Neutral Strip and southwest Kansas. Later, after the big storms of 1885-86 they moved their operations to Montana range. *Photo from the Original Robert E. Eagan Collection, Dodge City.*

Oliver M. Nelson, 1861-1957, came to Kansas and the Cherokee Strip as a boy of 16. He was a cow camp cook on the T5, a cowboy, a freighter, a stage "Jack," a squatter on land in No Man's Land. When the Cherokee Strip was opened for settlement he made the run and claimed a fine piece of land near Hennessey, Oklahoma. *Photo courtesy the late O. M. Nelson.*

Henry H. Raymond
Taken in the early
1900's. Arrived at
Dodge City in 1872
with Masterson bro
-thers,Bat,Jim & Ed.

Henry H. Raymond, 1847-1936, came to Dodge with the earliest buffalo hunters. He was a close personal friend of the Masterson family, living at Sedgwick, Kansas, where they lived. Raymond was the only man to answer the call to Dodge City of the old timers who came in 1872, at the 1935 Ham Bell Picnic. He was then 88 years old. His Diary, which he kept in 1873-4, tells of his trips with the Masterson boys, Bat, Jim and Ed across the plains, hunting buffalo. *Photos courtesy the Original Robert E. Eagan Collection, Dodge City.*

D. Welborn (Doc) Barton, was the first of the Texas Trail men to arrive at Dodge City and the last to leave. Barton spent his lifetime as a cattleman and lawman, remaining in Kansas after the other Texas men returned. *Photo courtesy the Original Robert Eagan Collection, Dodge City.*

The above photo of "Frenchy" McCormick, the Tascosa dance hall girl, was taken when she was 16 or 18 years old. "Frenchy" married Mickey McCormick, the Tascosa gambler. She was "The Last of the Girls of the Golden West," and is buried beside Mickey in the old Romero Cemetery at Tascosa. *Photo from an old newspaper.*

The late Bernard Lemert, age 87 when picture was taken on Crooked L Ranch, Meade County, Kansas. Lemert was foreman of the Sharp's Creek operation of the Crooked L Ranch in the 1889-1895 period. Astride the horse is E. W. McNaghten, Hutchinson, Kansas, present co-owner of the Crooked L holdings on Crooked Creek in Kansas. *Photo by author.*

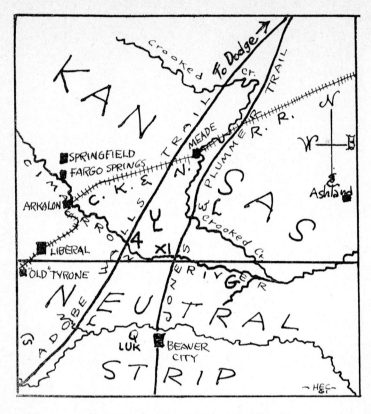

ARRIVAL OF THE RAILROAD

In the spring of 1887 the Chicago, Kansas & Nebraska railway survey crossed Meade County, Kansas, and the rails followed that summer and fall. It appeared to many that the road would head directly west to the coal fields at Trinidad, Colorado, and in doing so pass directly through Springfield or Fargo Springs, Kansas, on the Cimarron river. Instead, the railroad headed southwest, crossed the Cimarron at a point that soon became the vital cattle-shipping town of Arkalon (now a ghost site). The road then wound its way out of the Cimarron River valley and built southwest into "No Man's Land." By 1888, Liberal, Kansas, became end-of-track—and supply point for the ranches of the Southwest Cattle Range. The railroad got the big Texas and Neutral Strip cattle hauls.

exceptionally good price for it. The feed purchase offer was the clincher, and a period of peace reigned for a few weeks.

Oliver's youngest brother, Charles Nelson, came out to Beaver City about that time and they had a long visit. Oliver then went down to Chiquita Creek and started cutting fence posts and hauling them to Grand Valley where he stacked nearly 2,000 posts in the Silverwood yard, letting Silverwood and his wife who operated a grocery store, earn a small commission selling them. It was May, 1888. The railroad had now built out to Liberal, Kansas, and Scranage and his men took enough teams and wagons—and armed men—to move a carload of barbed wire which he had ordered and which now stood on the siding by the tent which served as station house until an empty boxcar could be located there.

After the railway car was opened for inspection, Scranage and the agent walked back to the hotel "bank," where Scranage was to make out a draft for the wire. The land shark wasted all the time needed for his men to load the wire on to their wagons and get out of town, then he returned to the car, making some sort of an excuse to the agent. When they got back to the car men, teams, wagons— and wire!—were gone. Scranage got into his buggy.

"Them are all desperate men," he told the agent. "So I wouldn't advise you to follow them down into No Man's Land for you might never get back from that lawless land. I'll see if I can recover your wire or get the money back to you later." With that he departed.

Oliver Nelson learned of this transaction and he at once thought of his 2,000 posts lying out in the open yard at Silverwood's. He had also quarried a good amount of the "magnesia rock," at white, soft rock that hardened when uncovered and brought out into the air, and which the settlers used to some extent as a building stone. The rock was unguarded at the quarry site, northwest of his claim about four miles, waiting for buyers. Everyone knew that Oliver had grubbed it from the earth and sawed it into suitable blocks for building. So Oliver straddled his horse, Old Paint, and headed for Grand Valley.

He stopped first at Silverwood's place. Mrs. Silverwood was crying when he approached. "Oh, Mr. Nelson, I'm so sorry I didn't get to sell your posts, but Mr. Scranage came and took them.

When I tried to stop his men he abused me fearfully, telling me to get in the house or he would cause me real trouble."

Nelson looked at the woman, knew she was telling him the truth. It was just like Scranage, he thought, to bully a woman.

"Don't you worry, Mrs. Silverwood," Oliver told her, "I'll make Scranage come back here, return every post he stole and apologize to you." Oliver noted that his voice was so filled with emotion he could hardly get it out. As he rode away he was amazed at the commitment he had made, yet he knew he would fulfill every word of it if he lived. His usually friendly blue-grey eyes were now flashing like the case-hardened steel on the Colts .45 that dangled at his belt. He had one purpose now in life, a settlement with the little tyrant who had stolen his posts, stolen the railroad's wire, and abused a helpless woman.

Oliver was a planner. He didn't risk everything on the turn of one card. He understood the long chances he must play in dealing with Scranage, so he carefully thought about the best method of attacking an enemy many times more numerous than his own forces and better entrenched in the business of violence than he ever hoped to be. That Scranage would show the white feather when faced up to danger, Oliver couldn't depend upon. Yet he knew that any man who would bully a woman must have a yellow streak up his tailbone, whether it showed plainly or not. Upon this judgment he based his campaign.

Oliver rode directly across country to a place on the river bottom where he knew Scranage was directing a man who was plowing furrows to define a claim. A newly-erected soddy stood nearby, and as Scranage saw Oliver approach he darted inside the house. Oliver dismounted at the door and banged on the cedar boards with his fist.

"Come out, Scranage, I want to talk to you!" He purposely dropped the title of "Mister" which all in No Man's Land used in addressing Scranage.

"Don't you dare come in," Scranage called from within.

Nelson lifted the latch, kicked the door open, and came inside, his six-shooter in his hand. As he stepped within, the land shark dropped a revolver to the floor at his feet.

"No," Scranage said, backing away from the gun.

Oliver paid no more attention to the gun on the floor. He had known that a Scranage man had once killed a settler who reached for a pistol dropped on the floor in just such a manner, had shot him with a hide-away gun while the settler picked up an empty six-shooter. It was good to know about such a trick, Oliver thought to himself.

"Scranage," Nelson said coldly, "you stole my posts at Silverwood's place and you treated Mrs. Silverwood shamefully. All right. Now you can pay me 25c for each post you stole, which is just what I had offered them for sale. And you will march right back to Grand Valley tomorrow and apologize to Mrs. Silverwood for your meanness."

Scranage batted his eyes like a cornered coyote. "But how will I get the money?" he asked.

"Just like you got the posts," Oliver responded.

"You'll just have to go and take them up," the wily land shark proposed, challenging the lone settler to undo the work performed by thirty men over a period of a week.

"You have a good team," Oliver parried. "You go take them up—you set them!" Oliver was getting angrier by the minute. He realized that nothing short of fear would force the wily thief to act. So he stepped to within a foot of the land shark and said evenly. "Now I'll be honest with you for the last time, damn your old soul, and I'm going to see that you're honest for once in your life with me. I want eighty dollars from you—within ten days. How you get it is no concern of mine. Just *get it,* if you value your life! I'll collect the rest later."

Scranage said nothing more and Nelson left him standing in the darkened soddy, thinking, wondering if the young settler would cool off or would actually search him out and kill him for his theft.

Nine days later Scranage rode up to Oliver's claim shack and handed him three drafts, two for $20 each and one for $40. Oliver promptly loaded a wagon with bones and some good buffalo horns to sell and started for Englewood. At Englewood he cashed the checks, found that he could not sell the horns so left them with friends to sell. Then he returned home. He had been gone five days.

When he opened the door of his shanty that evening he received the biggest surprise of his life. There was nothing within—dishes, table, chairs, bedclothes, rifle, stove, everything he had owned was gone. That night he slept in his wagon and the next morning drove over to his rock quarry. Again he was dismayed. There was not a cut rock at the place. He spent only a few minutes looking for "sign," the tracks that would tell him who had been there and stolen his rock. Then he touched up his team and drove up to Grand Valley to see if any of his posts had been returned. There was not a post on the place. Mrs. Silverwood, wringing her hands, told him that no Scranage man had returned a single post.

Oliver sat on his wagon seat in the Silverwood yard for a few minutes, collecting his thoughts. This, he knew, was the showdown. Scranage had called his hand while he was gone, had set his committmen and the compliant settlers upon him. Now they would be pressing him to leave the country for all time. Oliver realized that to act with force and violence might bring them all upon him, yet he realized that somehow he must act with decisiveness that would compel their respect and back them down. One man was no match for the entire Scranage complement of committeemen and servile settlers. His best hope lay in dealing with them separately and with skill, to cut each individual away from the whole of the Scranage apparatus. He had seen a dozen settlers driven off the land this way, one at a time. He had often felt that he should go with his puny strength to help them stay, to fight back. But it was a time and place where each man was independent and lived his own life, not horning in on the affairs of others. And the Scranage gang controlled many of the towns and had sympathizers on some of the surrounding claims.

To the small squatters, Scranage appeared to be an important man with heavy finance behind him. It was said that he had influence reaching to Dodge City and beyond, to the financier J. V. Ellison in Cincinnati, Ohio, in fact. So it would be no simple matter, concluded Oliver Nelson, to cross a man who controlled such a powerful organization of men who were proved killers and who could make murder in the Neutral Strip appear to be done as law enforcement. But there was no turning back now. He must meet the crisis or leave the Neutral Strip like a whipped dog. And Oliver had long since elected to stay and fight.

On his visit to the quarry, he had noticed the imprint of a man's feet in the sandy area near the rocky face of the cliff where the rock was quarried. The footprints were enormous in size. There was only one man in the area whose feet were of that proportion and he was a mean one—Texas Jack, he was called. Jack was a close neighbor to Oliver, but a Scranage sympathizer. Oliver immediately set out for Jack's claim, a barren shack on the plains. When Oliver rode up Jack appeared through the doorway, stooping to get through without taking off his big, greasy felt hat. Jack peered at Oliver from beneath craggy eyebrows and tossed a huge wad of tobacco from his mouth at Oliver's feet as he swung down from the wagon seat. Oliver came to the point immediately, throwing the big Texan off stride.

"Wa'll you left," Jack explained his action in taking the stone which was piled behind his house. "In our talk we thought you'd gone forever, knowin' how Scranage don't care much for you anyhow." Texas Jack tried to leave the impression that the fight was Scranage's alone and that Oliver was on the wrong trail in fussing with him. But Oliver refused to have it that way.

"Look, Jack," he said grimly, bristling up against the big fellow like a banty rooster eyeing a turkey, "I'm here for one thing and one thing only. I want a quick settlement about the rock you stole and anything else you took from my shanty. Now you do what you think will help you to live the longest. I'm fixin' to shorten some lives."

Oliver stepped back on to the wagon, took the lines and headed his team for the claim of another settler, a Scranage sympathizer, Buck Twidale.

Buck sat in the front yard on a rock, sharpening the blade of a broadaxe with a whetstone. He was a rough-looking man in buckskins, fringed at the legs and with the sleeves cut out of the jacket. His hair was long and his eyes red, as though from drinking, or loss of sleep. Oliver never left the seat of the wagon but challenged the settler.

"Buck, you've been stealing my rock. I saw traces of it on the trail here and there's some inside your shack, no doubt, maybe some other property of mine. Now I haven't time to look for it. I'm here for a quick settlement, and not necessarily a peaceful one. Get my rock and other property back to my shack at once or prepare yourself for a new life. That's all." Oliver didn't even wait for an answer but slapped the horses with the lines and wheeled out of the yard.

From Buck's, Oliver continued his rounds to the claims of settlers and supporters of Scranage whom he suspected of joining in the theft of his household goods. He knew he was accusing some who were innocent, but he knew that they would be soon putting their weight behind the return of his goods, rather than risk a fight with him for no reason. He wanted them to carry tales of a "showdown" to every corner of the area.

At Big Sam Edwards' shanty he ordered the settler to "Get the stuff back, Sam, or arm yourself for a shooting the next time you see me." Oliver knew the big man to be a coward, and he knew he would travel the length and breadth of the Strip trying to get others to help him stand off a Nelson attack.

From Edwards' place, Oliver rode to the village of Fulton. Though it was early afternoon and he had been visiting the community only since early morning, the news was starting to get around. Eva Cummings, 18, a friend of Oliver's, was the postmistress who relayed the gossip in the Fulton settlement and Oliver went there first.

"They say they got rid of you, Ollie," she laughed at the young settler when he entered the store. "They say they led you out of town on a jackass and that you'd never be back again." She was teasing, and Oliver knew it. But it irked him. Eva admired Oliver, and she knew him to be a spunky young man.

"Who told you that fib?" Oliver asked her.

"Oh, some of the Scranage men." Eva now lowered her voice, for another man had entered the store.

Oliver left and called at Jim Mitchell's house where he borrowed Mitchell's double barreled shotgun.

"Please be careful, Ollie," Mrs. Mitchell warned. She too had heard of the fight Nelson had launched on Scranage. At another friend's place Oliver loaded the shotgun with Blue Whistlers and borrowed a Long Tom cap and ball rifle to add to the Spencer rifle and six-shooter he already had along. He said goodbye to this neighbor, Jake Ingold, and rode to the Hardesty cow camp, where he found his paint horse in the corral.

"We picked him up for you, Ol', so you would have something to ride when you got back," Tom Hungate told him. "Seein' as how the rascals stole you out of house and home when you left, guess you may need him." Oliver tied the saddlehorse to the end-gate of the wagon and threw his saddle and blanket into the wagon. Then he talked confidentially with the ranch foreman.

"Tom, I may not get this job done, but I'm going to try. If anything happens to me, you claim my property and hold it until my brothers get here. Also see that these long guns get back to their owners. You can keep my forty-five for yourself. It's a pretty good gun."

The Hardesty foreman listened soberly to Nelson, for he knew the danger Nelson faced.

That night Oliver slept in his empty claim shack for what he thought might be his last night in No Man's Land. He wished his brothers were not all gone at the same time, Harry to marry the girl he had met at Desperado, Charles working on a cattle ranch in Texas, Delos to God knew where, and George back at Caldwell. They had heard rumors of a land opening to be held in Oklahoma soon, and Oliver had hoped the whole family might pack down that way and file on some decent farm land. Now here he was, alone, facing the greatest personal crisis of his life, and not a member of his tribe to back his play.

Oliver slept little that night, but he felt better with a clear-cut decison made and with the countryside aware of his challenge of Scranage and his organization. His position, he felt, would eventually draw the more timorous settlers to him, even though they might not appear openly. If he could survive the first few days of his campaign, he felt that outside help would somehow come to aid him—perhaps from the Hardesty camp or other cattlemen on the Beaver who had never accepted Scranage's ideas. But he knew that in the final accounting, it would be up to him to make the first assault on the unchallenged domain of George Scranage and the vigilantes.

Early the next morning Oliver scratched together some bread, bacon, and coffee. While he was eating Big Sam Edwards drew up to his door on a wagon, halooing for attention. Oliver stepped cautiously to the doorway, pulling down the double barrel shotgun on Edwards.

"Don't shoot, Nelson!" Edwards called out nervously. Then Sam unburdened himself. He had come to make his peace with Oliver, since the Hardesty cowboys had carried the news of Oliver's angry challenge to every shanty and ranch on the Beaver. "Nelson will shoot on sight any man who has robbed him," the cowboys told the settlers. "This includes Scranage, Big Mack, Mundell, and the rest," Tom Hungate had told the cowboys what to say. "Ol Nelson is on a rampage and so anyone wanting a peaceful settlement better see him tomorrow," the news went out.

It took only a few minutes for Nelson and Edwards to conclude their grievances, Edwards agreeing to go to the quarry and saw out and pile an equal amount of rock taken by him and delivered to Scranage. Nelson then set out to find George Scranage, armed to the teeth and angry as a bogged longhorn cow.

Coming to a line of fence Scranage had thrown up across a recently used trail, Oliver stepped off his horse, took out his wire-clippers, and cut a gaping hole in Scranage's new fence. Archie Picks, a Scranage man, plowing nearby with a pair of oxen with four-foot horns, came over to stop Oliver from crossing the field.

"You hunting trouble?" Oliver asked, drawing his six-shooter and putting a bullet into the sod a few inches ahead of Archie's toes. Archie stopped, stepped back to let Oliver's horse pass.

"No, I'm not hunting a fight," Archie said.

"Then you just keep on whalin' them bulls," Nelson advised the settler. "I'll take up my business with your boss, not you."

Passing Texas Jack's place on the way, Nelson scribbled a note and hung it on Jack's door. It read:

YOU BE AT HOME WEDNESDAY, JACK, AND PAY ME FOR MY ROCK WORK OR I'LL TAKE THE ROCK OUT OF THE WALLS OF YOUR HOUSE.

O. M. NELSON

At Buck's place, Oliver exchanged a few harsh words before the fellow promised to come by the quarry and work out the amount of his theft alongside the neighbor, Edwards. Farther on, at Billy Mitchell's claim, Nelson heard that Scranage had sent several of his best fighting men, among them Addison Mundell and Big Mack McIntosh, to stop the infuriated settler from wrecking Scranage's empire. "That'll be the end of me," Oliver thought to himself. But he couldn't show his doubts to others now, his course was set.

The following morning he rode up to Fulton, taking along the Long Tom rifle to shoot a wolf he had seen the evening before. A mile or so north he saw two riders going east and at an angle that would soon bisect the route he was taking. Dropping down behind a bank, Oliver studied the two. It was Tom Hungate and Big Mack McIntosh. They were riding toward Beaver City. Oliver quickly thought to himself, "Tom's help is better than to knock Mack out." So he let the Scranage lieutenant and gunfighter get away.

At the Fulton store and post office Eva Cummings greeted him. She leaned over the counter and laughed, then said confidentially to him. "The Beaver men won't come."

"What you mean, 'won't come?'" Oliver asked, "I've already seen one—Big Mack."

"He's ordered back," Eva told him. "The rest won't come. I know." Oliver was relieved. He headed at once for Scranage's headquarters at Grand Valley.

Scranage had a soddy at Grand Valley that he called his Western Land Office. From this point he penned such gems of advertising as the following, which appeared in the *Portsmouth* (Ohio) *Blade*:

CHEAP HOMES: McAllister and Scranage, locators of land in the Neutral Strip, Indian Territory, can give you the best situation and figures on land. See Captain A. J. McAllister on board the steamer *Louise*. Finest climate, best farms, purest water in the country. Titles clear and terms easy. McAllister and Scranage, Portsmouth, Ohio.

Scranage and McAllister could not, of course, give any sort of land title to property in the Neutral Strip. This fact was immediately recognized by Congressman Payson, (*Congressional Record*, July 25, 1888, Page 7, 546) when the Neutral Strip was before Congress for legislation; he remarked:

> Every man who publishes advertisements of that kind or is in any way connected with them is a thief and robber. It is an attempt on their part to secure from honest people of the country, under false pretenses, their hard-earned money.

Oliver Nelson was well-acquainted with these facts and with the dishonest practices of the Scranage committeemen. Furthermore, he knew the danger in opposing the land shark. Bennett's and Thompson's deaths had been only too recent for Oliver to forget, and he saw how the evil deed was whitewashed with a covering of legality, hypocrisy, and respectability. Now, as he paused in front of the Scranage office, he was determined to reach a final settlement, come what would to himself, for he had come armed, both morally and physically.

Scranage stood before the building as Oliver rode up, raking some grass seed into the sandy soil. Observing Nelson coming down the street, he dropped his rake and started for the doorway, then changed his mind and turned to face the irate settler. Oliver dismounted deliberately, dropped the reins, and motioned for Scranage to follow him behind the soddy, away from the spectators who stood at the front of the building.

When they reached the rear, Scranage started talking. "Nelson," he said, "you've been a thorn in my side ever since you come to the country. And you've cost me a heap of money. Now I thought I got rid of you when I gave you that eighty dollars. But you won't be bothering me much longer, I'll see to that. I had enemies at

Beaver. Now everyone's my friend. There was Thompson and Bennett—you remember them? You remember what happened to them? Well, I did that—not me personally, but my money and influence. Now if you want to end up like that, you just keep bothering me. . ." Scranage continued in monologue, along the same line, for several minutes. Finally he stopped, turned on his heel as though to leave. Oliver then spoke up, his voice showing his emotion, try as he did to conceal it.

"Are you through now? If you are, I want to talk."

"I'm through *talking*, yes," Scranage said. "But I'm not through with you, yet." He started away again, but Nelson's next words stopped him short.

"You point them eyes of yours at me, you old son-of-a-bitch, or I'll bust them both wide open. Now I came here for a knock-down, drag-out fight with you and all your damned tribe and I don't intend to leave without a settlement. I'm taking that sorrel mare of yours as a first payment. Call it damages if you prefer. But I'm also collecting every pound of that rock I dug and sawed and that you thieves stole while I was gone. I want my posts paid for. What's more I want every piece of my household goods put back or by God there'll be a dozen dead Scranage thieves sleeping under the sod within the week. Furthermore, I'll shoot on sight any Scranage man I catch on my property, including you, who comes there without my permission."

Scranage's hand twitched in his pocket, but Nelson's blazing eyes and his hand resting on his Colts 45 stopped any action he may have considered. Nelson's talk had perceptibly cooled the land shark's anger.

"All right," Scranage said. "Take the damned mare if it will satisfy you. Parks is plowing with her now."

Oliver made a few more caustic remarks, backed away to where his horse grazed, then keeping the horse between himself and Scranage led the animal away about eighty feet before mounting. He tipped his hat to the astounded spectators who had overheard much of the talk, then rode away.

In the meadow, Warren Park was unhitching the team from the

plow when Oliver rode up. Oliver sat his horse and told the settler what he wanted, and the deal made with Scranage.

"You're a God damned liar," Park said. "Why George Scranage is a regular wildcat and would have shot you in a minute had you talked that way to him. You'll take this mare over my dead body!"

Oliver had anticipated such a response from the big fellow. As he rode up he had noted that Parks had left the wagon tongue braced up through the ring of the neckyoke. Now he reached down from his horse, took the neckyoke like a baseball bat and swung hard at Park's head. The metal clip and ring at the end of the neckyoke hit Parks behind the ear, sending him reeling to the ground where he lay half conscious, the blood running from his head.

"All right, if that's the way you want it," Oliver said, dismounting and pulling the harness from the mare. He had looped his lariat around her throat and nose into a hackmore by the time Parks regained his feet. Parks staggered toward him, saying "I'm sick." Oliver watched the big man closely, knowing how well he would like to get his hands on Oliver's throat. As Parks came closer, Oliver again picked up the neckyoke.

"All right, Dad, I'll help you get in the wagon where you can lay down," he said, waving the neckyoke at the settler threateningly. Parks scrambled into the wagon with the agility of a squirrel.

"Now you think Scranage is such a wildcat, you just tell him who put that lump on your head—and tell Big Mack and Mundell, too!" Oliver mounted and left, practically dragging the mare behind him. Out of sight of Parks he changed mounts and rode east through the night, putting the mare in the D Cross pasture the next morning, safe from Scranage's thieving hands.

Back at Fulton two days later, Nelson walked in to the post office. Eva was leaning over the counter, talking to two customers. When they left Oliver asked, "Is there any news?"

"What do you call news?" Eva teased. She, like all others along the Beaver River, had heard of Oliver's tough talk to Scranage and the beating given Parks.

"Is anyone coming from Beaver City?" he asked her, quietly.

"I told you they wouldn't come," she said. A Mrs. Burns, a

friend of Oliver's, came in the store. She handed Oliver a box of .45 cartridges and paid for them. "Take these, Ollie, you may need them," she offered. Oliver asked her if she had any news of the committeemen from Beaver coming up the river.

"There's talk, that's all," she said. "But there's lots of that."

The following day Oliver was surprised and pleased when brother Charles appeared. Oliver had made no appeal to his brothers for help, but Charles had heard by the frontier grapevine of the trouble Oliver had encountered and had quit his job and come at once. The two went the next day to Grand Valley, going at once to Scranage's headquarters soddy. Taking a team and wagon, they immediately commenced loading the barbed wire piled at the rear of the soddy, the stolen railroad wire. Scranage soon appeared.

"I thought you settled with me once?" he said.

Oliver noted the inversion of the sentence. It was now "you settling with me." Oliver continued to press his luck. Stepping down from the wagon he faced Scranage.

"I did," Oliver answered. "Now I'm settling for Mrs. Silverwood, the Rosenbergs, Lem Moore, Charley Plymell, and others you've cheated or run out of the Strip!" Charles stood a few feet away, his hand on his revolver butt, eying two Scranage men who had walked up. Oliver had planned to take the barbed wire alone. Now he realized it had been an ambitious project, and he was grateful for Charles's presence.

When they had finished loading the wire, they pulled out to the west, to lead trackers off the trail. That night they doubled back, took a well-used trail where they could not be tracked through the dune sand and buried their wire in the Hardesty hay meadow, stacking hay over the spot.

Back at Oliver's cabin the next morning both were surprised when brother George rode in. Now Oliver was elated.

"We've got Scranage on the run now," he told George and Charles. "If you two will stay on a few more days to back my play, I'll settle his hash here in the Strip." The proposition pleased his brothers, and both agreed to stay.

Within the week other settlers commenced openly to rally to

the Nelson brothers' side. Backed by the opinion of the Hardesty cowboys and their foreman, Tom Hungate, the settlers decided on a party to celebrate their victory over the land shark and the committeemen and to make a show of force, at least the force of their opinion. Boyd, a popular town, was picked out as the point at which to celebrate, since it was about half way between Hardesty and Beaver and would show the committemen their power had receded, at least that far up the river.

The settlers and cowboys, their wives and daughters, danced until daybreak. When the dance ended that Saturday morning, every man came and shook Nelson's hand, complimenting him on his stand against Scranagism. "We're for you. . . We'll stand with you. . . Keep up the fight. . ." Oliver Nelson heard from nearly every mouth. Seventy years later, Nelson wrote:

> Before leaving Boyd, I believe I took hold of nearly every hand in the town.

No one has ever shown *why* George Scranage and the committeemen suddenly pulled out of No Man's Land. A few, of course, rushed to the opening of the Oklahoma Indian Lands. Some committeemen probably were among these. Charles and George Nelson went, staying at Beaver overnight. Scranage, at Beaver that same night, laid low. His team was stabled at the Norton barn. The following morning the fine team and the Nelson brothers were gone.

"I'll never see that team again," he told the widow King. "Those Nelsons are just a bunch of damned thieves."

But Scranage was wrong again. A few days later the team came back to the barn for feed. They had strayed and had been grazing near Beaver all the time, a settler told Scranage.

Scranage went back to Ohio, this time with a bone infection in his leg. He returned once, later, to Beaver and walked the streets on a cork leg. He tried to salvage something from his land speculations, but his power was broken, the committee dissolved, his hopes of a land empire gone with the hot south winds.

Oliver left later for the Oklahoma land rush, grabbed a claim, and was beaten out of it by a crooked lawyer. Later he made the rush into the Cherokee Strip, picked up a good claim near Hennessey. George and Charles worked on ranches from Texas to Montana, but Oliver elected to farm. Only once did he return to No Man's Land, this time to dig up the barbed wire in the Hardesty pasture. With it he fenced his property at Hennessey and there he lived, worked, and prospered for a half century or more, passing on to his reward at the age of ninety-six years at his home in Muskogee, still in full possession of his faculties and with a deep sense of honor, a great wisdom gathered over his long years and the independence that had been his outstanding characteristic for nearly a century on earth.

Nelson's struggle against Scranage had proved one thing, if nothing else. It had verified the expression used by Willis Peoples in his determined wolf hunt on Crooked Creek, that "One man with his mind made up is a majority."

To three social characteristics of his epoch, Oliver Nelson attributed the successful opening of the frontier by the pioneers. "The chief qualities we needed then are the same that are so sorely needed in government, in agriculture and in industry today," Nelson said. "Those qualities are *Honor, Industry* and *Economy*. Nothing Good or Great has ever been built without them."

Chapter VII

The Neutral Strip produced the most varied assortment of persons ever to assemble together, and what weren't produced in the Strip could be found in southwest Kansas. There was everything, literally, from Bootleggers to Benedicts in the new frontier community.

On Hog Creek, about 1885-86, there was a wide area between the banks and the bluffs along the stream where a ravine led down to the stream. In this area was a fine growth of timber, with much usable dead timber for firewood—or to keep a still heated up. Here, some young men built a well-concealed lean-to at the mouth of a cave, 40 feet by 80 feet in extent. And here they set up their still, with the coils cooled by the clear stream that gurgled down from springs above. This still soon became the source of supply for many of the towns in the Neutral Strip, for the liquor was tax-free, though it was bottled dynamite. Some of the stuff was hauled to Dodge, traded for cornmeal from which more of the fiery liquid was manufactured. The Kansas hypocrisy was at its greatest, and much of the booze was freighted north to Beer City, Garden City, and other points in southwest Kansas.

A cowboy once filled up on the liquid at the creek and rode in to Beaver City. There he bettered his condition at Jack Garvey's saloon. While he was inside, the boys on the street "highlifed" his horse, a practice that was considered particularly humorous in the old days. The puncher returned and mounted the fretting animal which bucked so hard the cowboy lost his hat. The boys on the street, real jaspers from the way it sounds, tossed the rider's hat into the town well. When the man finally got his horse under control and returned for his hat, they agreed to lower him into the well to recover it, at the end of the rope, in the bucket. The soak readily obliged and stepped into the bucket while the town jokers lowered away.

There was about seven feet of water in the well and after lowering him with the windlass they permitted him to soak in the bottom of the well, then brought him to the top, his hat firmly clenched in his hand.

Mounting his charger the cowpuncher touched him up with his spurs and dashed madly down Beaver's main street, past Jim Lane's road ranch to the Beaver River. As he hit the water they heard his voice come back to them on the wind.

"Farewell, Beaver, you old son-of-a-bitch!" he shouted. "You'll never see me again!"

And true to his words, Beaver didn't!

Lyman Savage, an old timer who knew as many stories about No Man's Land and its activities and people as any other resident, once told of the gang of horse thieves that headquartered for a while at Sodtown, about 1885. Their rendezvous was about two miles from Sodtown, which was two miles from the Texas line and a half mile west of the mouth of Coon Creek. Sodtown was the home of Al, Charley, and Lyman Parson, brothers who feuded with the town of Lockwood, promoted by a couple of Kansas boys, Chance Fish and Smith Ellis. There were about fifteen members of the horse thief ring, and they were led by the Chitwoods from Medicine Lodge, Jim and Kit.

One evening a vigilante committee from Kansas slipped into the Chitwood hangout on Coon Creek while the brothers were absent. They made Chitwood's mother prepare their supper, and had Bill Chitwood, another brother, serve it. They had stacked their arms in an adjoining room while they ate.

Bill Chitwood knew about when his brothers would return so slipped from the house and met them down the creek a ways, warning them of the committeemen at the house. The three Chitwoods then returned to their shack, got the drop on the committeemen, and after working their heads over with their own rifle butts sent them whimpering back to Kansas. Chitwood later came by Lyman Savage's house, offering the committeemen's guns for sale!

Later, Kit Chitwood was in a blizzard and froze his feet. The amputation left him a cripple. Once the Chitwoods were tried by Beaver City's committeemen, posing as law men. Only one of their number was found guilty, a man named Montgomery. Montgomery was placed on a cracker box, a rope around his neck tied to a wagon tongue. A committeeman kicked away the box and the man strangled to death. The Committee confiscated his team, wagon, and effects. The Chitwoods were ordered to leave that night, which they did, going to Texas.

B. E. (Medicine) Steadman, an old-timer of the Strip, added some information concerning the Chitwoods. Jim Chitwood, he said, once prevented a hanging committee from executing an old man named Fowler, whom they had accused of drunkenness in lieu of a better charge to rid the community of his opposition. When a committeeman, "Red" Wayne, said, "Let's string him up," Chitwood stepped up with his hand on his revolver and told the group, "You better not try unless you want trouble from me." His presence averted a tragedy, and the committee left.

Jim Chitwood seems to have had some Robin Hood qualities about him, and was once shot while laboring in another man's vineyard. They brought the doctor, Dr. Varden, blindfolded to Chitwood's hangout. The doctor was returned safely and was paid cash for his services. But he could never recall where he had been, so many times had they spun him around during the trip he had lost all sense of direction.

When Chitwood left No Man's Land, he first took his family to Texas, then he went to Idaho, later sending for them. He was elected sheriff of an Idaho county and made a good lawman. He shot a man over a woman there, but was exonerated for the act, so the story goes. "Chitwood and his family were no worse than the others in the Strip," said old Medicine Steadman.

George H. Healy and Frank D. Healy came out from Boston to Texas in 1878. Soon they were operating their KK ranch on the Beaver River, not far from the Chitwood hide-out. But they lost no livestock to the Chitwoods, so their relations remained amicable enough. Healy Brothers ranch was considered a gathering point for socials and dances in the early days of the Strip.

Once, when the Territorial Legislature had passed a declaration calling the Neutral Strip in fact free government range, Healy brothers invited everyone in the strip to a giant oyster supper at their place on the mouth of Cottonwood Creek. Though the invitations read "Mr. and Mrs. Healy request your presence. . ." it was a well-known fact that Mrs. Healy was, at the time, on a visit back east. Many attended and few thought anything of that fact, however, until later.

It so happened that Healy picked a night when old No Man's Land was to undergo one of its severest blizzards. The storm broke after about twenty-five couples had arrived. It was too late for them to return to their homes so the revelers stayed all night, dancing and enjoying themselves, though filled with anxiety about the storm.

The storm continued through the next day and night. The oysters gave out that night, the drinks by the following morning. Before the visitors could return home, the food had nearly given out. When the ranchers could get their horses dug out of the drifts and harnessed for the return trip, there was great concern for the big herds that ranged over the land. Cattle, they knew, had died by the thousands.

For many years afterward the event was known facetiously as "George Healy's Awfully Expensive Oyster Supper." How Frank Healy's name came not to be mentioned remains a mystery, for Healy Brothers also suffered great losses in the storm, and the party was as much his as his brother's.

George Healy later entered the mercantile business at Alpine, a boom town east of Beaver on Duck Pond Creek, where he also studied and practiced law. Frank served a term as sheriff of Beaver County when the job called for a good man to handle the job. The Healys are well-remembered in the old Neutral Strip to this day. They were good, sociable neighbors, good friends.

Among those persons who came to the southwest cattle range, moved across its vast panorama, and then disappeared from its scenes as quietly as they had come, were two young men who arrived at Dodge City one spring night in 1876 in a covered wagon pulled by two faithful horses they called Mustang and Cody. These

147

young men wore the raiment of the Benedictine Brotherhood and came from its headquarters at Atchison.

Fridolin Rosenfelder and Raymond Huber came to the wilderness of the plains to establish a monastery somewhere south of Dodge. At Dodge, the two met brother Andrew Allerman, who had arrived previously and had waited for their arrival at a nearby saloon, where he had sought shelter. Visiting cowboys proposed toasts to Brother Andrew and "set them up" to him on the bar. In an age and area when to refuse to drink with friendly persons was an insult to them, Brother Andrew sagaciously ordered a mild wine to which he would touch his lips, rather than refuse the courteous invitations. As the bartender served his wine, the cowboys laughingly accepted his substitute for the raw, red tiger milk which they drank with gusto but wry face-making.

The three Benedicts loaded supplies and headed south to Fort "Coffee." This was a point along the Fort Dodge-Camp Supply Trail where a square had been constructed of hundred pound coffee bags, re-filled with the sand and clay of the area. Some called this point "Redoubt." It was approximately twelve feet square and offered a modicum of protection from Indian attack for those caught out on the trail between the posts.

Here the two Brothers Fridolin and Andrew unloaded their wagon while the third Brother prepared to "hold down the fort" while the first two returned to Dodge for another load of supplies that had arrived at Dodge by train from Atchison. After returning from Dodge, Fridolin and Andrew found that Brother Raymond had scouted a lovely location for their monastery. It was on a promontory, not far distant from Fort "Coffee." The mesa had an almost imperceptible elevation from three sides and covered about three acres. Nearby Bear Creek offered a stream of cold, clear water for both man and beast. On the mesa top the Brothers erected a low, rambling sod building, with a cottonwood log roof, covered over with a plaster of clay, branches, and twigs. Atop the long ridgepole at the building's front they placed the white cross they had brought with them. They named their monastery in the wilderness Monte Casino. And for it they invited the blessings of the Lord.

148

At the foot of the mesa they planted a vegetable garden and improved the area with stone walks. In the valley below they cut hay and stacked it there on the meadow where it would be accessible to their team on cold winter days. By the end of October they were comfortably situated, well-supplied with potatoes, squash, and other produce grown in their garden. Green tomatoes hung from the soddy's ridgepole, tomatoes that would freshen and ripen from the vines by which they were suspended.

During the spring and summer months the Brothers had made the acquaintance of nearby cowboys from the Driskill ranch. One of the cattlemen had given them a longhorn cow to milk in exchange for vegetables that summer while another had supplied them with a half of a beef for winter eating. The irreverent cowboys, who personally learned to respect, even to admire, the gritty Brothers in their somber black garb, dubbed the new religious establishment Mount Jesus.

Father Oswald Moosmueller, who had come out from Atchison to oversee the work at Monte Casino, soon had to return to his abbey, St. Vincent's. In September, 1876, Father Innocent Wolf was elected Abbot, and this changed all plans for Monte Casino. Within a few weeks came instructions for the Brothers to abandon the project and to return to Atchison. It was a great blow to the hopes of the three Brothers who had performed the initial work. But they delivered their altar, which had remained unpacked on their wagon, to Father Schwembarg, a missionary of the region; they sold their hay and gave the balance of their produce to the nearby ranchers. Then they returned to Atchison. Monte Casino was abandoned forever.

Today, only an historical marker stands atop the mesa to mark the spot where the Brothers sought to establish a place of worship on the plains. It is said by those who know, that if you drive by the mesa in your car of an evening, stop and turn off your motor and listen carefully, that you may still hear the friendly voices of Brothers Fridolin, Andrew, and Raymond and the sound of their busy hoes as they labor diligently in their garden at the foot of the mesa.

One of the Driskill cowboys who knew the Brothers was John George. He was born July 22, 1859, in Comal County, Texas. His father, E. Ben George, was a Floridan, once removed to Seguin where he had married Mary De Weese, daughter of an old Texas family. The son, John George, came up the Western Trail with a Driskill herd in 1877 and stayed to work for J. L. Driskill & Sons in Clark County for several years. George also worked for Beverly Brothers and for George Anderson, Dodge cattlemen. He eventually established himself in cattle in No Man's Land as well as operating a large grocery store and becoming the first banker of Liberal, Kansas.

In 1877 Driskills operated on the range south of Dodge, their stock running on Kieger and Sand Creeks. Only six other ranches were in the area at that time: J. M. Day on Sand Creek; Hiram (Hi) Kollar, north of Mount Jesus on Bluff Creek; Henry Kollar near the mouth of Bluff Creek; A. J. Anthony and Sam Kieger on Kieger Creek; and Dennis Sheedy northwest of there several miles.

When George struck out for himself, he ran his T Bar T on the Beaver River. The brand is still in the family hands seventy-five years later! Together with Ludwig Kramer of the Half Circle Q and LUK brands, George went to Old Mexico in the summer of 1885 and brought up a large herd of Carletes steers. Because of the drought the cattle were cheap and the two men looked forward to some good profits. They brought the herds back that fall of 1885, just in time for the big herds to die in the snowdrifts along the Beaver River. The operation nearly broke both Kramer and George.

The following two years, George held a small herd of cattle near Nar Vico, New Mexico. He later brought about 400 head back to the Beaver River range, built a ranch soddy and some corrals on the north side of the river, and developed about 13,000 acres southeast of Liberal. Thereafter George prospered and held good luck hands the balance of his life.

Al Buchanan rode for George about this time and became his ranch foreman. Al trailed what is probably the last herd north to Nebraska range. This was in 1906. He moved his family to the little ranch near Mullin, Nebraska, on the great Sandhill range,

150

between the Middle Loup and the Dismal rivers. Grass was good and it was an open winter, but the terrible cold convinced Buchanan that he would never again leave the southwest cattleland, so he returned to stay. Al Buchanan ranged his own VVV brand as well as serving as George's foreman. He ran the last roundup wagons along the Beaver as roundup captain. Al passed on at a ripe old age in 1958 at Liberal, one of the last genuine old-time cowboys to leave for the Other Range. John George had preceded his foreman in death by several years.

One story about John George concerns itself with the establishment of the First National Bank of Liberal. This institution is dominated by John George's descendants more than sixty years after its establishment. The following article appeared in *The Southwest Daily Times,* July 2, 1960, Liberal, Kansas, in connection with the celebration of the 60th Anniversary of the bank as well as its removal to the new building at that time:

"JOHN E. GEORGE, Texas Cowman"

One pioneer banking institution of Liberal, The First National Bank, is still guided by the descendants of its founder, John George, a former cowboy who came north with a Driskell herd from Texas in the middle seventies, liked this area and decided to stay. The story of the founding of the bank is interesting.

By the turn of the century there was a small but unofficial banking group in Liberal. They made ranch and farm loans and served as well as could be expected. But the expansion of ranching and business in the region brought demands for larger capital loans. A Wichita banking house was approached by local businessmen and a request made that they send in a competent man to evaluate the needs of the growing community. One hot summer day a Mr. Paul Woods, formerly from South Dakota but now with banking connections in Wichita, arrived in Liberal.

Woods made a quiet but thorough investigation in the town and area, finally visiting the office of the Liberal News. He inquired of the editor, Ray (Skinney) Millman, if there was a man in the area "with sand in his craw and whose word you can tie to" who would be interested in helping organize a bank. Millman, knowing it would take a man with money, character and nerve to launch the new financial enterprise stared into space while his mind sought out such a man. He finally said:

"You rent a livery rig and be back here in twenty minutes and I'll take you to such a man."

Millman directed the driver to take the road to the George Ranch on the Beaver river, in the Neutral Strip. When they arrived they found George and his cowboys cutting white face cattle in the corrals. Sweaty and dirty, George dismounted from his cutting horse and Millman introduced him to the banker.

George listened attentively while Woods made his proposal. The rancher tugged at his mustache, carefully studied the young banker before him and asked a few pertinent questions. The proposition made good sense to him, since he understood the needs of the growing area.

"You want a bank in Liberal, eh?" he said. "Well, I know nothing about banking except to know that we need one in this country. So you deal me in. Let me know how much money you will need, so I can govern fall beef sales accordingly."

John George and Paul Woods shook hands. After a good supper at the George ranch home and night's rest, Millman and Woods returned to Liberal the following day.

There had not been a scrap of paper signed. But more than fifty years later Ray Millman said, when telling the story, "I knew that Liberal finally had a bank—for I knew John George."

John George was a hale and hearty and practical man who liked a good joke, but once had a joke played on himself that he didn't entirely approve. John McGovern, who lived in eastern No Man's Land, was the perpetrator. He was a young cowboy on the spring roundup with George. George was running the cook wagon, doing the cooking himself since the roundup cook had been ill for a day or two with food poisoning.

McGovern, riding for Kramer's outfit, thought it would be a good joke on George to unscrew the nuts from the axles of the chuckwagon. He did so, hiding them in the tall grass along the river nearby. When George started the mules the following morning a rear and a front wheel rolled off before he could stop the teams. From the ruckus made by George, McGovern realized that he had not correctly gauged the George temper.

That evening, the chuckwagon still sitting at the place it had

152

camped the previous morning, the wheels now put back on but unable to move without the wagon nuts on the axles, John George called the men to supper. He had been told by this time who the culprit was and intended himself to have a joke with McGovern carrying the laugh instead of himself. George had his belt and six-shooter on his hip and a huge Bowie knife stuck in his scabbard. He wore the gun during the meal, all the while bellowing that he was "going to shoot the son-of-a-bitch that messed up the cook wagon." George created such a scene before the campfire that no one could enjoy the meal. He strode back and forth, kicking up dust and ashes into their plates and faces and bellowing like a rutting bull. Unexpectedly, he pulled his six-gun and drilled three holes into the sod about five feet from McGovern's tin plate. That did it. The young puncher could stand the pressure no longer. He jumped from his place at the fireside, ran down to the river bank, and came back with the four axle nuts, handing them out toward what he thought was a very angry wagon boss turned cook.

"By God, John, I sure never meant to get you riled up so bad. If you'll just forgive me I'll see that the wagon is straightened out, the axles greased, and the nuts all on tight afore I hit my suggan tonight!"

John George bawled and pranced some more, exacted a promise that McGovern would help the cook out for the next week on the roundup for making his little joke. After McGovern's contrition, and having flushed out the perpetrator of the joke before all the men, George could no longer keep up his act of anger. He laughed and slapped the young cowboy on the shoulder.

"All right, Mac, but if you're bound to unscrew any nuts in the future, pick on something besides the chuckwagon!"

McGovern was relieved to know that he had not made an enemy of a good friend, and faithfully brought up firewood for the cook and aided him in every way thereafter on the roundup.

Later John McGovern ran a saloon in Beaver City and it was a hangout for the cowmen. In 1909 he was running a hotel at Ashland, also patronized by the cowboys. He and John George remained friends after George entered the mercantile business in Liberal, when Liberal was end of tracks on the Rock Island.

John George, "a man with sand in his craw," and "a man you can tie to," as the cowmen expressed it, died in July, 1931. In addition to a fortune, he left a good family name.

The name of Liberal, last town on the Rock Island railroad in Kansas, before it enters the Oklahoma panhandle, has aroused the curiosity of many persons. And it is a fact that probably four out of five people who live in the busy little metropolis have no idea how the town derived its unusual name. Here is the story:

Mr. Seymour S. Rogers, a settler of the early 1880's, influenced the naming of the town. When the railroad reached this point on the southwest high plains in 1888, and a few months later pushed across the line into No Man's Land, it was a focal point for servicing the great ranch country to the southwest, hitherto serviced by Dodge. There were estimated to be more than 200,000 head of cattle on the Beaver River range. Several old towns, such as Fargo Springs, Arkalon, Springfield, Vorhees, Oak City, old Optima, old Tyrone, old Hardesy, and others would soon die for lack of commercial trade with the ranchmen, largely because the railroad missed most of them. Other points along the railroad would see new towns such as Liberal, Kansas and Tyrone, Guymon and Hooker in Oklahoma, spring up.

As early as 1883, the area west of the present town of Liberal (that is the air base) had seen a small general store and a tent hotel build up into a small village at what is today the intersection of 2nd Street of Liberal and Western Avenue. This settlement, along the trail from Fargo Springs, Springfield, and Garden City to the cattle ranches on the Beaver, was called "Lib'ral" by the travelers and the cattlemen on the trail.

The *Fargo Springs News*, August 19, 1886, noted this fact in the following news story, picked up from the Garden City newspaper:

> Mr. S. S. Rogers of Liberal, a new town in the southwestern part of Seward County, was seen on our streets yesterday. He comes to prove up on his homestead. He says everyone in his neighborhood is happy and prosperous.
>
> —*The Daily Sentinel*

154

Mr. Rogers was at that time operating a small road ranch and general store at the location given above. His homestead was at the northeast corner of the 2nd Street and Western Avenue, 32-34, 33, Seward County, Kansas. At that time he had seven children by his first wife but was living with a second wife, a former Mrs. Mason, a French woman who later lived at Joplin, Missouri, who had two children.

Northeast of the Liberal "area," on the Fargo Springs Trail, lived another settler named Anders. Anders had a claim near the rounded hill that is the highest landmark on the flat plain between Liberal and the Cimarron River. Mr. Anders was then in the process of digging himself a well, since previously all water south of the Cimarron to the Beaver was hauled from Fargo Springs for drinking purposes. Since he expected to dig more than 100 feet to find water, Anders proposed to all passersby that he would give free drinking water to any who helped him dig or would work the windlass while he dug in the well. A few responded.

At the same time, Rogers was also commencing a well at his store and road ranch. Hearing of Anders' proposal he laughingly told travelers that when his well was completed "everyone can have all the free water they want, whether they work at the digging or not." As an enterprising merchant he realized that such an offer would bring trade to his store.

As though his promise had been heard On High, Rogers soon struck a plentiful supply of clear, cold, sweet water at a depth of only eighty-seven feet! Thereafter, when anyone needed water on the trail, they always stopped at Rogers' road ranch and well. When asked his price, after helping themselves to water for their teams and themselves, Rogers would laughingly reply, "Oh, just help yourselves to all you want at twenty-five dollars the bucketfull!" When over their surprise, and knowing that Rogers would not accept a penny for his water, travelers would usually reply, "Why thank you! That's mighty *lib'ral* of you, Mr. Rogers."

To this day, if you listen carefully when a resident of this area near Liberal, Kansas, pronounces the town's name, you will note that they always refer to it as "Lib'ral," just as the pioneers did when they thanked Rogers for water from his well.

155

In April, 1888, when the railroad reached the Liberal area, it missed Rogers' store and the little community around it by an even mile, passing through that area a mile to the east and a city block to the south. Soon the hotel moved to the railroad, then other businesses followed as the town-boom started and lots were sold by the score. Rogers did not move his store to the railroad but continued to live at the homestead location until he sold his homestead. About 1899-1900, according to Henry Tucker, Liberal businessman, John George bought the old Rogers store building and moved it into the new town of Liberal, locating it on "Quality Hill," just south of the old Court Brown and DeVoss residences. The building was later razed and used to build a newer building somewhere in the Harrison Circle region.

There has been much dispute locally at Liberal as to exactly where the Rogers Store stood at the intersection. Since Rogers' homestead was on the northeast corner of that intersection, it is reasonable to suppose the old well and store were at that corner. Aunt Bettie Lemert, ninety years of age in 1960, placed the well's location as she recalled it "in front of, west of, Rogers' store." That would place it about on the corner of the present Municipal Golf Course. She related a story of when she once passed the place in the years gone by with a friend, Beatrice Buckland. Mrs. Buckland remarked, "We should all get together and put a stone marker where the old well was located so future generations will know." But time passed, the raising of families took up the girls' time and energies, and the location remained unmarked.

Ray Millman, veteran newspaper editor of Liberal, once pointed out to the author that the old well must have been approximately fifty-five feet north of the place where 2nd Street *joins* the Western Avenue crossing, where the residencial corner house now stands. Burris Wright, old-time cowboy, recalled the location as being somewhat north of there and across the street. Once, while grazing cattle near there, a band of sheep passed by. Burris saw a young lamb fall into the open top of the well, now nearly filled with debris and old wire. He waited until the herder had passed, then peered into the debris at the top. He picked the lamb out and took it home on his saddlehorse.

"We had lamb stew for a few days afterward," he chuckled.

Frank Peacock, another old-timer, a settler and cowboy who has been a Seward County deputy sheriff for fifty years, recalled an incident of his youth that places the old well at still another place. With his father-in-law, W. T. Hollaway, an early settler of Stevens County, Kansas, Frank once rode by the location on a wagon. As they approached from the west, Hollaway pointed to the right side of the road and said to Frank, "There's where Rogers' old well was dug." He singled out the southwest corner of the intersection, the old Calvin J. Hurd corner, 6-35-33. Hurd was the first Liberal postmaster at that location, on May 2, 1887.

No one, to the author's knowledge, has yet placed the site on the southeast corner of that intersection (5-35-33) though it is likely that before the discussion dies away for good, that corner, too, will find its supporters.

At least one old-timer held that neither the town of Liberal, nor the Liberal Precinct, received the name from Rogers' Well. Lee Larrabee stoutly maintained that it was named by officials of the Rock Island Railroad. But Lee was never able to show why Rock Island officials would be out in that area naming a town nearly two years before the railroad was built in to Liberal Precinct or Seward County, Kansas!

Earlier, when the Springfield community refused to vote Rock Island railway bonds, the new railway, building west in the region (it was then called the Chicago, Kansas and Nebraska R.R. company), appeared to be heading west to the Colorado coal fields at Trinidad via Meade, Springfield, Woodsdale, and Richfield. To the disappointment of these towns the railroad swung southwest from Meade to Arkalon, where it crossed the Cimarron River. Lee Larrabee lived near Arkalon as a boy and worked there in a general store. The new town was named by H. E. Tenny, its first postmaster, after his father, Arkalon Tenny, just in time to make the first of the 1888 Rock Island maps. The town, at its peak, had nearly 3,000 residents. Most of the town was composed of residents from Fargo Springs, a town up the Cimarron about six miles, who had moved down to Arkalon to be on the railroad. Fargo Springs was named after C. H. Fargo, the Chicago shoe manufacturer who owned land in the vicinity. Fargo Springs had about 500 people at its peak.

Lee Larrabee was a diminutive fellow, weighing about eighty or ninety pounds. The story was told many times how Lee had challenged Ray (Skinny) Millman, the editor, to a duel with pistols at thirty feet. (Actually they were the best of friends.) Lee, so the story goes, was caught practicing with a six-shooter, firing at a two-by-four set up edgewise at a hundred feet. When asked why he was attempting to gain such skill and artistry with the pistol and told that no man on earth could be expected to hit such a target at so great a distance, Lee just kept on firing and said, "You don't know what I'm up against. If you think that's a narrow target, you ought to see Skinny Millman when he stands sideways in that printing house doorway!"

Once, when Lee had been in the hospital for several weeks for a serious operation, the author met him on the street and passed the time of day with him, complimenting him and noting that he had lost some weight.

"I still say I can whip any man that can get into my clothes," Lee bragged, hitching up his belt, his merry eyes twinkling at his joke.

George Ragsdale, who came up from Ochiltree County, Texas, and worked in John George's store, told of ordering a pair of Levis for Lee Larrabee one time. The waist measure sent in to the company was given as 22 inches. When the factory received the order they wrote back, asking for guidance, somewhat as follows:

J. E. George Company,
Liberal, Kansas

Dear Sirs:
   Your order for Mr. Larrabee's Levis received. Would Mr. Larrabee prefer one regular-size hip pocket sewed in the middle of the seat or two small ones, sewed to each side?
                                        Yrs resp. etc etc.

A Mr. Ihde once said, remarking on the thinness and size of Lee Larrabee and Ray Millman, "The two of them together wouldn't weigh as much as a ga'nted Shetland stud in breeding season."

Not long before Lee's final sickness and death the author prevailed upon him to write something for posterity, telling him that a light history of the Cimarron country was what he had in mind and that almost anything Lee preferred to write would be acceptable. A few days later Lee came into the newspaper office and handed the author a slip of paper upon which he had hand-written his material. "You can call this 'Lee Larrabee On Religion,'" he said. Here is the story he wrote:

Back in the 90's I read the Bible plumb through. Seemed in this one story about Adam, who was the first Man to be placed on Earth, that he needed a mate. So the Lord took one of Adam's ribs and made Eve. Now for some reason or other, they didn't get along any too well.

At any rate Adam wandered off somewhere. Took him some time but he finally returned.

Now when he returned Eve, like all women, was mighty suspicious as to what kept Adam away all that time. She kept nagging after him, asking what other women he had met up with and some such impossible questions, seeing as how there wasn't another woman on Earth but her. Still she kept nagging after him. Adam kept denying there had been any Other Woman, since, as he kept repeating to her, she was the Only Woman in his life, the Lord having made her from one of his own ribs.

A few nights later Adam lay asleep in bed. Suddenly he felt a tugging along his breast bone, then felt a warm hand going down lower, along his rib cage, feeling, investigating, first on one side, than on t'other. Adam awakened, and knowing there were no other Humans on Earth asked, "Eve, what in tarnation are you doing?"

Eve stopped her investigation immediately. "Honey," she said, "I was only checking on your story to be certain there wasn't another rib missing on t'other side!"

When Lee Larrabee passed on, the Southwest lost a wit, funsters lost a good companion, and all lost a good friend. May his genial personality and fun-loving soul rest forever in Heaven!

The name Ragsdale is an old and respected name in No Man's Land, the Ragsdales having come north from Texas in the Eighties. One story, still told, concerns Charles Ragsdale. In a time when no stranger, especially night rider, was trusted in that region, Charles Ragsdale awoke one night in his little soddy. There was a pounding on his door and a rough voice commanded, "Get up or I'll tear the roof off your house!"

Ragsdale aroused himself, grabbed the old double barrel shotgun from its peg on the wall, and poked its snout out the window. He could not see around the corner to his doorway, but the pounding continued. Charley took aim as close to the corner of the house as he could and pressed the trigger. The old gun roared, sending a scattering of buckshot out across the dusty farm yard. Charley then heard footsteps of his visitor receding in the distance, then the sound of a familiar voice coming back from across that person's shoulder.

"Don't shoot again, Charley," the voice fairly whined. "It's only me, Charley; it's Curley, your brother-in-law. I was just coming over to get your boys to help in the harvest!"

Charley Ragsdale sleepily recalled that his brother-in-law, Curley Hodges, *had* mentioned something to him a day or so before about getting the Ragsdale boys to help shock grain. So he put away his shotgun and went back to bed.

Curley Hodges didn't appear until well after sunup the following morning, satisfied to start the wheat shocking a little later in the day than he had first planned.

Joe Brown was a cowboy from the Indian Territory in the eastern part of the Oklahoma Indian Lands. He hired out to work for the Anchor D, west of Guymon. In his hurry to get to his job he forgot both his dog and his pipe, his two closest companions, leaving them at the ranch at which he had formerly worked.

During the first few days at the Anchor D bunkhouse, Joe mentioned to other riders how much he missed the dog and his evening pipe. On the third day after his arrival at about seven o'clock in the evening, came a scratching at the bunkhouse door. One of the cowboys arose, opened the door. Much to his surprise Joe Brown saw his dog walk into the room, and come over to him, laying his head in Joe's lap.

In his mouth the dog carried Joe's pipe, firmly clenched between his teeth, and in the pipe bowl was a note from Joe's folks. Joe read the note, filled the pipe bowl with borrowed tobacco, and petted his dog, all the while bragging on what a smart animal he had.

One rider, tiring of Joe's display of affection, finally spit into the stove, banged shut the door with his booted foot.

"Yes, he's a damned *smart* dog, all right. But you didn't tell us that he was also a damned *fast* dog, makin' that 400-mile trip out here in just three days and nights!"

The saloon, in the early days along the Cimarron, was the social meeting ground for the cowmen. No matter what old men wrote or related later in their lives in their efforts to cover up the youthful pranks or to protect their family's "good name," there was just a lot of purely "social drinking" in those old saloon days of yesteryear. When a man invited you to drink with him, it was the essence of bad manners to refuse impolitely. For it was a most friendly compliment he was paying you. You could, of course, politely decline on most any grounds you chose. But you never refused brusquely or made such a statement as "I don't care to drink with you." That is, unless you were ready for action. There was one thing all decent men sought to avoid, and most cattlemen and their cowboys were a decent sort. That was drunkenness. Drunkenness was the sign of a dull fellow then, just as it is today. No one loved the alcoholic—unless it was his deluded spouse. And most fellows didn't try to get drunk, they just wanted enough to have fun. Many paid for their excesses with the usual hangover, for all young men pay an exhorbitant price just to learn their capacity for hard liquor.

There was once a cowboy—and he was a good one—who never seemed to find his limit for hard liquor—or for beer or light wine, for that matter. His name was Bill Jay. Bill drifted into Lakin, Kansas, one day in the early Eighties. He was minus the first finger of his right hand, the wound being freshly healed. Bill said that the finger had been jerked off when he pulled down a big longhorn steer and accidentally caught the finger under a dally on the saddle horn. Another Texas cowboy who was present, and who recently had come from Dodge, observed that Texas men—and Bill Jay was one—were tie-fast ropers. This second cowboy opined that it hadn't happened the way Bill Jay said it had, and 'lowed as how a certain Dodge faro dealer had fared "wusser 'n Bill."

Bill Jay played a shrewd hand of poker, he drank lustily, he would stand up and fight any man who crossed him. He eventually became the foreman for John O'Loughlin on the Pigpen 7 ranch. He always stuck up for the Pigpen and for Hardesty's outfit, even after going to work for Huff Wright. Once, at a camp in No Man's Land where a group of rustlers met, Bill Jay accosted them at their own campfire and told them, "If I catch any O'Loughlin, Hardesty, or Wright cattle or horses in your hands, there'll be no trial for any of you. Otherwise I don't give a damn what you do here in the Strip." The outlaws left the next morning.

In a Liberal poker game in which John Bell, a one-eyed and partially-paralyzed poker player kept cheating him, Bill laid his six-shooter on the table and made that speech that was repeated all over the west for the next forty years:

"There's some cheatin' goin' on here. I aint namin' any names, but if it don't stop I'm goin' to shoot out the other eye of the son-of-a-bitch that's doin it!"

In 1896 Bill was getting along in years, though still riding. One cold morning he visited a friend down the creek who had bottled a batch of home-made wild grape wine. Following a two-hour visit with his old friend, Bill rode back along the road he had followed down from Hardesty. A gate on the trail that had been open when he came down was now closed. Bill's horse, not wire-wise and loping along half asleep, hit the gate, throwing old Bill on his head against a rock.

Friends found Bill sometime later. They rushed him to Liberal from where he was sent to Kansas City to a hospital. But it was no use, Bill died. Ironically, he was buried in a pauper's grave in that city.

Some cowmen from the Strip were in Kansas City a year later with their beef shipments. They knew of Bill's burial so they passed the hat and took up a collection with which they marked his grave with a simple yet distinguished gravestone. On it they had engraved:

BILL JAY—COWMAN
Died 1896

When someone back at Old Hardesty observed that Bill Jay would probably take his next drink in Hell, Jim Mahoney, who knew old Bill well and loved him, said, "If he does he won't find it any hotter than an August drink of Beaver River water from an oak keg laced alongside his Pigpen 7 chuckwagon."

Huff Wright, mentioned above, was named James H. (for Huff) Wright. He was born in Johnson County, Missouri, December 24, 1842. He died in February, 1915, after a long and eventful life.

In 1861 Huff's father passed away. Huff joined the Confederate army, serving with a company under Capt. Frank Cockrell, later a Senator. The company was surrendered to Union forces at Shreveport, Louisiana, and Wright was shipped back to St. Louis and discharged. The great lawlessness in his home country prevented him from staying there and he moved with his mother to Sedalia, where he dealt in livestock.

In 1866 Huff married Mary A. Maize, and the couple came west to Bent County, Colorado, in 1872. There he worked as a cowboy and in 1876 moved to the Neutral Strip and to the Texas panhandle. He established a small ranch at Bugbee, on Home Ranch Creek, later moving to Moore's Creek.

There were few ranches at this time between Fort Bascom and the Springer ranch in Indian Territory. Dodge was two hundred miles distant, across dangerous trails infested with Kiowa, Cheyenne, and Comanche Indians.

Mel B. Wright, Huff's brother, joined him in 1877. Later, neighbors like Asa Powers, Alfred Poke, and others came to the country and Bates & Beal established the Backward LX ranch about 1878. The Bar C was established soon afterward by Hank Creswell.

About 1883, Wright sold the Moore Creek ranch and bought a place near Dodge with Tom Bugbee as partner. The blizzards of

1885-86 cost the new firm 800 head of their best cattle and they also lost 150 head of saddle horses in forty-eight hours' time. The next spring Wright drove the balance of his herd to Hansford County, Texas, and sold to Harry McGee.

Wright then became interested in "town booming," seeing therein an opportunity to recoup his cattle losses. He located the town of Hansford, Texas. But he couldn't stay out of cattle, and by 1894 he had charge of the Coralitis Ranch in New Mexico with 75,000 head of cattle and 3,500 head of horses. Wright trailed many of these "Meskins" from the Rio Grande to Fort Hancock and there put them on cars for Colorado City, from where he had them trailed to the Two-Buckle ranch. There, they held them briefly, then trailed them out to ranches in the Texas and Oklahoma panhandles and to western Kansas.

In his later years, Huff Wright lived at Hansford with his mate of many years whom he always requested interviewers to mention as his invaluable lifetime helpmate. The couple lost their only child, Idrus, a girl, when she was bitten by a hydrophobia skunk on March 15, 1879.

"Uncle Huff" Wright had the widest possible acquaintance in the southwest cattle country. All men paid respect to his honesty and fair dealing. He was sixty-eight years old when he crossed over the Last Divide after a lifetime of adventures on the cattleman's frontier.

Herb Craig made himself known in the Texas panhandle and the Neutral Strip by his love of fighting. He loved to fight as some men love to eat. Herb was not a mean or vicious type, either. He seldom picked quarrels, but was one of those rare individuals who *could* fight and liked to show his prowess as a fist-fighter. Most cowboys, at least when drunk or angry, settled their quarrels with their six-guns. Not Herb. He preferred the manly art of self-defense—and attack!

As a lad, Herb moved with his folks from Wisconsin to Wichita Falls, Texas. There, he became, as he later put it, "range trained." In his early twenties he drifted north to No Man's Land and found a job on Hardesty's ranch. When Hardesty's men stopped Ab

Blocker's trail outfit from crossing the Strip without following their guide, Craig called it "a frolic for us punchers." Herb offered to fight any Texas trail hand, and each wisely declined. He laughed it off as a joke.

Herb Craig had superior ability, above-average mentality. He was a student, read a lot, and had a fine physique.

Tom Hungate was Hardesty's foreman and when Herb was a new hand he and the tough-minded but level-headed Hungate crossed lances. To settle their accumulated differences, they agreed to fight three rounds to see which was the better man and who would give and take orders. One round was to be fought each noon on three consecutive days of the spring roundup. Hungate never claimed to be a fist-fighter, but he would not let the young puncher's challenge go unanswered, for Tom was a young and physically fit specimen in his own right.

At their first noon-day meeting, with most all of the roundup wagons drawn up nearby, Herb Craig had everything his own way. He was stronger, more experienced, and better accustomed to fist-fighting; so he drove the roundup captain in a circle around the Hardesty wagon with vicious right hand smashes accompanied by left-hand uppercuts. Hungate was bleeding badly around the eyes, his face greatly swollen when the session was over. Many of the men felt sorry for the roundup captain, feeling that he would not show up for the next round of the fight on the following day.

The second day the wagon was camped on Chiquita Creek, and more than a hundred riders and other spectators came out from the towns and ranches to watch the affair. Though Tom Hungate had appeared to take a fearful whipping the first day, few noticed that Herb Craig had also taken a terrific walloping in the stomach from the roundup captain's short, choppy, and damaging hooks. So hard a beating had Craig's mid-section undergone, he could hardly mount his horse that morning. But the roundup captain had observed it. Now he figured if he could last through this second session against the free swinging and walloping Craig, it might be possible to hold him to a draw in the final session. So Hungate waited for no prompting but sailed into Craig's mid-section again with both hands and a will to win.

Craig tried hard to stop the vicious two-handed attack Hungate was launching upon him but could not keep the Hardesty foreman away from his painful mid-section. This day Herb did not get to use so many of his long, looping right hand blows with which he had so damaged Hungate's eyes in their previous round. At the close of the second round all admitted it was Tom Hungate who won. He had risen to the occasion and tied the match up 1-1. The third day's fight would decide the issue between the two men and the betting was now even. Stiff, sore, and bruised, neither man looked hopefully toward the task on the morrow.

That night Herb came to Hungate and stuck out his hand. "Tom," he said, "I'm willing to concede that you're the best man of the two if you're willing to close the issue and fight no more." Tom Hungate took Herb's hand in friendly fashion, but he looked thoughtfully at Herb Craig. To Hungate it was more now than a question of which of the two was the best fighting man. He had the inner feeling that Craig, physically, was still the master of the situation, even though it was Herb who was taking the initiative to end the scrap. But he knew that if he was successfully to run the Hardesty ranch and handle all the rough punchers who came and went from the place, he must once and for all establish himself as the toughest man in a rough outfit, the hardest character they would run up against.

"Herb," Tom told his new hand, "you're by far the toughest fighting man I ever met. You will probably whip me tomorrow for the second time, and that will mean that you can run the camp. But so long as I'm foreman of this work, and captain on this roundup, then no man can make me a challenge to fight and then not finish it—one way or another. If I didn't fight you tomorrow, every man on this work would be going around saying I didn't stand up against you."

Herb Craig nodded his head. He turned his heel, knowing he would have to end the affair some other way, yet show the roundup captain the respect he demanded. He walked out before the fire where the other cowboys lay around telling stories and visiting, exchanging their lies. Stepping before the campfire he called their attention.

"I'm saying now, and I'm saying it loud enough so any man can hear me, that Tom Hungate is the best damn fighting man in these parts. He's the best man that straddles a horse on this round-up. Now I'm saying further that I will never fight him again, come what may. Now any man on this work that questions Tom's 'sand' will have me to whip. Tom and I will never fight again. That's all."

The word was passed around to the other wagons the following morning and that settled the matter. No one ever accused either man—at least to their faces—of fearing the other. Tom and Herb became fast friends and remained so the remainder of their lives.

Herb Craig drank a lot, but was always sober when breaking bad horses, a feat at which he excelled. After leaving Hardesty's ranch, he ran a saloon in Beaver for many years, where he let liquor whip him and get him down. Finally, he went on the wagon for good. When he died, a friend pressed a small glass of medicinal whiskey to Herb's lips, hoping to help and comfort him. Herb refused to taste it and pushed it away.

"I took a pledge to God on my mother's honor that I'd never touch a drop again—and that's final," he whispered. With that, Herb Craig turned his face to the wall and went on with a parched throat and a clear conscience to meet his beloved mother and his Maker.

A good friend of Herb Craig's, and Tom Hungate's very best friend, was Jim Mahoney. Jim was the singer of the Hardesty outfit, with a fine baritone voice that was the envy of every man in the Strip and which thrilled the heart of many a school ma'am who came to teach in the area. Jim regularly rode the rough string for Hardesty's ranch, those horses that were too rough broke for the regular cowboys to tackle without having some meanness ridden out of them—the horses, of course, not the cowboys. Jim was originally from Boston, but don't let them tell you that easterners didn't make good cowboys, for some of the very best had come out from the eastern states to learn their new trade.

Jim Mahoney first drifted to Montana, where he drove stage. There, in some gun play, he killed a man and came on, as had so many before him, to the Neutral Strip. Jim was, himself, once shot up in a saloon brawl in No Man's Land. A favorite song Jim sang, according to Dick Quinn, went like this:

Range is gettin' grassy, winter's drawed its claws,
Calves are fat n' sassy, teasin' of their ma's,
Laffin' days are over, dreamin' days have gone,
No mo' life in clover, fo' th' roundup's on.

Come alive you fellers, hear th' foreman shout,
Drop yo' books an' banjos, fetch yo' saddles out,
Put away them card decks, wrangle up yo' traps,
Git chur spurs and lass' ropes, buckle on yo' chaps.

No mo' nawthern blizzards, weather's soft an' prime,
Nature's fairly yelpin' that it's Roundup Time.

Jim Mahoney once shot out the lights at Billy Bailey's saloon in Hardesty, not by hitting the lamp globe, as Billy later explained it, but by the concussion of the big 44 caliber Merwin-Hulbert revolver Jim always carried.

"Jim wuz too drunk to hit them lamps," Billy said afterward. "He jest blowed them out with th' breeze off'n thet big pistol o' hizz'n."

Dick Quinn, in the old *Hardesty Herald,* told of a trip Jim Mahoney and a friend once made on horseback to the OX ranch headquarters:

Jim and a friend once made a horseback trip to the OX ranch, up the river a few miles, with "two quarts of elocution" tied on behind the friend's saddle. The wild bronc, Old Sundown, stumbled while bucking and threw Jim's friend hard against a clay bank. Jim, accustomed to bronc's bucking under him every day, thought nothing of his friend getting throwed, but inquired anxiously when the action was over, "Did it break the bottles?"

Jim Mahoney sang at the dances, led the men in spontaneous singing at the roundup campfires, and was always a welcome figure at any gathering. When Col. Hardesty quit the range in No Man's Land and moved his herds to Montana, Jim joined a circus, driving six-horse teams in the parades.

168

Oddly enough, Jim was once shot by Cap Hungate, his best friend's brother.

John (Hooker) Threlkeld was so nick-named after Gen. "Fighting Joe" Hooker of Civil War fame, some say. Others say he received his name after an old cattleman on the Beaver River whose name was Hooker. Still others say he received his name by being such a "Hooker" of cattle, that is, top roper. Wherever he received that nickname, we know how the town of Hooker, Oklahoma, received its name. For it was named after John (Hooker) Threlkeld.

Hooker was born in Kentucky, November 13, 1846. He came west with his parents to Missouri. On May 15, 1864, he joined up with a freight outfit and bullwacked west from Omaha to Virginia City, Montana, with his two brothers. In 1873 Hooker came to No Man's Land where he spent the next thirty years in the saddle. He was foreman for the OX ranch many years. When the OX withdrew to Montana after the disastrous blizzards of 1886, Hooker was given their side camp on the Frisco, later the Tom Stratton ranch. That year Hooker married Hannah Davis of Greeley, Kansas. When Hannah's folks came to that region, Hooker yielded his ranch, the XX Frisco, they called it, to the parents, and he and Hannah went to open up a new place farther up the Frisco. They called the new ranch the Hooker Ranch. He hauled the lumber for his new home from Dodge and also built outbuildings of sod and stone.

Hooker was a big man, with raven black hair and eyes and the appearance of an eagle. He had much gold bridge work in his large, showy white teeth and wore many diamonds, large and expensive ones, as did his new bride. They made an imposing couple wherever they were seen together, for he was an outstanding figure and Hannah, nearly twenty years his junior, was a very beautiful girl. They had three children.

Old cowboys who have seen Hooker in action described him as one of the really great ropers of the day, a man who could ride quietly into a herd, drop a tight, small, and fast loop from either side of his mount and catch calves standing beside or under their mothers. This type of roping, more so than the sensational run-and-catch kind, accomplished the day's work on the range with speed and without ostentation. It was the sort of roping most highly regarded by the cowmen themselves.

Hooker's first wife died in 1908. In 1912 he was married again, to Miss Edith Calvert of Greeley. He died December 5, 1938, at Redondo Beach, California. Charlie Hitch said of him, following his death, "Heaven will be dearer to me since Hooker will be there."

When you drive through Hooker, Oklahoma, slow down, look around. Here is a town named after a man's *nickname*. Do you know of another?

Walt Naylor, when his cowboying was over, ran a livery barn at Liberal. In August, 1909, with Con Jackson, another old top hand, they journeyed to Kingman to a fair. Neither knew how good he still was, but they wanted to try for the loose change paid for bronc riders and ropers. By the time the show was over both had pleased the crowd and both had his pockets full of "jingle."

Walt was the first to compete. He tied a big, rough Texas steer in one minute and seven seconds! The *Topeka Capitol* said of the event:

> There was no Hippodrome business about the contest. The steers were from the Texas range and full of fight. The steer that Naylor roped hooked the pen gate down, hurling a heavy piece of timber twenty-five feet through the air, striking John McFall, a local cattleman, in the chest and inflcting a painful injury.

When it came Con Jackson's turn, he come out on a big, rangy, and tough bucking horse that turned Con every way but loose. Con scratched the big sorrel from his shoulders to his tail root, fanned the bronc's fiery brain with his hat, and when the ride was over—not a few second ride but after the horse quit bucking—he rode him over to the grandstand where he made the judges glad to hand him the first prize for a clean, hard ride.

Sam Johnson, a big Negro cowboy from the 101 Ranch down in

the Indian Territory, bulldogged a Texas longhorn with a six-foot spread of black antlers. The crowd afterward declared it was one of the best all-round cowboy shows ever offered in central western Kansas.

Con Jackson lived and worked on the southwest range for many years and passed over the Big Divide at Las Vegas, New Mexico, September 25, 1946.

Lewis (Brushy) Bush was one of the lesser-known characters of the Southwest cattle country. Most of his life on the range he received little publicity. He liked to work in peace and quiet along the Cimarron and Beaver watersheds, first for this ranch, then for another. In this way no one could tell exactly what Brushy was doing or where he was doing it. He was a fair hand but the men who worked alongside him knew he carried a bigger noose for himself than he would for his employer. Brushy always found work on the fall roundups, this annual event providing him with the opportunity to push a few big steers of Taintor's, Dudley's, or Day's up a blind canyon and there leave them to graze. This was what the cowboys called a "winter job," for it provided an unemployed rider with some beef to sell at Beaver City, Buffalo, or Optima right at a time when the cowboy needed money the most.

When Beer City sprung up from the buffalo grass prairie south of Liberal, "just a whisper across the state line," as Merritt Beeson put it, Brushy Bush made application to become Beer City's town marshal. He had heard about and known the Earps and Mastersons at Dodge and had learned from their school of law enforcement. Since he had essentially the same sort of citizens with whom to deal, that is, pimps and panderers, prostitutes and gamblers, thieves, cut-throats and outlaws, he took charge in much the same manner the Earps and Mastersons and other border lawmen advocated. He ruled with sawed off shotgun and six-shooters. No one elected Brushy. He simply appointed himself. His capabilities with knife and gun he offered as his highest recommendation for the job. His "protection" came high, but Beer Citizens accepted it—at least for a while. "Bush carried two revolvers; ate, drank

171

and slept where and when he pleased," a contemporary, Oliver Nelson, said of him.

The town of Beer City was a growth spawned by that virulent Kansas hypocrisy—prohibition. Beer City rose as an oasis on the desert to meet the need for cool beer, a shot of raw red liquor, or a taste of wine. But it brought in its train the wine and women and song, the slow horses, fast women and dice that follow the Jug, wherever it is not supervised and directed by an alert society. The townsite was never laid out, like Topsy it "jes grew." The main street started to run east and west, facing the Kansas trade, then commenced also building north and south. The melange of dance halls, saloons, redlights soon faced north, east, south, and west—every direction to catch new trade.

Many of the Beer City businesses were conducted in tents. There were no sidewalks, no crosswalks, no water or sewage system. There were no civic improvements of any kind. Beer City was just a sudsy, boozy spot on the plains—just pure froth.

The big stacks of beer barrels at the place gave Beer City her name, and she was never to have another. Huge swarms of flies of an August afternoon would settle around the barrels, lapping up enough of the sour, amber fluid that leaked through the open bungholes to keep them on a perpetual binge. Clouds of gray dust played back and forth across the bleak scene, rendering the faces of all the buildings the same, harmonizing sod-gray of the buffalo plains in dry time. The rows of wooden hitch racks in front of the buildings were paralleled by long windrows of manure, created while the faithful cow ponies awaited their masters' return from within the saloons and bawdy houses of Beer City. With hind ends atop the smelly mounds, the patient ponies would stand and fight flies by the hour, sometimes pawing more earth to make their pedestals even higher.

Brushy Bush regarded Beer City as his own private domain. When he "collected salary" he would patrol the streets, stopping into each place of business and sticking out a greasy palm. One cowboy who ran a saloon and knew Brushy before his Beer City career as lawman told how Brushy one time was caught skinning a settler's cow. Brushy promptly paid the settler off in solid metal—

lead from his gun. But Brushy's career at Beer City could only bring trouble to him for all Beer City soon grew tired of his graft.

The end came on a 4th of July. The town had planned a great celebration. No one in Beer City could care less for the 4th of July than did the Committee elected to promote the affair. It is possible that some did not even know why the 4th of July was celebrated in America. But the Committee obtained the services of two well-known fighters and wrestlers, Joe Low and Dee Hannah. Bob Davis was second for Low; Fred Oschner seconded for Hannah. A grand Masked Ball was planned for the evening following the wrestling match in the afternoon. There was great betting on the match—and Brushy Bush horned in at the last minute to hold most of the stakes, for 5 percent!

It so happened that Pussy Cat Nell, a local madame, had placed a high bet on Joe Low. She had entrusted Fred Oschner to hold the stakes until after the fight since he was an honest fellow, though personally favoring Hannah. In the hour or so preceding the match, Brushy Bush came in to hold the stake Pussy Cat Nell had entrusted to Oschner. The madame didn't like it a bit and so told Brushy Bush, who promptly beat her face in with the butt of his six-shooter, rendering her *hors de combat* for the celebration.

About a week after the celebration, Pussy Cat sat in the upstairs room of her house and saw Brushy Bush passing along the street just below her. Quickly seizing her trustworthy double barrel shotgun loaded with Blue Whistlers, those deadly little steel balls about an eighth of an inch in diameter, she poked the snout of the gun out the window and gave Brushy both barrels in the back of the neck.

When she stepped back to re-load, Bush was lying face down on the manure of the street, dead. But now the other folks of Beer City took up the battle and the crack of rifle and shotgun fire made the street sound like Gettysburg. When one group would run out of ammunition, another would commence firing into Bush's inert form. When they finally picked his bloody body out of the street and took it out onto the prairie for burial, there was not a whole bone in his body.

Brushy's body was buried somewhere near Beer City, amid the

bottlecaps and beer bottles that surrounded the old town. His grave is lost today in the wide fields of wheat and milo maize that annually cover the area, there on "the lone prair-e-e-e."

Beer City, the Sodom and Gommorah of the Plains, no longer reigns as Queen City of the Southwest Cattleland. Her trail ran out in the late Eighties. Nor is she, nor her erstwhile Marshal— Brushy Bush—missed by anyone.

Chapter VIII

Dodge City and Garden City were supply towns for the Cimarron and Beaver river regions before the Rock Island Railway drove its spikes down through the area in 1888 and helped establish Arkalon and Liberal as new supply points. During their first years, Dodge and Garden spewed up a whole passel of highbinders and saints. Most everyone who owns or has access to a TV set, a motion picture theater or a few comic books, has learned something about the Earps, Mastersons, Doc Holliday and the others—or at least think they know. Others like Neil Brown, W. H. Harris, Charles Bassett and Luke Short have had a share of such recognition. But few of the real solid citizens who lived through the early days at Dodge and Garden have made more than a ripple on the sea of ink used up by western writers and historians on the gunmen, lawmen and outlaws. As a consequence the Raths, Zimmermans, McCartys, Wrights, Bells, Evans, Olives and Sughrues, together with a score of old and really important families of the southwest, have yet to find their Boswells. So it is not surprising that one of the most monumental frauds of all is still remembered in Dodge while many of the upright citizens are forgotten.

This candidate for the future "Hall of Cowboy Shame" was known as Ben Hodges. For sheer humbuggery, Ben put all the old roisterers to rout. Don Benito Hogero, the Mexican population of Dodge called him; to the Negroes of old Dodge, who probably understood him best, he was referred to simply, but politely, as "Nigga Benjy." The rest called him Ben.

Ben Hodges was a beady eyed, weazened little fellow about five feet six inches tall, weighing one hundred and twenty pounds. He had come to Dodge with an early trail herd from Texas, some say with a Dewees herd, others say with Olive brothers. Robert M. Wright, a good authority, says Ben arrived not long after Doc Barton came, which would make Ben one of the really first up the

Texas trail. Ben was a black man, both from weathering in the southwestern sun and from mixed racial heritage. He spoke Spanish like a Mexican, but he had both Negro and Mexican blood lines. No one knew or pretended to know Ben's age, but he was probably in his late twenties when he reached Dodge.

In the late Seventies or early Eighties, the cattlemen of the Cimarron region heard with great interest that Mexican heirs had revived an old Spanish Land Grant that comprised most of the range land south of the Arkansas river to the Canadian, west of the 101st Meridian to the Picketwire. This was range land upon which the 101 ranch, the OX, Prairie Cattle Company, and the ranchers on the Neutral Strip, along the Beaver River had thrown thousands of head of cattle. It was now reported that the rightful heirs of this vast tract of old Spanish land were being sought in Texas—and from the very vicinity where Ben Hodges' family originated. Soon Ben was describing himself as a co-heir to the lands, and following a trip to Texas Ben arrived back at Dodge and presented himself to Dodge City officials as both claimant to the Land Grant and the representative for the other San Antonio heirs.

At first the little fellow's pretentious claims drew laughter, then some local lawyer recalled having seen a document in Ben's possession which truly appeared to be the power-of-attorney of the rightful heirs in Texas. Another lawyer or two went along with the idea, and some interesting speculations resulted, amid great laughter, over the many-faceted case presented by Ben's claims. Fun being a scarce item on Dodge streets at that early time, many more citizens, businessmen, and officials began to buy Ben's case, some with hard cash money.

With his new-found prestige, Ben very cleverly worked most of the southwest cattlemen into his plan, exhibiting a canny natural talent for organization and publicity work. Most of the cattlemen went along as insurance against calamity in case that Ben's claims actually bore fruit and he did become the legal custodian of the powers such an enormous Grant of land might entail. Now when Ben needed a saddlehorse, a fine pair of chaps, a silver-plated six-gun or gold-inlaid spurs, all he needed to do was to mention his need among the cattlemen and ergo!—his wants were filled. Not all, of course, were fooled; many went along for the simple pleasures of the ride.

Ben's newly affluent state began to have an effect upon the businessmen of Dodge, and more of them climbed on Ben's financial bandwagon, extending him credit to come and go through their stores, take what he liked and pay when he wished. Ben was soon enjoying a one-man Credit Binge. As one businessman or financier would watch Ben's ascending star being supplied for free from a competitor's store he would enter the competition and supply added fuel to the flight. Soon the little fellow had soared majestically into a grand and mystic financial orbit that was fantastic to see.

The jokers behind Ben drew up endless petitions, affidavits, and claims, setting forth in full Ben's claim to this fortune in range land. All these papers the little fakir faithfully recorded at the Ford County court house. He proudly exhibited the series of claims to Dodge visitors and they, in turn, fanned the flame of his publicity from the Cherokee Strip to the Purgatoire. Those waddies who had known Ben on the trail howled with glee at his audacity and effrontery and further pushed his claims wherever possible for them to do so.

Eventually Judge Sterry of Emporia, a leading Kansas lawyer, impressed by Ben's paper assertions, undertook to press Ben's claims in court, the judge himself financing the litigation in hope of a rewarding future. The case dragged along in the court and finally came to the attention of the higher courts.

By this time Bob Wright, H. M. Beverly, Chalkley Beeson, I. P. Olive (whom it was said once threatened to hang Ben for stealing Olive cattle), Martin Culver, and other reputable Dodge citizens were requested to make some personal recommendations to support Ben's character and claims in the eastern court. They responded, and of course Ben's claim was immediately thrown out of court and the little cowpuncher narrowly escaped prosecution for fraud, such a downgrading did they give him.

But while this litigation was in process, Ben made hay in his own green meadows, for his name had now become well-known and important in Dodge, and he borrowed all he could on it, cooking up many other schemes and deals.

About this time the U. S. Land Office was moved from Larned to Garden City. Coincident with the move, a great fire in Dodge destroyed the Wright & Beverly store and the four-ton safe dropped through the burned street floor and into the basement. The huge iron box fell on its doors, precluding anyone from opening it until it was uprighted again. In this fallen safe the clever Ben Hodges found natural material to further implement his schemes.

Sometime previously he had written the Gray County treasurer, asking for a detailed listing of all land open for settlement through Garden City or U.S. Land Office. The treasurer had obliged, listing some thirty-two sections of land in Gray county. Armed with this listing, Ben now sought out the U.S. Land Office at Garden City, asked for the Land Commissioner and told him that he, Ben, held a total of thirty-two sections of land in Gray County which had been filed on by his cowboys. Showing the Commissioner his long and legal-looking list, Ben warned him not to throw open a square foot of this land. The signed affidavits to the land, given him by the cowboys, Ben stated, were now in the burned safe at the Wright & Beverly store at Dodge. He would, at the proper time, Ben told the Commissioner, have the safe restored and the documents removed, though Ben slyly intimated that these valuable documents *might* have been destroyed by fire. Ben spoke so authoritatively, waving about the long list of Gray County homestead lands, that the U.S. Land Commissioner never tumbled to the fraud.

With his land papers, Ben now appeared at the Dodge City National Bank and explained to the president, a newcomer, of his land holdings that had been temporarily tied up because of the Wright & Beverly fire. He asked the bank president for a letter of credit, suggesting that he get in touch with the U.S. Land Commissioner at Garden City for the details of the matter. A great name-dropper, Ben made such an impression on the banker that he left with a letter of credit *testifying to Ben Hodges' ownership of thirty-two sections of good, Gray County land!* Acting on impulse, Ben asked for and received two more letters of credit from other Dodge financial institutions. The letters showed the lying and cheating "Nigga Benjy" to be ". . . sober, industrious, very economical and a man of his word."

With his letters of credit, Ben now rode down on to the Beaver and Cimarron Rivers and bargained for thousands of head of cattle on the range, at "spring market price." It was fortunate that the cattle market increased greatly that spring, making it impossible for Ben to comply with his contracts. So no livestock changed hands, and no-one was hurt in the razzle-dazzle he had created. Ben had by this time exhibited some of the traits and qualities that in other men had made them titans of finance, the lords of our economy, entrepreneurs, ex post facto abra cadabra—at least while they were succeeding. For he had learned *how to get hold of and manipulate other peoples' money!*

Ben Hodges now rode on complimentary railway passes, dressed like a cattle baron, and cut a wide swath in banking circles. He carried on through his lawyers (he could hardly sign his own name) a wide correspondence with financial houses in Omaha, Kansas City, and St. Louis. He completely bamboozled businessmen and cattlemen alike, John Lytle, Martin Culver and others like Bob Wright shaking their heads at such duplicity and chicanery. "It was surprising how an ignorant darkey could make such a stir out of nothing," Robert M. Wright wrote many years later.

Don Benito Hogero's life in Dodge was filled with episodes that were ludicrous, laughable, comic, tragic. He made one brief excursion into politics, circulating a petition to Governor Morrill asking for the appointment as Livestock Inspector at Dodge City. It was like a wolf asking to guard the sheep pen, for Ben was known to be one of the cleverest cow thieves in the region in earlier times. But in his petition he set forth all his services to the Republican Party, many commendable, if unperformed, acts being listed. And of course everyone signed the petition for "Nigga Benjy," businessmen, saloonkeepers, cowboys, dance hall women, the gamblers—that is, everybody except one small group of men. It was a great joke. Everyone had a big laugh.

But Bob Wright, Print Olive, Beverly, Culver, and the others who knew Benjy best had to pull into the breech and head him off again, lest the innocent governor award the goat a cabbage patch to watch over and care for. They reported Ben Hodges the most competent cattle thief in the region, and their veto killed Ben's chances in politics. And he never forgave Wright and the others for standing between himself and a cattle kingdom.

Old Ben Hodges died at Dodge City at St. Anthony's Hospital during the summer of 1929. But he was an aged and mellowed Ben Hodges, whom everyone had forgiven for his frontier frauds. His trail ended at Maple Grove Cemetery, where they tucked him in within shouting distance of the graves of his old neighbors, the Wrights, Bells, Beesons, Hardestys, and Olives.

"We buried Ben there for a good reason," said one of his pall bearers. "We wanted him where they could keep an eye on him."

Ben Hodges, they later found out, was the bastard son of a colored trooper of the old 9th Cavalry, which was stationed at San Antonio at the appropriate time. His mother was the daughter of a good Mexican family of breeding at San Antone. Ben had no claim to wealth or to land except his own collossal nerve, which served him well for many years, pulled him out of obscurity into the limelight and gave him an opportunity for an interesting and adventurous life. He earned an "E" for Effort.

So much for Don Benito Hogero. May his rascal bones rest in peace!

Another character of Cimarron country was Jesse Evans, a hard-bitten young cattleman who lived in north Texas and New Mexico. Evans stood five feet and an inch in height and weighed 150 pounds. But what he lacked in stature he made up for in gun savvy. In April, 1876, when Evans was twenty-three years old, he spent a few days in Dodge City, transacting business. He was well-known on the streets of Dodge, and in the custom of the day, no one inquired in to his affairs. He went about his business soberly and industriously, and at the end of two weeks had gathered together a band of fifty cowboys, giving particular attention, in his hiring, to the experience each had had with pistol and rifle. A "bonus" would be paid, he told them, in addition to the "forty a month and found" which would be paid for the job of moving a herd of Meskin cattle out of New Mexico to Dodge.

When his men were gathered, Evans pulled two chuckwagons by Rath & Wright's store, loaded the necessary provisions, tossed the men's bedrolls on top, and headed southwest to the Texas panhandle. There, at Evans' headquarters, they spent a few days gathering and breaking out a remuda of 300 head of saddle horses. Jesse Evans now outlined the job to the men. They were heading for the Pecos Valley, he said, where they would gather 20,000 head of cattle which were to be purchased by Evans and Hunter from John Chisum, the noted cattleman of the region. Hunter would take care of all the negotiations concerning the sale and pay for the livestock, Evans said. His part of the bargain was to receive the cattle at the Chisum ranch and make delivery of them to the Santa Fe stockyards at Dodge City. There the men would be paid off.

John Simpson Chisum was at that time one of the best known cattlemen of the country. He owned the Fence Rail brand and the U brand, or Muleshoe as some called it. He also used a distinguishing ear mark called the Jinglebob, where a three inch strip of flesh at the bottom of the calves' ears was slit and allowed to dangle down alongside the head at each side. Chisum had driven cattle out of Texas for other Texas ranchers as well as for himself. He would obtain the power-of-attorney from the ranchers whose cattle he handled so that he might sell or trade these animals without going into a lot of extra trouble venting brands or perhaps rebranding an entire herd. His practice was to give the rancher a simple receipt for his animal or several animals in the form of a note, with his promise to pay. These he made out in duplicate, keeping the second copy for himself and giving the Texas owner the first copy. He would then take the cattle to New Mexico, hold them on good range until they were grassed out a year or two, then send them up to the Denver market for sale to the mining camps or deliver them to buyers on the Wyoming and Montana ranches for further growing out and fattening.

That was Chisum's theory of business. But it often slipped and he would fail to make restitution to the Texas owners who were left holding his little slips of paper. His business practices soon came to be known to them as "a mouth full of gimme and a handful of much-obliged." Chisum became wealthy and influential, his South Spring Ranch becoming one of the show places of the Southwest. He marketed livestock in Dodge as well as at Denver and army forts on the frontier. Chisum had his enemies, and he had his friends. He employed such notorious characters as Billy the Kid to keep people "friendly," though Billy later turned on him and quit him.

The previous year, 1875, Chisum had been sued. Tom Catron, an energetic lawyer who was later district attorney, filed the suit against Chisum for Texas clients. They claimed that Chisum did not own the cattle that he sold from his range. Chisum answered his summons to court, produced his power-of-attorney papers given him by the very people who had brought the suit. The suit was forthwith dismissed. It made Tom Catron and his Texas clients look foolish. John Chisum laughed long and loud at their discomfiture. But neither Catron nor the Texas cattlemen forgot.

The following year Robert Hunter, Evans' new friend, developed a plan by which they thought to harness Chisum's greed to work for them. Hunter made a trip to Texas alone. There he bought up every cattle note of John Chisum's that he could find, paying as little as a nickel on the dollar for them to the Texas cowmen who despaired of ever realizing a penny on them. Hunter then contacted Catron, the lawyer, and Catron brought Jesse Evans into the plan. Evans was told to recruit the toughest assortment of gunmen that he could find at Tascosa and Dodge for this work, for it would be no picnic to deprive John Chisum of a big herd of cattle if he should get his dander up.

At his ranch, Chisum met Hunter and Catron with a smile. Cattle prices were up, and he looked forward to making a fine sale on the big, full-grown, and fat steers he had acquired during the panic of 1873 as yearlings. Chisum played the good host for the next two days, showing his guests the ranch, making everything pleasant for them. Within a week after their arrival the cattle were gathered and Hunter looked them over carefully, studying the old Texas brands on them, comparing them each night with other papers he concealed in a black handbag he had brought along with him. When the cattle had been thoroughly studied and tallied and some turned back for reasons not given to Chisum, Hunter and Chisum came to a financial agreement on the sum total to be paid for the herd. There were more than fifteen thousand cattle included in the sale.

That afternoon Jesse Evans and his chuckwagons appeared on the horizon and he and his fifty hard cases camped, as agreed, about two miles from the Chisum ranch headquarters. That night Hunter and Catron rode out to the wagons and talked with Evans. Evans assured them that everything was in apple pie order, his men ready to move the cattle out in five big herds when the monetary agreement with Chisum had been fulfilled. Hunter studied the men with Evans. He agreed they looked like the kind who could move the cattle, whatever Chisum's personal whims should be when he had settled up with him. For he had never seen such a tough aggregation of gunfighters in one group in all his life.

"Be ready in the morning," Hunter told Evans, then he rode back with Catron to the ranch.

The following morning Hunter and Catron walked over to Chisum's offices at the ranch, carrying the black satchel with them. Chisum, his lawyer, and his ranch foreman met them and together they stepped into the office.

"Here's your money, John," Hunter said casually to Chisum who sat at his roll-top desk. He set the bag at Chisum's right hand. "Jesse Evans has fifty cowboys who are ready to start the drive as soon as the cattle are turned out." Hunter unsnapped the lock on the bag.

John Chisum nodded, signed the bill of sale that had been worked out previously between himself and Hunter, then turned to the black bag. Hunter picked up the bill of sale and carefully put it in his inside coat pocket in his wallet.

Chisum now opened and peered into the black bag. He looked up angrily at Hunter.

"Is this some sort of joke, Bob?" he asked.

"No, it's no joke, John," Hunter answered him. "Those are

183

your own notes—surely as good to you as cash money, are they not?"

Chisum pulled out a handful of the papers—his promissory notes left with the Texas cattlemen three, four, five, and six years before and never paid. The facts came quickly to him. He turned to his own lawyer.

"Counsel, can they get by with such a swindle as this?" He handed his lawyer a sheaf of the crumpled notes. The lawyer studied them carefully, looking at the signatures closely.

"This is your signature, isn't it Mr. Chisum?" He handed John Chisum a note, then another, and another.

"Yes! Yes! They're all my signatures," Chisum answered testily, "But are they *legal*—can they do this to me—*legally,* I mean?"

The lawyer nodded. "Yes, there's nothing you can do since you signed the notes yourself and have also signed the bill of sale."

Hunter and Catron waited to hear no more. With a hasty farewell, they stepped out the door, mounted their saddlehorses, and signaled Jesse Evans and a dozen of his riders to ride into the ranch yard and back to the corrals where some of the big steers had been held for them. Chisum followed them out the door, stepped into his waiting buggy, turning his back on his lawyer who stood in the doorway, his jaw still wagging. Chisum's foreman stepped into the buggy beside his boss. "Drive me on out to the herd," Chisum ordered. A half dozen Chisum cowboys stood along the bunkhouses, waiting, without instructions, as the buggy whirled past them.

Jesse Evans opened the corral gate and turned the cattle out. Then he rode with six of his men to the hill country back of the ranch where the remaining herds were held on the grassy slopes, signaling his men to bring them along in the order he had previously planned.

John Chisum sat is his buggy east of the ranch house where the herds would cross a stream as they left the Chisum ranch. As Jesse rode by the buggy he tipped his hat to Chisum. He heard Chisum give his orders to his foreman, "All right, Henry, let's get the sons-of-bitches off of *my* grass." Jesse Evans smiled to himself, but he had a feeling of contrition.

When Hunter and Catron overtook Evans that evening on the trail, Evans was laughing and slapping his chaps with his glove.

"The old bastard took his beating like a champion," Evans said, laughing at the manner in which they had used Chisum's greed to trap him.

"Yes," said Bob Hunter. "I wonder if you or I could do the same?"

One character of old Dodge City, and one of sound timber, was William B. Rhodes. He came to Dodge from Wisconsin in 1885 and worked for Bob Wright as his foreman on the Crescent W ranch for several years. Later he worked for the Fitzgerald ranch and after that, when he was older, he became a Dodge policeman for twenty years. Rhodes was a tall, broad shouldered man, very powerful; and his claim was that he never had to shoot a man to arrest him. He operated on the same principle as Tom Smith had at Abiliene, Kansas, for Smith was a lawman whom Rhodes greatly admired.

Rhodes and his family lived in a little house on the corner of Vine Street and First Avenue. The house had a history of its own, since it had been built in Abilene in the early cattle-shipping days and had once housed Tom Smith, the Abilene town marshal. From there, after the boom, the house was taken down and moved to Salina. From Salina it was moved to Ellsworth, and when the cattle boom ended at Ellsworth the little house was moved again, this time to Fort Dodge. There it was occupied by Charles F. Tracy (later to be heard from in No Man's Land) and after that by John E. Tappan. When Bob Wright was the post trader at the Fort, he too lived in the little frame house for a short while.

When Bob Wright helped start Dodge City, up the tracks west about four miles, James Langton (another old cattleman) stayed in the little house with his sister, who was a delightful entertainer and musician, it is said. Finally, the little building was moved to Dodge City. During its many years of existence such figures as President Rutherford B. Hayes, Gen. William Tecumseh Sherman, Gen. Ulysses S. Grant, Gen. Phil Sheridan, General Miles, General Forsythe, and Generals Custer and Pope were entertained within its walls.

It is no wonder that, living in a house whose very walls and echoes must have given off the music and voices of history, Bill Rhodes became one of Dodge City's greatest "carriers" of the legends and stories that have become Dodge history. Rhodes found himself relating Dodge history to others and always trying to interest others in the rich folklore of the old cattle days. In later years, when he became old and could no longer take the active life as a policeman, "Dad" Rhodes, as everyone called him then, became a guide on Boot Hill. This was long before radio, TV, newspapers and magazines had made the stories of Dodge household common-places, as they are today. Nor would Dad Rhodes have liked the manner in which the stories of his old town are oftimes related on the screen and pages of print today.

Sitting high on the seat of the old Chuckwagon, 'way back in the Dirty Thirties, Dad Rhodes would clear his voice, then regale visitors with the real facts about the Cow Capitol of the World. He told them firsthand, and those who heard them from his lips enjoyed the vicarious thrill that comes from hearing a tale told firsthand by a man who has participated in much of the history he relates.

"I don't tire of telling the stories of Old Dodge," he once said, "for most of the folks who came here to visit are new to the place. They hear something from me that is different from what they expect to hear. It is just too bad that so many liars have become historians of the southwest cattle country. The really true stories are just as interesting, and in most cases are of more consequence and importance, than the fibs they tell. I get a lot of questions, but I'll say this: The folks from New York, New England, and other eastern points are not half as green as they were about the West a few years ago.

"Once in a while I find someone who expects an Indian raid as soon as the sun goes down, but most of them feel convinced that *real* Indian trouble won't start until they've reached the Rocky Mountains!" At that jibe, Dad Rhodes' eyes would twinkle.

"Seriously, though, everybody expects to find a museum on Boot Hill when they get here. That ought to be the next objective. We should build one up here and I'm already campaigning for it!"

Dad Rhodes liked to tell how Pete Harding lost a fine little cream colored saddlehorse named "Cookie." He had Cookie's body hauled to Boot Hill and there interred him *with his shoes on!*

Thirty years or more have passed since Dad Rhodes launched the campaign for a museum on Boot Hill. Today, could he visit there, the cockles of his heart would be warmed by the big museum atop the hill, the Boot Hill cemetery, and the many mementoes of an earlier age. But his eyes would bulge from their sockets when he looked down the slope, to see at the bottom the very image of the Old Dodge he knew as a young man, recreated in the Replica of Front Street, through which pass scores of thousands of visitors and townsmen annually. The Beeson Museum Annex, housed within the Replica buildings, would please him as nothing before, for within its walls he would find the stories, the artifacts, and the pictures of his own age, when the Cowboy was King.

Dad Rhodes had one story he liked to tell visitors. It went something like this: When the cattlemen withdrew from the range, many cowboys settled on homesteads, married school ma'ms, and gave up their festive life. One cowboy who did so was Dad Rhodes' friend, Terry McCracken. At first there were no schools for the McCracken children, and when Terry finally took his two boys, aged seven and twelve, to their first school, he asked the teacher what subjects they might be taught. The teacher went over the curriculum rather hastily—reading, writing, arithmetic, spelling, algebra, trigonometry—there would be many subjects as they developed and school facilities and courses improved, she said.

"That's good enough for me," Terry responded enthusiastically. "Just load this here older boy up with all that Triggernometry you can find. He's the poorest shot in our entire family!"

Dodge City remembered Dad Rhodes. On one section of the river today, his name is perpetuated by combining "Will" and

"Rhodes" into the pleasant-sounding Wilroads Gardens, a spot near Dodge that is now and will always be restful and charming to live in or to visit, just south of the Arkansas River.

Dad Rhodes would have liked that.

Ham Bell was a Dodge Citian who lived a full life on the frontier and was completely passed up by the western scribes. The truth is, Bell lived too long for them to corrupt his life story, doctor it up, and make him into a two-gun sheriff or U. S. Marshal —both of which he had actually been! So they left Ham Bell's interesting life story out of their books, though Bell probably had arrested more criminals than all the rest put together.

Ham Bell was more than just a Dodge lawman. Like Bob Wright, Print Olive, Jack Hardesty, Arthur Gorham, Doc Barton, and many others of that older generation that made Dodge what she was, Ham Bell was strictly a self-made man in an age when to be self-made meant that a man had red blood in his veins. Bell came from Pleasant Valley, Maryland, where he was born Hamilton B. Bell on July 31, 1853. He journeyed west to Great Bend, Kansas, accompanied by a cousin. At Great Bend he drove a livery rig for Poole and Bell Stables. Later he worked at Brinkman's Lumber Yard. He served for a time as assistant police officer under Jim Gainsford and was a deputy sheriff under George Moses. In 1874 he came on west to Dodge.

Ham Bell erected a small livery stable in Dodge, a low-roof soddy with a wagon yard behind and a pole fence forming a corral for the ox teams and mules. When the Texas trail herds started coming in over the new Western Trail in 1876, Bell built a new and larger building of wood. It was located where the Godfrey Auto Works was later located in the 1930's, south of the tracks. Bell named it The Elephant Stable. Under this name it became famous to all trail drivers who put up at Dodge overnight. On the front of the building was painted a huge running elephant, carrying in its trunk a banner that was emblazoned with the inscription in letters a foot in height, "H. B. BELL." Across the entire width of the building ran a sign, "LIVERY STABLE." In a small shed at one side of the entrance was a blacksmith shop. At the other side was a windmill. The building was about 60 x 120 feet in size and in its large haymow as many as fifty drovers and cowboys would bunk when the Dodge hostelries overflowed during the height of the cattle season in June, July, and August. Perhaps another fifty would be bedded down in their tarps and suggans in the wagon yard at the rear.

In the office of the old building, around the pot-bellied Army stove, booted heels would rest after being in the saddle all day, and many were the stories told, of Indian raids, of events along the cattle trails or battles between the Blue and Gray. Ham Bell heard them all, and it goes without saying that it is a shame no one sought to record the many true stories Bell could have related had he been pressed and invited to do so.

Here at Ham Bell's wagon yard, Texas trailmen could literally "see the elephant and hear the owl holler," as they expressed it.

In later years Bell built a brick structure at the same location as the Elephant Barn, which he sometimes referred to as "my white elephant." Here he engaged in the furniture business and in the undertaking establishment he operated for many years. As to the latter enterprise he once said, "The motor machinery business drove me out of the horse and buggy business and though I tried I was never able to again catch up with the modern stream of life. I made up my mind then that it would take the change to Everlasting Life on the part of the human race to catch me again in a business which would completely play out, as the horse and buggy livery business did."

Ham Bell served Dodge as an alderman for four terms; as Ford County Commissioner for a year; as Ford County Sheriff twelve years. Bob Wright wrote of Bell's service: ". . . he made many trips into No Man's Land alone, each time returning with his prisoner."

In 1884, after U.S. Deputy Marshal Harry T. McCarty was murdered, Bell filled his office for twelve years under all administrations. Genial, warm-hearted Marshal McCarty was killed in the Longbranch Saloon. He was chatting with a friend, a Mr. Jackson, at the bar, when a half-drunk desperado called Thomas Roach snatched McCarty's revolver from its holster. After twirling the weapon to show off, Roach pulled the trigger, the bullet hitting McCarty in the groin. Bystanders immediately shot Roach down, not killing him, however. It was not known whether Roach's foolish act was accidental, was the result of drunken bravado and wanting to show off, or was a planned murder. Most observers thought it accidental, for snatching the pistol of Marshal McCarty, and not in fun, was regarded as "sure death." Nor did the drunken man, whose real name was Thomas O'Haran, have any grievance against the lawman. He was given twelve years.

Ham Bell had also been a deputy under Ford County's first sheriff, Charlie Bassett, an over-all record of years of law work that overshadows the work of the prominent TV marshals. And it may be added that Ham Bell accomplished his duties over these many years without having to shoot down or kill a prisoner, a source of great pride to him for the balance of his life.

In addition to his law work, Bell served as Dodge's mayor from 1912 to 1915. In 1909, trying to keep pace with a growing community and a technical society, he built a garage and sold the first automobiles in Dodge! Keeping abreast of the times, he later built a two-story brick building on Chestnut Street (re-named, alas, Wyatt Earp Boulevard) and at this location he sold auto supplies, maintained a hearse and ambulance, sold fish, and kept a pet store. Bell appeared capable of doing almost anything he set out to do, and in 1927 he constructed a brick building at 209 West Spruce Street, which he later thought was 'the most interesting spot in Dodge City.' It was a larger and more elaborate pet shop! Here, he enjoyed his final years.

For many years Ham Bell had dealt in land, cars, and insurance, invested in town and ranch properties, cattle, and the pets for his pet shop. He had buried most of the old pioneers he had known from youth—Chalk Beeson, Print Olive, Jack Hardesty, Bob Wright, Brick Bond, A. J. Anthony, George Rieghard, John Riney, Doc McCarty, George Hoover, H. L. Sitler, most of the personnel of the Cowboy Band, and not a few of the "bad" men who were buried on Boot Hill and later moved to Prairie Grove Cemetery. As a mortician, Ham Bell had learned to look upon Death as a part of Life, the closing chapter, nothing to fear, something only to expect and to become reconciled to at the end. His sympathetic understanding helped many who parted from their loved ones at the grave, to which their beloved dead had ridden in the horse-drawn and later motor-drawn vehicles provided by Ham Bell.

Ham Bell probably knew more cattlemen and law officers by their first names than any other man in the Southwest. He made quiet, private, and personal loans to many old friends who were down on their luck, rarely charging them interest and failing to be repaid by many of them. In his years as a law man he arrested every sort from youths just entering a path of crime, many of whom he turned back to the straight and narrow, to psychopathic killers. Like many of the men of his age he feared no man, but could rarely steel himself to serve foreclosure papers on a widow or an old friend, usually delegating this distasteful duty to a deputy. When Print Olive's widow, Louisa Olive, was losing her town properties by foreclosure following her husband's murder at Trail City, Colorado, Bell, an old friend of Print Olive, took every precaution to avoid hurting Louisa Olive or offending her. He made every effort to see that she obtained the highest prices possible for the town lots which she sold to provide for her family of small boys.

When Ham Bell was in his eighties the annual Ham Bell Picnic became a city-wide attraction. Old folks who had known Bell in youth were getting scarcer and it was now their sons and daughters who carried on the tradition. Since the birthday fell in July, on its last day, the weather was often too hot for the old people to attend. Bell then thoughtfully arranged to hold the picnics in September. As the years passed and Ham passed a white-thatched 88, he fast began running out of old friends, only their sons, daughters, and grandchildren remaining to attend the picnics.

Before one of the last picnics, Ham Bell was reflecting. "I hope to live several years more," he said, then paused and flicked an ant from the bosom of his shirt. "I love everyone, especially western Kansans. I thank the Lord for much which I have to be thankful for, since He has been with me all my life—and He's gotten me out of some pretty rough spots, too!"

On his 91st birthday, July 31, 1944, Hamilton B. Bell greeted friends down town in Dodge at his pet shop and "waited on trade" as usual. Following his death in 1947 the author was talking one day with Ida Olive about writing of the old pioneers of Dodge City. "If you're going to write about some one," Ida said, "write about Ham Bell."

"I remember him for many kind things he did," Ida Olive continued, "and for many kind things he said to others. But probably the best thing we remember him for was that he always laid a floral tribute on the casket of anyone who passed away in Dodge City."

Matt Brennan has long since left the Neutral Strip where he rode for several ranches. He passed on many years ago in Montana. Brennan was remembered by Bernard Lemert who rode with him and bunked with him in the rain on the roundup of '84. Brennan later left with a trail herd from the Half Circle S and a story later came back about Brennan and his experiences in Montana.

Claud Carter, a Nebraska man, needed a spot on which to sell whiskey to the cowboys, so he established the town of Ekalaka, Montana, in 1885. Ekalaka never boasted a Boot Hill, but near a rocky butte a graveyard of sorts was eventually started. Not one of the Ekalaka residents, however, died a natural death. The first to go was bitten by a rattlesnake; the second was drowned; the third was a suicide; two perished in blizzards; two died of bad horse accidents; then came the death of Black Sam. Here is where Matt Brennan came in.

Black Sam was actually a white man, that is his skin was white, when not too dirty. But his heart was black as a tar pit. He was a Texas man, as was Matt Brennan who had worked with him and knew him. Black Sam rode into Ekalaka one winter evening and announced his intention to get drunk and raise as much hell for a week as was possible for one man to do. Then he bellied up to the bar and began. This continued for six days.

Jim Hagen's wagon, JJ Ranch roundup. The cook and the ranch foreman establish a "fight scene" for the photographer the cook keeping the foreman at bay with a long butcher knife. The wrangler scoops out a helping of beans from the pot. In the background is the "gather" of cattle while in the right foreground stand the horses of the remuda in their rope corral. The wagon is piled high with the bedrolls of the cowboys, with an unfolded tarp on top. *Photo by R. W. Day, Doby, Kansas.*

The above shows branding time on the plains. No corrals, a fire made of sagebrush and cowchips. Two men to ride and catch calves; two men to "wrestle" them; a fire and iron tender; a man to "run the irons," and a couple or three men to hold them down. *Photo by R. W. Day, Doby, Kansas.*

193

The JJ Up and JJ Down was originally the Jones Brothers outfit. It was later sold to Prairie Cattle Company, the largest cattle outfit on the Southwest Plains.

The above picture shows the JJ at roundup time having dinner at the wagon. The time is about 1887, southeastern Colorado or in Neural Strip. *Photo by R. W. Day, Doby, Kansas.*

Beaver River roundup—spring of '87, camp on Clear Creek. Tentatively identified in this old photo of Ludwig and Frank Kramer's LUK and Quarter-circle Q ranch outfit are as follows: Third from left, Robert McFarland; 4th Mr. Masston; 7th "Lengthy John" Halford; 11th (behind horse) "Fletch"; 14th Ludwig Kramer; 15th (standing afoot) Bernard Lemert; 16th Al Buchanan; 17th John George; 24th Col. Perry (of Perry Brothers); 28th Rube or Perry Chilcott. *Photo courtesy the late Bernard Lemert.*

COWBOYS ON CHIQUITA CREEK ON ROUNDUP OF 1884
The above shows cowboys of the Hardesty Half Circle S
Ranch during the roundup. The boy at the right is B. M.
Lemert who rode his first roundup that year. At the extreme
right is Tom Hungate, roundup captain. The small boy at the
left is said to have been called the Backward LX Kid, a friend
of Lemert's.—*Photo courtesy Bernard M. Lemert.*

An unidentified group of southwestern cattlemen and settlers as they meet to enjoy a "social." A typical three-day event
would start on Friday night with a dance, continue all night.
After a good rest Saturday morning, the party would continue
with a dance until not later than 12 o'clock Saturday night. All
would gather at church meeting the following day, Sunday. The
meetings would end and the "social" be over by Sunday eve.
In this group an Englishman, very much resembling Rud-
yard Kipling, sits in the center of the group. There were many
British investors in the cattle industry of the Southwest at that
time. *Photo by F. M. Steele, Beaver, Okla.*

RUINS OF THE OLD DR. REGNIER HOME
IN DALLINAS CANYON, NO MAN'S LAND

This big rock home was done in the grand style, offering many advantages theretofore never seen on the southwest cattle range. Now a heap of ruins it lies at the left side of the canyon road as one drives north from the Cimarron River. The Regnier-Labrier-Rowan feud ended in tragedy with the death of Bill Rowan and the wounding of his brother Charles. *Photo by Author.*

Boss Neff II, son of Jake Neff and grandson of the famous old Neutral Strip rancher, Boss Neff, stands on the site of Old Hardesty, holding a metal relic from the old Hardesty school house. The original town of Hardesty is about four miles northeast of the present town of that name. It was named after the Hardesty Brothers Cattle Company who held range in that area. Boss Neff later ranched in that vicinity and his heirs still own land near there.

Arkalon, Kansas, on the Chicago, Kansas and Nebraska Railroad, became a famous shipping point in 1887 when the railroad selected that point on the Cimarron River to make its crossing. Herds from the XIT, Backward LX, the Turkey Tracks, Westmoreland-Hitch and other big shippers drove their trail herds to Arkalon instead of Dodge City. As the railroad built on to Liberal, then to Old Tyrone in the Neutral Strip, Arkalon lost this lucrative traffic, withered away. Today it is only a ghost site of yawning basements and sidewalks. *Photo by Author.*

"The Grangers." Above, a typical pioneer and his family stand in the farm yard before their new home "on the Plains." He has brought his fine team out before the camera to show that he is a "propertied" man, well able to care for himself and his family. Pioneer life on the plains was rugged indeed. An old verse of No Man's Land tells how:

> "Pickin' up bones to keep from starving
> Pickin' up chips to keep from freezing,
> Pickin' up courage to keep from leaving,
> 'Way out West in No Man's Land." *Photo by Day, Doby, Kansas.*

197

The OX Ranch Headquarters, Beaver River, No Man's Land. It was here that the love affair between Emanuela and her cowboy sweetheart blossomed, but bore no fruit after he was drowned on a Trail Drive in the waters of the far-off Platte River in Nebraska. Emanuela had the old buildings enclosed with a stout, barb wire fence. There it has stood now for more than eighty years, looking out across the Beaver River, about three miles northeast of present Guymon, Oklahoma. *Photo by author.*

The great Anchor D ranch of the Neutral Strip was later called the Stonebreaker and Zea and was also called the Schumaker Ranch. Originally it was operated by E. C. Dudley and Son. Dudley was a Boston man with a marine background. Originally the brand used was a Double Cross. The significance of the brand was distasteful to Dudley and he formed his own brand—a brand that stuck for many years—the Anchor D. The ranch headquarters was west of present Guymon, Oklahoma, about 20 miles, and the Dudley range was of many sections from Kansas state line to the Texas panhandle and for miles along the Beaver River. *Photo courtesy Burris Wright, Liberal, Kansas.*

Three-C jerkline outfit. Henry Dotson drives a six-mule hitch into Old Optima to pick up freight for the CCC Ranch. The popular Bee Hive is shown just behind the lead mule's head. *Photo courtesy the late Burris Wright, Liberal, Kansas.*

Fred Taintor had his ranch headquarters on Taintor Creek, a small stream northeast of Beaver City, Neutral Strip, which flows northeast into the Cimarron River. Taintor branded with a GG. His brand was picked on by the rustlers who sold to the Beaver City and Kansas town markets. In 1883 rustlers ran 300 head of Taintor steers over into the Kansas range on Crooked Creek, held them for several months, then sold them at Dodge City. This group of rustlers were later apprehended by the cattlemen's organization in that area and hanged without more ado. Taintor ran up to 30,000 head of cattle it was said. *Photo courtesy the late Bernard Lemert, Liberal, Kansas.*

An old photograph, published in the *Guymon* (Oklahoma) *Observer*, April 27, 1950, shows a group of old-timers who, reading from left to right, are as follows:

Back row: Con Jackson—Con and Perry Bright used to catch mustangs, break and sell them. Burris Wright, son of Charlie Wright, attorney and cattleman (Burris' story appears elsewhere in this volume); Boss Neff, see his story elsewhere in book. The fourth figure was identified to the author as Jim Herron but since then Bill Antrim, 87, pioneer citizen, has stated the likeness is of himself. C. R. Miller stands at Antrim's left. Next in the picture is Charlie Hitch whose story appears elsewhere; then Curt Richards, who worked on the CCC Ranch on the Beaver; Bill George, a cousin of J. K. Hitch and Charlie Hitch is left in front. Next is H. S. Judy, who worked in the first bank in No Man's Land and later at Guymon. He knew scores of cattlemen by their first names; next is Lee Larabee, also mentioned elsewhere in this volume; Bill Ewing, who with his brothers Link and Lew were well-known cowboys and finally established their on ranch on Palo Duro. Bill went up the trail to Montana with a Kramer Brothers herd when the range was gone in No Man's Land; next is the only lady in the picture, Bertha Loofbarrow, according to what Burris Wright told the author. She was the daughter of Judge Loofbourrow, well known jurist of old No Man's Land. Jim England, right, is squatting on his hams, cowboy style. He worked for the CCC ranch several years and had worked for most of the ranches in No Man's Land at one time or another. Later he had a small ranch for himself and was in business at Guymon.

One night Black Sam stepped back from the bar and announced that he was through, was "going to cash in his chips" as he termed it. The other punchers in town laughed at his statement, but Black Sam contended his days were over, he was ready to cross the Divide. That night they put him to bed in Whit Terrill's Hotel, a metal-coated refrigerator of a building that brought most guests down to the lobby by four o'clock in the morning to stand by the big stove, beat their frosted hands together, and try to thaw themselves out. The room in which they put Sam was called "the school section" by the cowboys, and was a large, barn-like upstairs room where all slept together without the benefit of room partitions. After taking a few more swigs of whiskey, Black Sam finally dropped asleep.

About midnight, Matt Brennan, who was punching cows on a nearby ranch, came in. Finding all beds taken, he crawled in alongside Black Sam. Matt complained loudly to Black Sam about sharing covers and permitting him at least a third of the bed, but Black Sam never moved an inch.

The following morning Matt Brennan arose early. "That rascal of a Black Sam is the coldest and stiffest son-of-a-bitch I ever slept with in my borned days. I never want to share a suggan again with the likes of him," Brennan said.

An investigation soon proved why. Black Sam was stone dead!

Earlier in the week, they now learned, Sam had made a confession. He had committed a murder in Texas. His younger brother was now serving a life sentence at Huntsville for his crime. No one bothered to communicate this intelligence to the Texas prison system, so Black Sam's debt to society was paid by his brother.

The cowboys pondered whether Black Sam would pay for his sins in Hell as they tucked him in by the big butte. Matt Brennan thought not.

"Sam was so much like the Devil himself that the chances are that the two will pair up when Sam reaches the Pit," Matt told friends, then shivered as he recalled the frigid tailbone he felt on Black Sam that night in the school section of Whit Terrell's fleabag hotel, when the mercury in the thermometer stood at forty degrees below zero.

A story of the lost trails of the Cimarron would hardly be complete without mention of Robert M. Wright, and his proper place in the history of that area. Bob Wright was born in Maryland, September 2, 1840. At the age of sixteen he came west. He worked on a farm at St. Louis, then made four trips across the plains to Santa Fe by freight wagon, bullwhacking, and two other trips by stage. On these trips he learned much of the Santa Fe trade, learned buying, selling and trading as a way of life. Later he contracted hay cutting and hauling, wood and grain freighting, buffalo hunting and hide-buying. In 1867 he was appointed sutler at old Fort Dodge.

Robert M. Wright was president of the town company when Dodge City was founded in 1872. He was in business at Dodge for many years, was a noteworthy citizen, and later operated the Crescent W. Ranch south of Dodge, his cattle ranging from the Fort Dodge Military Reservation to the Cimarron.

Wright left many mementoes of his life in Dodge, chief among which is the lovely Wright Park on the north bank of the Arkansas River, at the end of the river bridge. It is a place of rare beauty and charm on a spot that was once only a part of the treeless river bottom, "south of the Deadline."

He was in several partnerships, such as with Charles Rath and with H.M. Beverly. The former, Rath & Wright, opened up the buffalo hide business when the hunters poured south of the Arkansas into the forbidden treaty lands to shoot off the remains of the southern herd. Rath, according to Wright, handled more buffalo hides than any other man of the time, and few hunters killed more of the big animals than Rath, said Wright about his partner. Rath spoke all the Indian dialects of the Cheyennes and Arapahoes and was the best on the plains in talking "sign" with the Indians.

H.M. Beverly, the other partner of Bob Wright, was another man of worth and character. Beverly was born in King George County, Virginia, in 1826. He was raised in Kentucky. When the Civil War came, Beverly enlisted with Texas troops and served the Confederacy as a lieutenant. He married Fannie C. Skiles in 1850 and engaged in the cattle business at Ellsworth, Great Bend, and Dodge City when the Texas trails reached those places. At Dodge he met Wright and engaged in the mercantile business with him. Beverly owned the BV brand for many years and was an officer in the Cattleman's Association. He was in business at Trail City when that little trail town "budded, blossomed and died." It was Beverly who brought Print Olive's body back to Dodge for burial after his murder by Joe Sparrow at Trail City.

The full story of Robert M. Wright and his businesses and his partners would require a large volume and would pall the feeble achievements of the Dodge lawmen who are today so important to fiction writers and television screens. Bob Wright did write some of his story in the work *Dodge City, The Cowboy Capital*, the most accurate study of old Dodge City yet written, and the foundation work for anyone attempting to write of the old cowboy capital. Bob Wright helped build Dodge City into a respectable city on the plains, and in doing so he created a deep and abiding respect for his name among the citizens of Dodge City and the Arkansas Valley.

"Buffalo" Jones was a name known to all men and women of the Cimarron region, to Dodge City and to Garden City, in the Eighties. He was the king of town boosters, an early, one-man Chamber of Commerce for Garden City and other towns along the Arkansas River. But he was more than this.

Charles Jesse (Buffalo) Jones came to Kansas in 1866. He was a nurseryman and the treeless plains convinced him that the first thing needed was shade trees. So with elm, hackberry, walnut, and cottonwood shoots, this Johnny Appleseed of the prairies entered business at Troy, Kansas. The locust plague (grasshoppers) of 1867-68 cleaned out his nursery stock. Now married and the father of a small daughter, he moved to Bull City, in Osborne County, Kansas.

In Bull City, Jones set up as a small rancher and as a locator for homesteaders. His Yankee soul was revolted by the tons and tons of buffalo meat left rotting on the prairies by the hide hunters. Jones had hunted buffalo for food, but this waste convinced him that without aid coming to them from some quarter, the buffalo would soon become extinct. As his mind groped with this problem, the thought came to him that cross-breeding with the domestic cow might preserve all that was good in the buffalo and combine it with the gentle qualities of the domestic bovine for posterity. He believed that a new, reinvigorated species of animal, the cross between the buffalo and cow, might replace on the plains the huge animals now facing extinction. This remained with his thoughts, though his activities turned to other fields for a few years.

In Bull City he found few opportunities and in 1879 he moved to Sterling, Kansas. There he carried mail, acted as a realtor and homestead locator. At this time he became interested in the promotion of Garden City, a settlement on the Santa Fe railway, west of Dodge City about fifty miles. To this end, Jones helped secure the U.S. Land Office for Garden City and built an entire business block with the lovely building stone from the quarry at nearby Kendall. This block included the famous *Buffalo Hotel.*

Through his successful years, Jones had spoken out wherever he could gain an audience for protection of the buffalo. Only a few of the big humped animals remained in the breaks of the Canadian and Beaver rivers, and Jones preached the value of saving them wherever he went. He said:

> The buffalo is constructed for the fitfull climate of the High Plains region of western Kansas. His flesh is more nutritious than eastern bread or meat. He is disease-free. His hides make excellent robes and winter coats. The buffalo cow's milk is richer than your dairy cream. The buffalo hide is an inch thick on head, neck and shoulders, quite ample protection to face the most terrible blizzards of the plains. His under-fur is softer than swan's down. His carded fleece weaves into blankets, hosiery and cloth fabrics that would be fit for any king. What other animal has so many graces, so few faults? Why, the American Bison is a work of God!

But Buffalo Jones was pleading a lost cause.

Jones was elected to the Kansas Legislature and went to Topeka in his $500 buffalo-hide coat. There, on the floor, he pleaded the buffalo's cause. He returned from Topeka when his term was over and again turned to booming such towns as Ulysses, Leoti, and Ravanna—most of them ghost sites today. He entered into the formation of river irrigation projects, and the Arkansas River bottom blossomed. But always in the back of his mind was the plight of the few remaining buffalo, fewer than fifty head remaining of the southern herd. These were all that were left of the estimated 60,000,000 head of the big humped animals that grazed on the North American continent when Columbus made his discovery of the New World!

Buffalo Jones, in November, 1888, acquired the herd of buffalo raised by Warden Benson of Stoney Mountain, N.W. Territory. There were eighty-three head in this herd, and Jones shipped them to Garden City, Kansas, where he turned them in with his herd of about fifty buffalo he had acquired the previous May when he organized the *Chicago Times* expedition and went to the Neutral Strip and Texas panhandle to rope buffalo calves taking along a supply of carrier pigeons to relay his reports back to that newspaper! Earlier, in 1886, with two companions, Charley Rude and Newton Adams, Jones had ventured to No Man's Land and there captured seventy-five small buffalo calves during the month of April. Now, on his buffalo ranch at Garden City, Jones began the experiments in controlled breeding that were to result in the hybrid calf of a buffalo bull and a domestic cow which he named the "catalo."

Jones found some of his theories right, some wrong. The first cross he found was the most difficult to make, the "catalo" readily breeding back either to buffalo or domestic bovine, which was unlike the hybrid mule which usually ended the process between jackass and mare. The experiments were interesting and useful, and were watched by all the cattlemen of the area, hoping for a successful cross that would present them with a durable, disease-free, buffalo-beef animal that could successfully replace the buffalo on the prairies and be at least as easily handled as the longhorns from Texas.

During these experiments Jones decided to teach a pair of young buffalo bulls to work. To this end he constructed a strong, two-wheeled cart with huge freightwagon wheels and a heavy foot break. The wagon was equipped with a massive, hardwood tongue. To it Jones harnessed the two young bulls in a manner so that they pulled the wagon with a yoke. But the young animals proved so headstrong and hard-mouthed to bridle bits that he was given some dizzying rides. With a companion who always helped him, Jones worked out a special system of controls. He built heavy leather halters. To the sides of each he fastened heavy ropes, bringing them back to the driver's seat. He ran a stout wood jockey stick between the buffalo's heads, from one halter to the other. Then he built rein-holders, two large spool arrangements that were actually miniature windlasses. Around each he started the rope that led to the buffalo's halter on that side. By turning the windlass crank, he, or his companion, could wind up the buffalo's head until the animal could not move, thereby not injuring its mouth, as the bits previously did, but simply slowing down one side of the cart while the other side moved ahead. This gave the drivers a control of direction as well as determining the speed at which the animals could travel. As a matter of fact, Buffalo Jones could well lay claim to America's first "power steering," for such as it was. But the whole arrangement was unsatisfactory, for the wild buffalo could not be tamed and driven like the domestic ox. So eventually Jones gave up the experiment, satisfied to ride behind a pair of good horses or mules.

In 1890 the southwest Kansas boom ended on a dry note—drought. With mortgage foreclosure, an exodus of settlers began. Low cattle prices and other recession factors worked against Buffalo Jones as it did all men in the area. So Buffalo Jones sold out and quit, later starting another buffalo ranch at McCook, Nebraska, about 1891-92.

Jones' experiments with the wild buffalo focused his interest on other wild animals and their possibilities. He had found that human beings were deeply interested in viewing his wild buffalo, as they had shown when he took six pairs of the animals to England and put them on Lord Leland's estate. So in 1893-94 Jones made a trip to the Arctic regions, there roped a dozen head of musk oxen with the idea of bringing them back alive to the United States to exploit. But the Esquimaux of that region had a different idea. They raided his camp one night and slit the throats of all the animals. Later he learned that it was against their religion to allow the beasts to be taken from their native haunts. Disappointed, Jones returned empty-handed.

In 1899 Jones completed his autobiography. It was titled *Forty Years of Adventure,* and the book found good sales. In 1901 he set to work inventing a water lift to irrigate lands higher than the stream flow. His efforts brought him much attention, but little money.

In 1902, Theodore Roosevelt procured an appointment for Jones as warden of Yellowstone Park, a position he held for the next four years. In 1906 Jones again started planning another buffalo ranch, this time on the north rim of Grand Canyon. At this time he became acquainted with the writer Zane Grey, and he led Grey on a mountain lion hunt, roping the big cats out of the trees after the dogs had treed them. Their game they turned over to zoos and parks.

In 1910 Jones set out for Africa, this time to rope and tie hartbeest, warthogs, eland, cheetas, zebras, and rhinos with a lariat! He returned with practically every specimen he sought, including lions and tigers. The next two years, Buffalo Jones followed the lecture circuit, telling of his experiences with buffalo, in the north lands and in Africa.

In 1914, Jones sailed again for the Dark Continent. Following his return from this latest safari, he again set forth on the lecture circuit. But he had contracted malaria fever this last voyage, and it stopped his lecture tour in the middle. So again he commenced work on his water-lift for irrigation, but still without achieving success. In 1918 Jones suffered a brief illness and on October 1, he died at the home of his daughter in Topeka.

One old pioneer of Western Kansas, upon hearing of the death of Buffalo Jones, removed his sweat-streaked Stetson, ran his hands through his thin gray hair, and remarked, "Most of us came west to grow up with the country. Not so, Buffalo Jones. He came west *to grow the country up!*"

It was true. In the west with its developing mores, there was always the wide-open invitation to individualism and individual expression. There, on the plains, creativity found some sort of outlet. The need for improvisation generated a race of inventive men such as the world never saw before. Individuals as dissimilar as Wild Bill Hickok and Dr. George Washington Carver were growing up on the plains at the same time, springing from fresh, new land as naturally as prize roses spring up from a patio garden prepared and suited to their purpose. No two individuals were alike, in fact, were as un-alike as the cumulus clouds that rise in great towers in the heavens over the prairie land, then sweep majestically across the western scene, many-layered, no two traveling at the same speed, yet all going in the same general direction.

No where in the west was there one to match the strange, many-faceted, industrious, ingenious Buffalo Jones. He was the man who set out to save the buffalo from extinction, and his work helped others after him to understand the plight of the great beasts, and help them to survive in this modern world. It is fitting that he wear, forever, their name, a name to which he ascribed integrity, power, beauty, and utility. He matched their own fine qualities, did Buffalo Jones.

Chapter IX

The initiative and versatility displayed by the pioneer people have often been mentioned, yet too seldom have the simple improvisions they learned to make on a wild and ofttimes unkind frontier been shown in detail. Sometimes when these "simple" improvisions are given study, they turn out to be quite complex measures that were of necessity taken in order for the newcomer to the high plains to endure. As in all matters pertaining to survival, those who failed to adjust either left the country and returned to a more favorable clime, or they perished on the plains. An example of one who endured was a Scotsman, a youth named Alexander McLeod.

McLeod came west and established himself on the pristine prairie land northwest of Dodge City at the head of Pawnee Creek. He liked the region with its widespread carpet of succulent buffalo grass. Near the creek, he dug himself a hole in a clay bank and made his claim. He put in a sheet-iron stove, hung a tarp for a door at the mouth of his cave, built a bunk for a bed at the rear on which he stuffed gunny sacks with hay for a mattress and used a buffalo robe for his cover. He had neither friends nor money when he moved in. He owned no livestock of any kind, so he pondered how he might convert this ocean of grass to a livelihood for himself. McLeod knew that he had no chance to weather any long spell on this open range without income and food from some outside source, and there were no other humans for several miles around him. To prove up on his claim he must live on it, but living on it under his present circumstances, he knew, offered only starvation as his reward.

Nearby ran the Texas cattle trail, where it now turned northwestward from Dodge City, heading for Ogallala, Nebraska, then a main point for shipment on the Union Pacific railroad as well as supply point for the Indian Reservations in the north country.

Watching this trail, McLeod observed that it was the practice for many drovers to kill the new-born calves on the bedground rather than slow up the herd with them tagging alongside their mothers. Finding the tiny creatures' bodies on the bedgrounds, a 45 bullet hole in their heads, grieved the Scotsman. One morning he appeared before daylight, asked the trail boss if he might have the calves born that night—alive. He told the trail boss he could feed them and it would enable him to start his own herd. The trail boss, a man who himself hated the hard practice of shooting the new-born calves, was very willing to let the calves live and be taken by the young settler. But he was skeptical that they could be kept alive.

"They cain't live without mother's milk," the Texan told McLeod.

"They can'na live without *food*," McLeod corrected him. "An' I think I ha' foon a way to feed th' bairnees something—but na' milk."

The puzzled trail boss expressed his sympathy and hope that McLeod could keep the calves—and himself!—alive, then pushed the herd away from the bedground leaving six small, weak calves.

McLeod had borrowed a neighbor's wagon and team for the occasion. He hastily loaded the calves and pulled out for his claim. There, he put them in a small sod pen he had built alongside his dugout. In a copper-bottomed boiler he had brought with him, he put an armful of buffalo grass he had cut with his pocket knife. Into the boiler he poured a few quarts of water, set the boiler on his little sheet-iron stove and brought the water to a boil, stirring the soggy mess slowly as it cooked. After twenty minutes of slow boiling he drained off the liquid, straining it through a piece of cheesecloth. This was the liquid which was to replace the cow's milk in his ward's diet. He named it "Hay Tea," or "Prairie Tea." It was rich, succulent, nutritious—but it had a bilous green color. And would the calves drink it?

For a few meals, McLeod was obliged to force-feed the lukewarm liquid to the calves. They would pull back, turn their tiny heads to avoid the strange, unfamiliar mixture, then stand

and bawl hungrily for their mothers' milk and for her warm, friendly tongue to lick and caress them.

At first a few calves died. But those that survived would soon follow the young Scotsman around the yard, bawling now for Hay Tea! As McLeod brought a few of the older calves to their weaning period he started them grazing, and he soon found a sale for them. With his first cash income he bought a lame longhorn cow from a trail boss. The cow had calved and lost her calf. This cow he converted to saving the weaker calves that he brought from the bedgrounds. His calf herd soon numbered nearly a hundred calves, about twenty of which had been weaned and now grazed on the surrounding range.

This ownership of a hundred calves and only a single cow soon brought McLeod to the attention of Texas drovers, and the trail herds that had formerly bedded their herds only a short distance from his soddy now undertook to make their bedground farther distant! They doubled their guards at night, too! The new settlers who had moved in to the neighborhood laughed at McLeod's predicament, but they helped to assure the trail bosses of McLeod's honesty and his system of maintaining new-born calves on Hay Tea. So the thrifty Scotsman added almost weekly to his herd.

When the Texas herds were forced by legislation to give up their trails across Kansas, McLeod traded some of his half-grown animals to Ham Bell for a livery stable. The young settler prospered at his new business and eventually owned three stables and a feed business as well as proving up on his homestead. He married a fine young Scotswoman and she helped him in every venture he undertook.

Alexander McLeod worked for the Santa Fe railway as an inspector and still later as a bridge and building contractor and painter. He worked with the crew that relined the Raton Tunnel in 1904.

In later years the McLeods moved to California, as had so many of the earlier successful Kansas settlers before them. Such people gave Kansas its never-fading bloom. The ingenuity and versatility they had shown was indicative of the Spirit that settled the West.

In speaking of weather, Mark Twain said that "everyone talked about it but no-one ever did anything about it." That was the way with the Texas Tick. It cost the new land thousands of head of livestock—that is, until an Oklahoma man came along and did something about it.

Albert Dean was an Ohioan by birth, born December 27, 1840. He came west and worked cattle, being familiar on the southwest cattle range in the days of the great cattle drives out of Texas. He spent many years in Oklahoma, having a nice ranch northwest of Gutherie, between Lovell and Mulhall. But his great work was done for the southwestern cattlemen against their greatest natural enemy—the Texas Tick. It was another case of frontier improvisation, the versatility to apply homely, home-grown remedies to the problem at hand and gaining a victory for an entire nation.

The Texas cattle were unaffected by the tick, but when the tick transferred itself to other domestic cattle it brought death in a matter of days. One night Dean was milking a longhorn Texas cow. He noticed that her udder was covered with a mass of black ticks, one of which would now and then fall into his milk pail. A side of fresh bacon hung in a nearby tree to prevent cats and dogs from gnawing it. Dean decided the greasy bacon might help heal up the udder and teats, which were raw from the tick bites, so he sliced off a piece of bacon and greased the udder and teats.

He noticed that when he greased the udder that the ticks immediately fell off—dead. The following morning when he milked, the udder was free of ticks and commencing to heal. Dean took a large slab of the bacon fat and rubbed it over the cow's back, head and limbs. A day later he noticed she was practially free of the Texas ticks.

Albert Dean continued to experiment with his bacon grease cure for ticks on cattle. After considerable success he wrote to the Department of Agriculture at Washington, telling of his experiences. His letter led to an acquaintance with officials, and he was later given an appointment as director of the Department of

Animal Husbandry at Kansas City. There he launched a research program on tick fever and planned an eradication program.

Dean soon had perfected a dipping vat, actually an extension of his bacon grease cure but with improved medicinal additives and a lower-cost oil for the dipping. His studies now proved that the Texas tick, put on a healthy domestic cow, brought about a rise in temperature on the third day and brought death to the host by the ninth or tenth day. Only the Texas longhorn remained immune to the tick, but the Texas cattle remained the carriers of the tick, therefore a danger to all other cattle.

The Texas tick actually had been responsible for the shifting of the earlier cattle trails (which led first to Missouri, Iowa, and Illinois) to a position farther west at Baxter Springs, Kansas, and later to Wichita, Abilene, Ellsworth, Newton, Dodge City, and finally westward, clear out of the state of Kansas.

The lack of a permanent trail north from Texas brought about the pleas on the part of Texas drovers for a National Cattle Trail which would come north on the Western Trail, turn west at Camp Supply and follow the Beaver River to a point where it could swing north, in Colorado, up the Colorado-Kansas state line to Nebraska, the Dakotas, and the Yellowstone. Such towns as Borders, in Kansas, and Trail City, in Colorado, sprang up to meet the needs of drovers on this trail. But their boom was short-lived. Settlers, barbed wire, the Big Die Ups, inaction in Congress to authorize such a "national" trail, all these things acted to kill the new trail out of Texas and the idea died a'bornin'. But the principle for destroying the Texas tick and new techniques for application of the greasy medication which did the killing lived on.

Vat dipping soon destroyed other pests and predators on cattle, it was found. Newer techniques for the application of the mixture out on the range were soon discovered. Today, on most American pastures where cattle range are devices such as the one called "Old Scratch," patented by Bill Kirk. The device invites the cattle to lean against a soft, pliable, medicated rope and scratch that very part of their anatomy which itches most. Needless to say, that itchy part is the egg-pocket where the nits of the parasites are laid. The medicine kills nits and eggs as well as the adult tick, if he be present. And the animal does all the work, leaving the ranch owner free to undertake newer, more vital tasks.

Albert Dean was cited by most of the cattlemen's associations of the west for his efforts that led to the elimination of Texas ticks.

A second enemy to the cattle industry, and one more dangerous to Texas cattlemen who owned only the tick-immune Texas cattle, was the screwworm. Born from the eggs of blowflies deposited in the navels of new-born calves or under the tails of the cows, the worms would eat out raged holes under the skin of the unfortunate animals, causing the deaths of thousands of head annually. Deep-branding in late summer, during the hot weather of late August and early September on the southern plains, often opened the hides of the luckless beasts to the screwworm and endangered entire herds of cattle. Oliver Nelson told how an inexperienced manager had the men of the T5 in the Cherokee Strip brand in August, which brought on a screwworm epidemic in the cattle. Seven hundred head of the deep-burned brands were isolated and doctored with crysilic ointment, a compound of tar, carbolic, and other medicines. They would dig "a pint of grubs out of a steer's back, put in a quarter of a bottle of salve, turn the critter loose and catch another," Nelson said. He told how a strip of hide a foot long would dangle down, leaving a hole two inches deep on the animal's back. They tended the animals until frost came, but 400 head of them died. Strangely enough, the usually wild steer displayed little temper or desire to fight during this treatment, the worms apparently having already debilitated them.

The screwworms could be as dangerous to man as to his cattle, though this was not generally known by the cowboys who doctored the cattle. One bizarre incident occurred and is mentioned in the *Dodge City Globe,* November 19, 1878, wherein death was brought about to a cattleman by the worms.

HORRIBLE DEATH

Mr. Allen Robertson, brother of Jason Robertson of this place, was buried here last Saturday morning. Mr. Robertson came recently from Paul's Valley, C.N., and while on a trip to Sherman for lumber to improve his place, with his team, his nose bled considerable, after which he lay down under his wagon to rest and sleep awhile, and attracted by the blood on his nose, the fly which deposits the screwworm, it is supposed, deposited the germs (eggs) in his nose.

After he came to Sherman he complained considerably of pain in his nose, but did not know the cause, but supposed it was a catarrh from which he suffered occasionally. The pain began to get worse, when a physician was called in, and it was found that he had screwworms in his nostrils, and they had probably worked their way into his lungs.

Several worms were taken from his nose, but remedies were applied too late, and he died after severe sufferings.

To return to more pleasant subjects, and to the initiative displayed by pioneer cattlemen and merchants in their approach to business and banking and other pursuits of a mundane nature, but on a raw frontier which lacked the usual tools and facilities for carrying on these useful practices, we turn to the manner in which merchants resolved the problem of a lack of banks to carry on their commerce.

Texas drovers, following the Civil War and for many years afterward, were skeptical of Yankee currency and preferred gold in settling for herds sold to buyers at the northern railheads. The gold they usually put under false floors in their wagons when returning to Texas. It was a risky cargo to carry and it was not long until many Texas cattlemen began to accept bank drafts. This worked fine—except to a new cowtown, like Dodge, that had no bank. So the buyers were compelled to find some alternate.

R. A. Houston of Gonzalez County, Texas, for many years retained an interesting document showing how the Dodge City firm of Beverly & Wright solved this problem of doing business with the Texas men, though living in a town unsupported by a local banking establishment.

These big general merchandise stores then handled almost everything a drover could ask for—harness, clothes, saddles, guns, food, powder, wagons, whiskey, and so forth. Their mammoth volume of business forced them to install immense iron safes to avoid armed robbery.

Now most of the Texas drovers did not desire to carry large amounts of gold coin through the outlaw-infested Indian Territory to their Texas homes. The Dodge merchants had, by this time, established their own credit with eastern suppliers, and most drovers had had some small credit dealings with the merchants and found them trustworthy traders. So the merchants commenced to issue acceptable drafts on themselves, just as a chartered bank might do.

The papers retained by Houston, mentioned above, are the accounts of one such transaction of 1883. It was sketched in *The Cattleman* magazine, Fort Worth, Texas, a few years ago. The amount shown in the transaction is $53,267.50 and involved a trail herd sold by Burnett & Syers, drovers. The debt was settled by a sight draft of $35,000.00 and a 30-day draft for $18,267.50 issued by Beverly & Wright. The itemized statement of the transaction showed the following amounts paid for particular classes of cattle:

1-year-olds	$30,705.50
2-year-olds	13,319.00
3-year-olds	5,872.50
75 Saddlehorses	2,700.00
Mules	180.00
1 yearling steer	15.50
Chuckwagon	90.00
Walker Horses	385.00

The latter item was probably for some horses privately owned by some member, probably the foreman, of the outfit. But the point of the story is to show the manner in which ordinary cattle-men-merchants like Beverly and Wright met the problems of their day with ingenuity, initiative, and great and good common sense. The demand made upon them as buyers of these herds was truly big business, even for today. For the men of that time, the problem of raising such huge sums to pay for scores of trailherds that arrived in a two or three month period in the summer, one herd upon the heels of another, must have seemed almost insurmountable. Wisely, *through building up their own credit, they reduced the southern demand for gold.* Our financial leaders today might well study their actions and the entire nation profit from such study.

What happens to men when their source of livelihood becomes extinct? What happens to men whose profession for which they have long trained dies? I am thinking of an old friend, Burris Wright, whom the author carried to his grave in December, 1958. Burris was then seventy-nine. He was born September 2, 1879, in Wayne County, Iowa, coming to the southwest with his parents and their family in 1887.

Burris' father was Charles Wright, the well-known attorney and former Beaver County, Oklahoma, county attorney, who also ran cattle, having the Th (Trassas) brand registered in his name on the Beaver River in the late Eighties. And there Burris, at the age of nine or ten, took up cowpunching together with his brothers Ray and Carson.

Charles Wright first had moved to the budding town of Vorhees and there, on the main street one day in 1888, Burris and Ray Wright had watched as the young man Tonney, the only survivor of the Hay Meadow Massacre, a bloody incident of the Stevens County Seat war in which four men were shot down in cold blood by Sam Robinson and his posse, rode down the street almost unconscious on his blood-soaked horse. An old man, a Mr. Vanier, caught the lad, let him down from his horse, and sent Ray Wright riding to Lafayette, another nearby boom town, for a doctor. Tonney lived and told the story of the infamous event.

When Vorhees died, the St. Nicholas Hotel was razed by the Wright family, its timbers moved to a location south of the town of Liberal, just east of the site of Beer City one mile. There, a fine ranch home was erected from the ruins of the hotel and there the Wright family lived for many years. Carson Wright died in 1941, after punching cows for many years. He had worked for Lee Howard a good many years, Howard having the distinction of shooting the last buffalo in No Man's Land.

217

Ray and Burris went to Arizona and there punched cows for Bill Green on the A Dot ranch near Bisbee and Naco for several years. Ray later became a supervisor in a mine, but Burris continued following the cow trails in Chihuahua, Mexico. The Spanish words and phrases, learned through these years, dripped from Burris Wright's lips as naturally and as easily as a prairie shower falls and were a part of the many stories he told of those days when he rode the open range.

But the range cattle industry died, and Burris later moved back to Liberal, Kansas. "The business as I knew it was all over," he said. "There was no use trying to bring back the dead."

Burris once told of a big herd that approached the Rock Island stockyards at Old Tyrone from the southwest, after watering at Shade's Well. The engineer on the train blew several sharp blasts on the whistle to hurry the railway workers who were sanding the livestock cars. The noise of the whistle stampeded the approaching herd, scared the other animals in the pens and chutes. Half the cattle in the pens broke out and mingled with the cattle on the plains surrounding the yards.

"It was a mell of a hess," Burris said. "It took the cowboys three days to get the mess straightened out."

Once the cowman Tyler refused to have his cattle loaded and pulled out by Engine No. 470 because of its poor mechanical condition. Another shipper, glad to get his stock on cars, cheerfully accepted the old engine. The second shipper was delayed four days en route by the old engine having trouble, was passed up by Tyler's train hauling his cattle and the market fell off 3c a pound by the time he got his cattle to the Kansas City yards.

He told Tyler later, "Being in a hurry cost me about three thousand dollars, but I collected $2,500 damages in a lawsuit, so I don't feel so bad about it any more."

Burris Wright told the story of Will Leahy, who became a successful cattleman and shipped many cattle to market. On one trip, Leahy happened to attend an art exhibit at the hotel where he was staying. One painting, with Southwest motif, showed Indians playing cards on a brilliant Navajo blanket. That night

218

Leahy persuaded himself that he would make an offer of $25 for the painting.

The next day he visited the art dealer's offices at the hotel, told him of his desire to own the picture. The dealer gave Leahy a "bottom price" for the picture—it was $3,200.00!

Leahy later told Burris, "I hardly looked back. I damn soon decided to put my money in cows, something I knew at least a little bit about."

The painting was an original by Frederick Remington and later sold for $10,000.00, the cowboys told Leahy afterwards.

Burris Wright was the product of an age when to recite a verse with a theme about the west, cowboys, bad horses, or cattle before the bar of a saloon meant an instant invitation to participate in a free drink. Burris knew many of these interesting, clean, and entertaining verses, and those who knew him well will always remember him best reciting some old ballad of the plains concerning a bad horse or a cowboy making a particularly good ride. Though Burris considered himself somewhat in the same cut as Holmes's "Last Leaf upon the Tree," he left a rich heritage for those who had known him and heard his stories of the great free range of another day, peopled with brave and courteous riders on the finest horses, long before barbed wire and tractors came along to ruin the land.

The author will best remember Burris with his voice lowered in a conspiratorial tone as he would recite some old ballad from the plains country:

> I'm ridin' Old Paint, I'm a leadin' Old Dan,
> I'm off for Montan' for to throw th' hoolihan' . . .

So with others who received much from this old cowboy and who wish him a happy trip to the Other Range I say, "Adios, Burris. Viaje con Dios!"

Chapter X

When ranches were few and far between in southwest Kansas, a man named Peacock had a ranch on Cow Creek. He was friendly with Satank, the great Kiowa war chief, or he would never have lasted long. Peacock sold the Indians whiskey, and Satank ordered his braves to leave the ranch alone when on raiding parties. This arrangement, however, caused Peacock to cache his whiskey everywhere possible, for the U.S. Cavalry troops were continually searching for it in an effort to jail Peacock for illegally selling alcoholic stimulants to the red men.

One day Satank stopped at the ranch and asked Peacock to give him a letter of introduction to the wagon bosses on the Santa Fe Trail, so he could beg supplies without having to fight for them, the Kiowas being a poor people.

"Tell 'em I heap Great War Chief," said Satank. "Ask them give much *woha* and chuck, best in shop."

Peacock turned the chief over to another man at the ranch, one who could write and did some of the little bookwork that was needed at the ranch headquarters. The fellow composed a "Letter of Introduction" all right. It read:

> This is Satank, the biggest liar and scoundrel on the plains.
> What he can't beg from you he will steal. Kick his lazy ass
> out of your camp, for he is no good.

Satank, of course, was thrown bodily from the first two camps where he showed his note. He sought out an interpreter who decoded the message for his primitive mind. What Satank heard didn't please him.

Satank took the trail to Peacock's ranch, picking up many small bodies of young warriors as he rode along. Arriving at the ranch early in the morning, he told his friend Peacock, "Get out of beds. Hide firewater in creek. Many soldiers on trail behind us looking for you!"

Peacock quickly gave orders to hide the whiskey, then with his men gathered atop the watchtower, field glasses in hand to watch for the arrival of the troops. From his position below, Satank shot Peacock off the watch tower. Then his warriors turned to and killed and scalped every man at the ranch excepting one sick man who was asleep in the kitchen woodbox and was overlooked. The Indians then burned most of the ranch and disappeared.

It didn't pay to tell an Indian the truth about himself, especially the Great War Chief, Satank.

John O'Loughlin arrived before the first buffalo hide hunters along the Arkansas River valley. He established a trading post at Lakin, north of Wagon Bed Springs, in 1872. That winter the first cars were pulled over the tracks of the Santa Fe from Atchison to the Colorado line. The following spring he was firmly established at his post when Billy Dixon, John Goff, "Hoodoo" Brown, Bat Materson, and others hunting north of the Arkansas stopped at the post for supplies. They were then planning to head south of the Arkansas into the forbidden "treaty lands."

Railwaymen, Indians, cattlemen, and travelers on the new route west were soon trading at O'Loughlin's. After Indians burned out Thomas O'Loughlin's trading post at Pierceville, in 1874, John O'Loughlin's was the only post between Dodge City and Granada, Colorado, where the tracks ended. He handled everything for the western trade—Sharps and Henry rifles, powder and ammunition and shot, groceries, wet and dry goods, lanterns, broadaxes and saws, cutlery and whetstones. When Guy Potter built a railway eating house at Lakin, O'Loughlin supplied him with his beef and groceries. Later, Fred Harvey, who achieved national fame with his Harvey House chain restaurant operation, bought Potter's business and it became the original Harvey House.

When the big buffalo shoot was over and the country turned to cattle, John O'Loughlin commenced operations at Wagon Bed Springs. He ran the Pigpen 7 ranch and the Open A Half-bar 7, the first under his own name and the second under the name of O'Loughlin & Company. His postoffice was still Lakin, though his cattle ranged from the Arkansas to the Beaver in No Man's

Land. In later years the Wagon Bed Springs ranch, the NE¼-S33-T30-R37, Grant County, Kansas, became the property of Harry Joyce, O'Loughlin's foreman. These springs were the first water the Santa Fe wagons found after leaving the Cimarron Station crossing of the Arkansas on the Dry Route, called by the Mexicans *Jornado del Muerte,* or "journey of death."

At the old springs was a Conestoga wagon bed which had been sunk down into the springs to form a wall around the water, and outside of which had been sunk many rocks to give a better foothold in the muddy ground for animals and men alike. From this old wagon bed came the springs' name.

Though the great storms of 1885-86 hurt the O'Loughlin cattle operation, it did not break up the ranch enterprise, and with Bill Jay as foreman the Pigpen 7 continued for many years.

Another pioneer whose life and activities were most diversified was H. P. Myton, who served three terms, 1878-1880 and 1882 as Ford County clerk. Myton was personally acquainted with almost every cattleman in the southwest during those years of the open range when Gluck & Myton's A Bar M cattle grazed along the north fork of the Cimarron.

Myton served as a deputy sheriff under Bat Materson for a short period and was also a commissioner for Ford County, Kansas. He was appointed register of the U.S. Land Office at Garden City and was re-elected to that position three times. He later served in the Kansas Legislature, beating the popular "Buffalo" Jones for that office.

Myton once shot and wounded a Mr. Stotts, an outgrowth of a political hassel of that time. But most cattlemen remembered him as a public servant who was always capable and ready to serve their best interests.

Myton later went to Indiana and was there elected vice-president of the Indiana Electric Railway which operated lines at Elkhart and Goshen. In 1897, President McKinley appointed Myton agent for the Ute Indian tribe and he went to Utah to serve. The town of Myton, Utah, now bears his name and that place, incidentally, is also the spot at which the former Dodge City editor, D. M. Frost, lies buried.

H. P. Myton died at Salt Lake City in March, 1945, at the age of 88 years. He was one who contributed greatly to the orderly processes that were much needed in the youthful days of the southwest, though like many others he once resorted to the six-gun himself for satisfaction of a point of law.

Chalkey Beeson is still one of the best-remembered citizens of Dodge City and the Cimarron country. Beeson was born in Salem, Ohio, April 24, 1848, and reached Dodge almost by accident.

He came west at an early age and was driving stage between Colorado Springs and Denver, about 1870-1875. He had made something of a reputation in Colorado as a musician. During this period of his life he loaned a friend some money, taking a deed to some Dodge City property as his security. When the friend failed to pay, Beeson boarded the Santa Fe and came to Dodge to see what his friend had wished on him. It wasn't much. Dodge was half way between being a buffalo hide center and a new cowtown. Property values were exceedingly low. But something about the men who made up the town and the breezy aspects of the new village itself prompted Beeson to stay. So he stayed for the term of his life and was buried in Maple Grove Cemetery in 1910, not far distant from both Print Olive's grave and that of Jack Hardesty, both of whom had ranched nearby on the Sawlog with him.

The larger ranch operation for which Beeson is best remembered is the Beeson & Harris spread, south of Dodge. They branded with a COD and their cattle ranged along Sand Creek. The great storms of 1885-86 finished their cattle operations, but their big branding irons can still be seen in the Beeson Museum at Dodge City.

Chalk Beeson traded for 80 acres of land near Dodge, south of the river. There he built a fine home and there he lived for many years while he operated the Longbranch Saloon with his partner, W. H. Harris. That there was nothing passive about the pioneer of Beeson's time is shown nowhere better than in his own life. He was always busy, always trying something different. Though principally a businessman and a livestockman, with music as a lifetime hobby, he was also selected by his friends to represent Ford County twice in the legislature, in 1892 and 1896.

Beeson accompanied the Grand Duke Alexis of Russia on his great American buffalo hunt; he organized and led the Dodge City Cowboy Band which played at the National Convention of the Cattlemen in St. Louis in 1884, captivating all with its melodies and songs; he served as a lawman and was with the posse that captured one of Doolin's men and wounded another after the bank robbery at Spearville.

Chalk Beeson was a Mason, and he was largely responsible for the erection of Dodge City's first Masonic Hall. He worked for all civic improvements, but he is probably best-remembered as a good neighbor and a friend.

Al Olive, son of Print Olive, who passed on recently at the age of 84 on May 19, 1960, told of Chalk Beeson's accidental death. Beeson was thrown from a horse and on August 16, 1912, died of his injuries. Al Olive, who had punched cows most of his life, was then dealing in horses and working on town jobs, such as draying. He had traded for an excellent young animal and broken the horse to the saddle. Beeson saw the horse and admired him, making Al a substantial offer for him. Al knew of one or two bad qualities in the horse and told Beeson he would prefer to keep him and work these traits out of him; but Beeson wanted the horse and, since Beeson was a good horseman himself and could train the horse as well as anyone, Al sold the horse.

On Tuesday, August 6, 1912, Beeson was returning from the Richland Township polls where he had been to vote. He was riding the horse Olive had sold him. On the return trip he passed by a gravel pit where some men he knew were working. Beeson "built a loop" and pretended he was going to rope one of the men, much to the enjoyment of all. But in some manner the horse became excited, got the rope under its tail or was spooked and started to pitch. Caught off guard, Beeson was thrown up on the saddle horn, then was thrown to the ground where his head struck a stone. He died the following Saturday at 4:30 a.m.

Al Olive deeply regretted the matter, since Chalkey Beeson and his own father had been good friends and he had, himself, attended school with Merritt Beeson, Chalk Beeson's son.

Merritt Beeson, together with his wife and daughter, retained many of the artifacts left by Chalk Beeson and added to the collection through the years until they have, today, the largest collection of genuine Dodge City relics in existence. Their main museum is south of the river bridge, on U.S. Highway 283, east of the old Beeson mansion, and on the land left by the Chalk Beeson estate. An Annex Museum in the buildings of the Front Street Replica at Boot Hill provides tourists and visitors another less satisfying look at some of the antiquities of "Old Dodge." Merritt Beeson did not live long enough to finish an important work he had undertaken, the cataloging of the names that appeared in the *Dodge City Globe and Livestock Journal* through the middle Eighties. This catalog, incomplete as it was, was greatly helpful to the author when he sought information from Beeson in the preparation of this work, and the genial countenance of Merritt Beeson will remain with him always.

Victor Carson, another Dodge Citian, passed away at Dodge in March, 1940. He was 84 years old, had lived in the Cowboy Capitol or on nearby ranches for more than sixty years. He arrived in Dodge in 1879 at the age of twenty-three years, and was one of the last of the old-time cattlemen to go.

Carson was a Swede and had immigrated to the United States with his family at the age of eight years. After residing elsewhere for fifteen years, he reached Dodge and entered the retail meat business. Later he established a fine ranch on the Arkansas River, just east of Dodge. He branded with a Half Circle V, and Carson's Market was for many years the chief source of supply for meats in town.

An interesting sidelight to Carson's operations was the leasing of his market to Print Olive, a Texas cattleman who lived in Dodge and had ranches on the Sawlog and the Smoky Hill Rivers at that time. Carson introduced Olive to a man who had worked for him by the name of Searcy. Searcy wanted to remain in the retail meat business, so Olive agreed to make him a partner. Searcy was to run the market in Dodge, which was leased from Carson, and Olive would supply the beef from his ranches.

After nearly a year had passed without Olive and Searcy making a financial settlement, Searcy disappeared. With him went $10,000.00 of Olive's beef which had long since passed over the retail counter at the Olive & Searcy Meat Market. There was some rent due, as Searcy had taken every penny in his path. Carson, a fair man, told Olive to forget the rent money, since he had lost so much money by the partnership and since he, Carson, felt bad about making Olive acquainted with Searcy in the first place. But Olive, with the old-time cattleman's sense of honor, paid up the debts of the partnership and took his licking without openly whining. But it was this loss, even more than the blizzards of 1880-81 in Nebraska and the bad storms in Kansas in 1885-86, that finally broke Print Olive.

Carson, who knew Olive's past, and that he had "killed his man" for rustling several times over, said later about the matter, "Ay would pittee th' man Searcy, should Preent Olave discover his whereabouts!"

Carson pioneered in irrigation farming on the Arkansas River, turning the lowlands into alfalfa and feed-growing areas for his cattle. His son, Walter Carson, worked with him in building his irrigation projects, and the family knew great sorrow when Walter was buried in a landslide while working on a ditch.

Like the other cattlemen of the day, Carson was versatile and he was ambitious, turning his hand to every good project in the valley that needed his hand. He was one of Dodge's civic leaders; he was a financier in the construction of the terminal elevator in 1939, and he helped bring many improvements to Dodge City.

Oliver Nelson and his brothers, living on claims in No Man's Land, once lost some horses. This happened about 1887 or 1888. Many, many years later, Oliver told of his experience in locating the horses and getting them back. For its sly, good humor, if for nothing else, it seems worth repeating. Here is the way Nelson told it:

This happened when I was on my claim in No Man's Land on the Palo Duro. Brother Delos had six ponies that would run all night and hide during the day. They strayed and were lost. They were stolen Indian ponies that he had traded for. As he was fresh-married, and couldn't leave camp long nor go far, I told him to look for them on water, southeast; I would look for them on water to the north.

Someone told Delos that Meade Center Bill was seen driving such a group of ponies north. I took the north route and inquired along the way at the Elzie Pile ranch on the Cimarron. They told me yes, the horses were a half day ahead of me. At Fargo Springs a young fellow approached me and asked, "Are you hunting something?"

"Yes, I am," I said.

"What is it?" he asked.

"A man," I said.

"What kind of man?"

"I am hunting an observant man," I told the youth, "a man that notices every bunch of stock that goes by here and observes the man who is driving them."

"Well, sir, you are looking at just such a man," the youth answered me.

We sat down on a bench and I described the horses to him—a stallion, two mares and two colts. He immediately said they had passed through there the previous afternoon. I said to him, "I've described only five of the horses; now you describe to me the sixth horse in the bunch."

A crowd had gathered by that time and one man said, "By Joe, you've got him there, stranger. He's the damnedest liar in town, but you've caught him!"

Everyone looked at the youth and I told him, "Go ahead. Describe the horse."

Finally, the young fellow blurted out, "A little brown *gelding*."

"You don't know much about horses," I said. "No stallion would allow a gelding to travel with his herd of mares and their foal. You'd never see such a bunch together." The boy looked befuddled. Then I told him.

"It's a golden dun mare with a light mane and tail." I turned to the crowd. "Has anyone seen them around here?"

Everyone shook his head and they all laughed at the boy. I turned back to our claims, found the horses on Chiquita Creek, 25 miles south.

Chapter XI

"No-Law Strip is the latest and most appropriate name for the neighboring territory on the south. They have no law and seem to want none. Its population is increasing daily by the acquisition from the lawless element of surrounding states and territories. Murders are of daily occurance down there, but the first case of punishment for crime committed has yet to be reported from The Strip."

Garden City Sentinel, May 1888

Old No Man's Land sheltered many outlaws in the early days, probably many more than most residents of that area want to recall. It was no fault of the residents of that land, the cattlemen or the settlers, for without law of any kind except that which each man made with his six-shooter, the land was bound to attract all the footloose young men who were wanted elsewhere for some breach of the law as well as many hardened criminals who sought comfort from their pursuers in the lands adjoining the Beaver River. One of the most notorious outlaws who found shelter in "The Strip" for a while was Jim Talbot.

Not many cowboys turned outlaw, but there were those few who did. And Jim Talbot was one. He first came to prominence in the Cherokee Strip in the late Seventies. Not a great deal is known of his early years, but he is believed to have been a Texas boy who came up the cattle trails to Wichita, Ellsworth, and Hays. But Talbot's rise to notoriety began on the day in December, 1881, when he appeared in Caldwell, Kansas, with a woman he said was his wife. The pair took quarters in the upstairs of a second-class hotel on the creek bank. Soon the couple were joined by a half dozen hard cases, who all packed shooting irons on their hips and among whom were Bob Johnson, alias Doug Hill; and Mel Slocum, also with an alias. These two had formerly held cattle on Quartermaster Creek in the Indian Territory for a man named Koch, and neither cowboy was considered a bad man at the

228

time. The group soon rented a house to live in down at the old red light section of town and thereafter led a riotous life.

W. N. Hubble was mayor of Caldwell, having defeated Mike Meagher for the office. He appointed a half-dozen deputies, all good men and not afraid of a fight, to prevent the Talbot Gang from taking the town apart. There were some small quarrels but Talbot showed no disposition for a showdown, merely bailing his men out as they made the Caldwell Can from time to time. Finally, Talbot was jailed and that brought on the showdown.

Talbot should never be accused of cowardice, though fool he may have been. He picked the day, then strutted up and down the main street like a fighting cock, telling the marshal's men, "Hide out, little ones, hide out if you value your lives!"

There are those who believe that Talbot was just getting the innocent off the streets before the battle, but there is little in his character to credit that effort. As he issued the challenge, he and his men paraded down the street in the best hooraw fashion, shooting out the window panes and eventually drawing the fire from the marshal and his men who lay concealed among the alleyways and beer barrels of the town.

Soon other citizens joined with the marshal's forces in the gun-talk against Talbot's men, and the heat became so severe on the griddle of the main street that Talbot and his boys took refuge in the livery stable. As the gunfire became more deadly, the Talbot gang saddled up and prepared for a break-away. During this final phase of the battle, Mike Meagher, the former sheriff and another well-known citizen, George Spears, were killed. It was never known which side Spears had favored, so mixed up had become the battle lines.

Talbot and his men ran for the Indian Territory and, following a few adventures of the flight, holed up in a log shack near Deer Creek, in a deep canyon. There a posse from Caldwell surrounded them, but the outlaws escaped in the night by climbing a precipitous canyon wall to safety.

When the posse returned to Caldwell, many rumors were going the rounds concerning Meagher's slaying. Some said there had been a feud between Meagher and Talbot over the slaying of

Talbot's half brother, George Flatt, who was shot down in cold blood on the streets of Caldwell on June 19, 1880. William Horseman, the city marshal, was later tried for the crime but found not guilty. Ironically, Flatt's first child, a son, was born five days after his father's murder. Talbot's cousin was also said to have been killed by Meagher, who ran a saloon in Caldwell.

Jim Talbot finally reached California, after finding No Man's Land, Texas, Kansas, and Oklahoma's Indian Lands too hot to hold him. In a few years he was a foreman for Marks & Newfield, ranchers of Mendicino County. There, on June 8, 1898, he again fell afoul of the law.

Talbot had been drinking with an acquaintance, a townsman, at the bar of a saloon in Ukiah. The jeweler, for such Talbot's acquaintance was, insisted on discussing the merits of the quick draw as opposed to the precise aiming of a weapon in a gunfight. Both men were armed. Talbot, now going under the alias J. D. Sherman, tired of the meaningless chatter of the townsman, jerked out his six-shooter, and put a neat hole through the jeweler's head. To the other men in the saloon, the question of quick draw-versus-slow aiming seemed settled for all time.

The shooting brought about a preliminary trial which resulted in revealing the actual identity of Talbot, outlaw wanted at Caldwell, Kansas, for murder. Talbot was found "not guilty by reason of self-defense" by the coroner's jury. Dissatisfied with such whitewash, the district attorney immediately filed charges against him, brought him to trial, convicted him, and sentenced him to San Quentin. From there the case went to the Supreme Court of California and Talbot won a new trial.

Now the sheriff, Johnson, corresponded with Caldwell officers, and took Talbot back to Caldwell for trial, thereby saving the state of California some money. But miraculously, at Caldwell, Talbot won his freedom!

In the meanwhile, Talbot's wife had eloped with a man named Bryce Vallele. Talbot trailed them, ran the man away; some thought he might have killed him. He brought his wife back to the ranch.

One August night in 1896 Talbot was returning from Covelo,

after buying supplies for the ranch. About fifty feet from a gate that led into a lane leading up to his ranchouse an asassin lay in the bushes with cocked gun. As Talbot stopped the team at the gate, the assassin fired, his first shot cutting Talbot's spinal cord after striking him in the throat. Two other men, Bill Williams and Charles Felton, had been similarly murdered in recent weeks and it was thought Talbot's death might be connected to the lethal activities of the night riders of the area. In addition to Vallele, who may still have been alive, there were many others who would have enjoyed seeing Jim Talbot dead.

So ended the career of another southwest cowboy who took the wrong trail. He had tried to take over one of the toughest little towns in the west with only six men to help him and had ended up hiding in the piney hills of California. Sudden death sought him out, as it does all of his kind, and destroyed him.

When granger law began to supplant the cattleman's law, many dry gulchings took place on the high plains. Oliver Nelson told how he once almost dry-gulched Tom Hungate, his friend, during his fight against Scranage.

Hungate was riding in the same direction with "Big Mack" McIntosh, a Scranage henchman. Nelson had told everyone in the neighborhood he would shoot on sight any Scranage men caught in his vicinity. Nelson, at a distance and armed with a Sharps 50 caliber, saw that the riders' trail would just about cross his own trail at an arroyo down which he was riding. So he dismounted, laid in wait for the pair to pass by where he could shoot McIntosh.

As Hungate and McIntosh drew near, entirely unaware of Nelson's presence, Nelson debated with himself about the matter. He knew that he would have to kill Hungate, too, for he would immediately take up the fight against an unseen assailant. "Tom's help would be worth more than to knock Mack out," Nelson reasoned. He permitted the two to pass by.

Not so happily concluded was the affair between the Rowan boys and the Labriers (pronounced La-brees). Will and Charles

Rowan had some trouble with a neighbor, a Dr. W. L. Regnier (pronounced Ray-neer). Regnier had come west to No Man's Land in 1896-97 from Illinois and settled in Dallinas Canyon, north of the Cimarron River crossing. Regnier, so the story goes, had shot a daughter's suitor before leaving Illinois. He had three sons, John, Louis, and Roy, and four daughters. One of his daughters, Sarah Regnier Condit, lies buried in a recently improved grave east of the road that leads north up the canyon. She is said to have died in childbirth, her baby and her husband surviving her. She was born July 7, 1872 and died August 18, 1906.

Will and Charles Rowan ran some 7JK-branded cattle in that area. One day they stopped to cut through a fence, reputed to have been erected by Regnier on what was considered, at least by the Rowans, as Rowan property. From high on the rimrock above, two rifles commenced firing. Will Rowan was struck in the upper arm and painfully wounded. Brother Charles was hit in the shin bone of the leg, making a most painful wound. The bullet passed on through his stirrup fender and into his horse's body.

Both of the horses were wounded and now ran madly, Will's horse carrying him in the direction of the figures on the rimrock above the valley. The men above mounted their horses and ran. Regaining control of his horse, Will turned and rode back to where Charles had stopped his own horse.

"Look at those cowardly bastards run," Will said.

Charles suffered greatly from his leg wound, but as soon as they returned to the ranch a Dr. Lane, a woman doctor of the area, dressed their wounds. Will borrowed a saddlehorse from a neighbor, Hughes, and set out for Trinidad to have the broken bones in the arm set. He had lost much blood and was very weak for such a trip. Blood poison set in and on April 28, 1903, thirteen days after the shooting, Will Rowan died.

Charles Rowan, unable to set his horse, had stayed at home and fared better. The night following the shooting his horse came and stood by his bedroom window and nickered. The next morning the faithful animal was found dead. A post mortem examination of the saddlehorse showed that it had been killed by a 30 caliber bullet, the one that went through the saddle fender into its belly. The bullet was such as was fired from a Springfield army rifle and it was known that the Labrier's owned such a rifle and that John Labrier knew how to use it.

John Labrier and Dr. W. L. Regnier were araigned for the murder of Will Rowan and for assault with intent to kill Charles Rowan. The trial was held at Beaver City, Oklahoma, and the two men were convicted and sentenced to fifteen years imprisonment.

On an appeal to the Supreme Court of Oklahoma, a reversal of the case was secured by the defense and the case remanded for new trial. Continuances were given from year to year until 1910. At that time Judge Loofbourrow, who had been interested at the initial trial, disqualified himself and since a qualified judge could not be found dismissed the prisoners.

The *Cimarron News*, April 14, 1910, stated the case:

While we may never know who is guilty of the killing of Wm. Rowan, we feel that the action of Judge Loofbourrow will meet with general approval, as it would not benefit anyone for another continuance and the trials were causing the county an awful expense.

John Labrier a few years afterward was living and working in Arizona. There, he fell from a scaffold, breaking his neck. Dr. Regnier died within a few years. Both men left good, substantial families behind them.

Near the old Regnier place had been the headquarters of the OX ranch, at the confluence of the Dallinas and the Cimarron River. Another old ranch in that vicinity was the Wilson ranch, west of there in Pat Canyon. An old cowboy who was riding that country when the Rowan boys were rimrocked told of finding several 30 caliber brass cartridge jackets on the ledge above as well as several cigarette butts at the location. When he checked the matter, he found that though John Labrier smoked it was always a pipe and Dr. Regnier never smoked at all! He estimated the distance from the rimrock ledge to where the Rowan boys were hit at about 400 yards—which was good shooting distance, even for army men at that time!

Burris Wright, whose father Charles Wright was the Beaver

County attorney, was once asked what he knew of the event.

"Labrier was convicted practically on circumstantial evidence," he said. "It was generally known that he was a top shot and wanted to see Bill Rowan dead. But Bill Rowan was a tough *hombre,* too. Who was to blame? *Quien sabe?"*

So there we must let this frontier tragedy rest.

Alexander McCoid was one of Seward County's most respected pioneers. He was born in Belfast, Ireland, February 11, 1851, and came to Providence, Rhode Island, as a child with his parents. When a young man, he moved west to Vernon County, Missouri, and there, on October 5, 1880, he married Miss Alice Foster. The young couple learned of new land in the west, so came on to Kansas in 1885. There Alex McCoid lived to the age of 99 years.

The McCoids settled on a pre-emption and tree claim southwest of Springfield, on the Cimarron River, selecting a location between the O Cross L ranch and the LV ranch, the latter being the James K. Hitch Alfalfa Land and Cattle Company holdings, just northwest of McCoid's claim. Alex McCoid first planned to grow garden produce for sale to the ranchers and new settlers, but he soon learned the problems of dry land farming and the uncertainties of vegetable production in drought years. So he soon entered into freighting, hauling commodities from Garden City, on the Santa Fe line, down to Harwoodville (Old Fargo Springs) and Springfield.

McCoid was made a trustee of Springfield township and before long he purchased some good cattle and put them on his place. He got along well with the cattlemen neighbors and was respected for his industry, honesty, and economy.

A few years after McCoid settled on his claim, another settler took a nearby claim. He was soon known as "Pie Belly" Davis because of an enormous gut which hung well over his belt, almost concealing its buckle. Davis was a slump-shouldered man, a loud mouth, and something of a bully. He soon fell into the bad graces of the neighbors around him.

Trouble soon came between McCoid and Davis when cattle belonging to Davis broke down the fence and got into McCoid's hay stacks. Later, when Pie Belly Davis's cattle destroyed a half-acre vegetable plot belonging to McCoid and from which Mc-Coid's family was planning on taking most of their produce for winter canning, McCoid equipped himself with a stout club. When Davis rode along, the much smaller McCoid "gave him the business end of the club," as the story is told.

Davis was a large man and a fighter when he found an opponent as small as the diminutive Alex McCoid. So a lively club battle issued a few days later, Davis catching McCoid by the throat finally and attempting to strangle McCoid. Alex McCoid got the worst of the deal, this time.

The final meeting between the two men, and the one which most folks remembered, came when Davis rode by McCoid's place one day with a long "blacksnake" cattle whip looped around his saddle horn. The two men had words, and Pie Belly Davis took down his whip and attempted to blacksnake the small and tough McCoid. McCoid pulled the bigger man off his horse, then, as Bernard Lemert described the battle, "McCoid suddenly remembered something he had brought along for just such an occasion, pulled out this metal object, and with it shot a big hole in Pie Belly Davis's head, hitting him squarely in his big mouth."

There was a "hearing" of sorts, sometime later. The prosecutor attempted to impanel a jury, asking several men (including Lemert) to serve. All declined, stating that they knew too much about the quarrels that led up to the shooting and that their sympathies were strictly for Alex McCoid. Finding it impossible to bring a jury together, McCoid's plea of self-defense was accepted and upon the prosecutor's recommendation the case was dropped.

Lee Larrabee threw additional light on the affair when he told of the appearance of a son of Davis about a year or more after the shooting. Young Davis spoke with several men of the area and a couple of attorneys about reopening the case. The concensus of the men was, when they conveyed it to the son, "your father got what was coming to him. You had better drop the matter and try to forget it as an unfortunate tragedy." The young man took the advice and left without causing the county added expense with a trial that was certain to end in a complete acquittal for McCoid.

This was the "granger justice" that replaced the rule of the six-shooter and the vigilante justice that was frequently applied in cases of theft and murder by the cattlemen of an earlier period. It was only a quasi-justice, but better than the rule of force that had dominated the Cimarron region for so many years since the days when the buffalo hunters arrived.

Chapter XII

One pioneer settler in No Man's Land told how he and his brothers established their claim by digging a hole in the ground, roofing it, then digging a well 200 feet deep. Then, looking around themselves for work that would bring in a few dollars until they sold their claims to some buyer "who was certain to want a claim," they saw the immense white covering of buffalo bones that dotted the prairie about them, left by the hide hunters of ten years before. So they stacked up huge piles of the buffalo bones and waited for a while, for "a railroad was certain to build right by the place where the bones were stacked!" But the railroad didn't come.

That was the way it usually happened. "The railroad went off in another direction from what we expected and our town died."

When the Rock Island Railroad reached the Cimarron in the spring of 1888, several towns that had grown up on the high plains hoped for the line to come directly to the spot where they had planted their town. Springfield and Fargo Springs in Seward County, Kansas, were two of those towns. Springfield nestled like an eagle, high above the Cimarron River on the tableland north of the river. Fargo Springs people had chosen a beautiful location close to the fine big springs on the north bank of the Cimarron. The two old towns were almost directly north of present Liberal, Kansas. As today's towns seek industries, they sought railways.

If the Rock Island (it was then known as the Chicago, Kansas & Nebraska Railway Company) built west from Meade, Kansas, to pick up the coal business at Trinidad, Colorado, it seemed almost certain to build through Springfield. If it elected to build southwest, into the Neutral Strip, to pick up the Texas cattle traffic, then either Fargo Springs or Liberal seemed to have a good chance of getting the railroad near to the town. As it turned out the railroad crossed the Cimarron six miles lower than Fargo Springs, and that town picked up bag and baggage and moved to the railroad crossing of the Cimarron. There they built a town and called it Arkalon, naming it after the postmaster's father. This town became an important shipping point for cattle, but because of the Texas tick restrictions, it was still not possible to pick up Texas tick infected cattle in Kansas. So the railroad pushed on southwest, passing within a mile of that settlement known as Liberal (which promptly emulated the other people in moving their town to the railroad). The railroad built on, just over the line into the Neutral Strip.

There, at the end-of-tracks, the railway company built a large stockyards with seven loading chutes able to hold several thousand cattle. This installation enabled many north Texas and Neutral Strip ranches to put cattle on the cars without the hundred mile drive to Dodge City from the Strip. It saved labor, preserved the fine flesh of the cattle, and gave the great ranches of the southwest a market right in the strip, for many buyers now came out to track's end to buy.

One of these large ranching enterprises that had been in both Kansas and the Strip for many years was the Westmoreland-Hitch outfit. Oddly enough, it was an unrequited love affair that brought young James Hitch to the southwest.

The girl of the story was Arminda George of Tennessee, an aunt of the Hitch brothers, James and Charles, a sister of their mother. When Arminda was in her late teens, she was wooed by a Bob McElhany, a fine young man and neighbor to her family. But there was another youth, too, and Arminda found it difficult to make up her mind. Bob McElhany was an ambitious young man and could not stand to wait without a decision in the matter there in the Tennessee hills. So he left and went west, to Springfield, Missouri. He planned to return and claim Arminda after he had made a success.

Bob slaved for several years, finally became the town's banker. But after two years of waiting, Arminda married his rival. Later, word came back to Tennessee that Bob had married a Springfield girl. But the two sweethearts never forgot each other. And time moved on.

Young James K. Hitch, fifteen years old, was living in the Tennessee community that McElhany, the Springfield banker, lived in years before. He, too, yearned to leave the sheltering hills and strike out for himself in the golden west. So he talked with his aunt Arminda, now a woman with a family of her own. She heard him with deep sympathy and understanding.

"Yes, Jimmie, I know just how you must feel. Other young men have felt like you do. Now here's a plan for you. Go on out to Springfield, Missouri. There you will find Bob McElhany, an old—well, an old friend of mine. He was once a restless youth like yourself. Go to him. Tell him I sent you. He will find work for you and help you."

That night Jim Hitch wrote on his old school slate this message:

I am going to Sprinfield, Missoury. I had to take the ten dollars we had in the savings for train fare. I will pay it back. I will write you where I am.

James K. Hitch

He propped the slate up on the kitchen table, put a few items of food in a sack, and left. Years later when asked why he had not waited and told the family what he was going to do and say goodbye to them, he said, "I hate to admit it, but I just couldn't stand to tell them goodbye."

Charles Hitch, Jim's younger brother, recalling the incident of the slate years later, said, "It was such a message as we'd never had before—almost like reading a death message to know that Jim had gone."

When Jim reached Springfield, Mr. McElhany was out of town. So Jim found work in a wagon factory. The day after McElhany returned, a Mr. Henry Westmoreland, a wealthy patron of the bank, was in town, and McElhany asked him if he needed a bright and ambitious young man. Westmoreland said he did, so he doubled Jim's wages from what he was making at the wagon factory and took him to work for himself.

Jim Hitch soon met Mary Westmoreland, the daughter of his employer. Their ideas were alike—Jim asked and Mary said "Yes." So they married.

239

About 1876, Henry Westmoreland and his two sons, Ben and Billy, and son-in-law, Howard Langston, drove a herd of 1,500 cattle from Springfield to Barber County, Kansas. There they found free range. When Westmoreland returned, he asked Jim Hitch if he would like to take a herd to Kansas to put on the free range. Jim liked the idea but had no money. So Westmoreland took him to the bank, co-signed his note for 200 head of cattle. The following year, early, Jim bought 500 more cows and calves and headed for Barber County. He was now launched on the career of cattleman, one he was to follow the balance of his life. In their Barber County soddy, Mary worked with him, cooking for the men and attending to the hundreds of tasks required of a woman on a ranch. They prospered, and their first child, Della, was born there in their soddy.

By 1882, as settlers moved in to Barber County, Jim Hitch decided to move to the Crooked Creek range, west of there. But here, too, he found range becoming crowded, the Cimarron and Crooked Creek Cattle Company, Chain C brand, already running as many cattle as the range would stand. So once more Jim Hitch moved in his quest for good grass, this time to the south bank of the Cimarron, about twenty-five miles northwest of present day Liberal, Kansas. Today, the Hitch Land & Cattle holdings are some of the largest in the county.

Jim and Mary Hitch prospered here. Each fall the men made a beef drive to Dodge City with big, grassed out steers.

On March 1, 1886, Charles Hitch arrived to start work with his brother Jim. Charles was big-eyed, inexperienced in cattle work, willing, and just thrilled to his finger tips to be starting on the road to become a cowboy. Jim Hitch was now in the process of adding more range for his growing herds, since he had been buying up some of the winter-starved cows that had survived the bad winter of the previous year. Several of the cattlemen had already quit after taking serious losses. The cows were a sorry looking lot, tails and horns and ears frozen off. But Jim Hitch knew that if he could bring them through another winter they would bring good calf crops for several years to come for him.

So Jim sent Charlie down to Coldwater Creek, on the Texas

line. There, Charlie and the men completed the new soddies they had started building. They also put up a lot more winter feed in anticipation of a hard winter—which is exactly what they had. It was a wild, new, and eventful life for Charlie Hitch, and he stayed all summer on the Coldwater, herding cattle and learning the ropes from the Mexican *vaqueros* and the other cowboys of the ranch. He learned fast, and he was to love this life for the next fifty years.

In September, when haying started, Jim came down with a crew of men. That fall he promised Charlie a trip to Dodge with the beef herd. A trail drive to Dodge City! Charlie had read about it, but he had never dreamed he would ever live to experience it.

That week Charlie helped clean up the mess wagon, greased it good, helped make hobbles for the night horses of the remuda. Some of the horses that had not been ridden since spring were tried out, "just for size." It was a big show for young Charlie Hitch, and he noticed how every cowboy dug down into his war-bag for his best shirt, his fanciest silk or linen 'kerchief. Each rider washed out his fanciest gambler-stripe pants, polished his faded and worn boots with lampblack from the lantern globe, oiled his saddle and bridle, and cleaned up his six-shooter. They always wore their six-guns in town, even though they carried them with their bedrolls on the chuckwagon during the drive.

"Cookie," in return for their help in cleaning up the wagon on which he would make his trip to Dodge, cut every waddy's hair and shaved each man, some of whom had worn their hair long since the previous fall. He also fixed up a delicacy they all, enjoyed, a fruit-pudding affair which he called "Son-uv-a-bitch in a Sack," and all ate their fill of it. Then one morning early Jim Hitch called them and every man rolled out, saddled up, and the cavalcade of wagon, remuda, and cowboys headed down the Cimarron to the big steer pasture, west of Fargo Springs, on the south side of the Cimarron.

It was the first of November, and frost had nipped the grasses and ended their growing season. The air was clean and sharp, and the sage was heavy with its silvery seed. The horses were eager and tossed their heads as they fought for more rein, the cowboys' unused spur rowels clanking and ringing to the horses' dancing feet. When they struck the river, Jim Hitch "told the riders off," sending some upstream to search the canyons and brakes for stray cattle, turning others southward across the flat land to round up the grazing steers. By eleven o'clock the circle riders were all in, each bringing several hundred head of grass-fat steers with him to the redezvous point below "the Springs," about where Arkalon would rise in the next two years and the railroad build its bridge across the Cimarron. There the wagon boss ordered the herd across the river, which was running a clear stream between high banks, for the river at that time was not the wide, sandy wash it appears today, extending almost a half mile from bank to bank.

Once across the river, the cattle were allowed to drink and graze on the north bank while the cook prepared a noonday lunch. At two o'clock the cattle and men had rested and eaten and the wagon boss ordered the drive to start. That night they made a dry camp.

The following day they camped on water at Stump Arroyo, where they joined the Fort Bascom Trail which soon met the Jones & Plummer Trail which they would follow on to Dodge. Since cattle bedded better when away from water they "made a dry camp each night and moved on water." The longhorn cattle "ran some," as Charlie Hitch put it, that is, stampeded at night, but after the first two or three nights the drive simmered down to routine and was over far too soon to suit the young cowboy, though the others were happy to reach Dodge.

The last water they crossed was Mulberry Creek, south of Dodge, where a small store was kept at the point where the Adobe Wall Trail branched off from the Jones & Plummer Trail. It was called "Dugan's Store." The next night they reached the Arkansas River, crossed, and threw their herd of 1,500 head of steers into the pens of the Santa Fe railway stockyards, two miles east of the town.

Here, Howard Langston, the Hitch boys' brother-in-law, stayed to load the cattle since he would accompany the shipment to Kansas City. The rest of the men, late though it was, roped their best horses from the remuda, put on their best clothes, and headed for town. The chuckwagon was left at the Elephant Stable wagon yard for the night.

Even before they reached Front Street, they heard shooting. Then they saw some cowboys riding wildly up and down the street near the Santa Fe station, several with young women riding astride behind them, their skirts flying in the wind, their shapely legs, silk-stockinged and with wide colored garters showing plainly as the wide-eyed Hitch cowboys rode by them. Some of the cowboys were getting pretty drunk, others were just feeling exuberant and in fine alcoholic spirit. One young man was hardly able to stay on his horse, and still another, together with the woman riding with him, had fallen to the street and there lay in the dust laughing almost uncontrollably at their misfortune.

Several riderless horses ran madly up and down the street, their reins flying in the air except when their hooves stepped on them, bringing them to a sudden head flinging halt. One rider lay sound asleep in the street, his head pillowed on his arm, the manure and dust covering him as the others galloped by his body, shouting and firing their guns.

Jim Hitch didn't allow Charlie out of his sight, and Charlie complained that he couldn't have fun like he had expected to have at Dodge with the others. But Jim Hitch was older, wise and experienced. The rest of the Hitch outfit was free to do what they pleased for a day or two, and with one exception, "Cookie," they tied into the first dance hall they came to.

After a day or two of roistering, Jim Hitch called an end to the ball. They loaded the chuckwagon with winter provisions and pulled out of Dodge City early the next morning.

On this particular trip back home, the Hitch outfit ran into trouble. At a fence gate, a big wooden one, erected by settlers across the trail, they were refused passage through the claim. Jim Hitch was in no mood to argue with the settler at the gate. He took the axe from the chuckwagon and started to cut down the gate, which was wired shut. The settler remonstrated with him, then called the sheriff from Meade, who was at a nearby ranch.

243

The sheriff overtook the Hitch outfit a few miles farther along the trail.

"The trial lasted ten days," Charlie Hitch ruefully recalled many years later. "But we came clear." The outfit then returned to the Coldwater for the winter. All through the winter months the cowboys would talk of their experiences on the beef drive to Dodge, talk of the dance hall girls each had met, what they said, where the girls claimed to have come from, how they got started in their nefarious trade. The cowboys would never understand the painted women they met in the old Cowboy Capital, but they savored each tall tale the others would tell of their experiences with them. And the tales would get bigger and bigger when the snow fell and more time was spent in the bunkhouses.

In December, 1886, the Hitch outfit moved all their livestock down from the Cimarron range to the Coldwater where they had plenty of feed and water. The soddies were comfortable, even for that terribly cold winter of 1886. Of special interest to young Charlie Hitch that winter was the fact that Josie Westmoreland, Mary Hitch's sister, came along. Charlie eyed with great wonder and satisfaction this pretty sister of his sister-in-law.

"I had my eye on this prime lassie since the first time I saw her, not long before," he wrote many years later. "I was a young boy, and I got mighty lonesome for feminine companionship." By this time, Charlie Hitch could look back and realize why brother Jim had kept an eye on him while in the old sin city of the plains, Dodge City. So it was not long before Charlie asked Josie to marry him. And it can be honestly said, "They lived happily ever after."

Conditions following the winters of 1885-86 became better for the Westmoreland-Hitch company as it did for all others, though they had suffered grave losses. But his brand had survived, because of the wisdom of Jim Hitch in preparing as much winter feed as possible and keeping a tight drift-watch by manning line camps all winter and throwing the cattle back to the Coldwater range when they drifted south with the storms. When Charlie Hitch came out to the line camps that spring, Jim Hitch told him they had skinned 500 head of their own dead cattle.

244

"Jim was a fast skinner," Charlie said. "He would skin the head and legs, then jerk the hide off with a team of horses. You had to work fast, for the dead animals were starting to putrefy."

On top of losses from the storms, they now were in debt to the banks. But the cattle business, with the shortage of stock occasioned by the great Die Off on the western plains, was looking better, and their creditors didn't push them. "It will be better next year," they said.

In 1888-89 came a big drought in New Mexico. The cattlemen there "moved out to grass and water," many coming to No Man's Land. Huff Wright was then managing the Carletes ranch in New Mexico with its many thousands of Meskin and Texas longhorn cattle. Wright was a friend of the Hitches. Later, Wright boomed the town of Hansford, Texas, against her rival, Farwell. When a tornado tore Hansford to pieces, Temple Houston, son of old Sam Houston, inquired if Huff Wright had been in town that day. Told that he was, Houston said, "I'll bet that tornado lost its best 'eye' when it bucked up against that stubborn fellow!" But Wright was not too stubborn to sell the Hitch boys these CS Connected cattle at $7.00 per head.

The Hitchs branded most of these New Mexican cattle with Jim's brand, an O on the right hip, and put Charlie's new cattle brand, a 7 Bar, on some of them. The Westmoreland-Hitch cattle they branded with the LV. Then Jim and Charlie rode down into the Texas panhandle to look for new cattle range. There, they saw grassy prairie as far as the eye could reach in all directions with nothing to mar the landscape but an occasional bunch of grazing antelope. Near what is called today Hitchland, Texas, they found what they were looking for.

There, on the great flat plains they came to a broad lake of fine, fresh water. Thousands of wild geese, curlews, ducks, plover, and big whooping cranes covered the water. The curly buffalo grass beneath the horse's feet was fully five inches in height and as thick as the fur on a beaver. "I don't suppose it had been grazed since the buffalo left," said Charlie. The brothers turned back to Coldwater, after taking heed of their position and directions. They borrowed every cent they could get at the banks and bought more of the cheap, droughted-out cattle from New Mexico and put them on the Texas range.

The following spring they erected a big windmill on the west side of the lake. Their cattle spread out over the Palo Duro Creek range, the Coldwater range and other streams running into the Beaver River. Westmoreland-Hitch was now running eight to ten thousand head of cattle. It was a most profitable time and the families enjoyed the good life.

The Hitch women-folk were refined and cultured people, and as their menfolk worked and planned for economic success in their ranching enterprises, the womenfolk worked to bring civilization to the wild, new country, to give it schools, churches, and the other advantages of an older and more settled society. Before many more years passed, Henry Westmoreland, the patriarch of the clan, died at his home in Guymon, Oklahoma, in 1909 and James K. Hitch became the head of the operations.

Among the members of the Hitch outfit were such cowboys as Walt Naylor, who broke horses and rode the rough string; Allen Walker, all-around frontiersman, cook, cowboy, and freighter for the outfit; Forrest Lowe; George Walters; Paul Dean and others. They served faithfully and it was not too many years until James Hitch's boys, Henry and George, were doing a man's work in the saddle. Both are hale and hearty men, today.

As the railroad built down from Meade, Kansas, to its crossing of the Cimarron at Arkalon, Dodge City became less important as a supply point for the ranches of the Southwest range. Good-sized stockyards were built at Arkalon, where the Chicago and Rock Island decided to cross the river. The Hitch outfit now drove to Arkalon and herds from the western end of No Man's Land now shipped many cattle from this point, including outfits like the JB's who loaded 10,000 head at Arkalon in 1888. Arkalon eventually boasted a population of 3,000. But it was doomed from the first, for the railroad soon pushed southwest to Liberal, where that town and community gathered up the dissonant groups from old Springfield which withered on the vine and from Fargo Springs, which also had died. Soon, Arkalon residents were offered choice lots to move to Liberal, and when the latter town became the county seat, Arkalon's years were marked. Its final death blow, came, of course, many years later when the railroad changed the river crossing and built that flood-proof, high, steel bridge, "The Samson of the Cimarron," a few miles east of where the U.S. Highway 54 also makes its crossing of the wide, sandy-bottomed stream.

Upon reaching Liberal, the railroad soon built on across the line into No Man's Land to pick up the Texas cattle from the XIT, the Backward LX, the Turkey Track, the Cross L, the LIT and other really big and important cattle ranches of the Texas panhandle, as well as the many ranches operating in the Neutral Strip. It was said that in 1884 there were 200,000 head of cattle on the Beaver River range alone. This was most lucrative business for a new railroad.

At this new end-of-tracks, a new town sprung up. It was called Tyrone. The present town of Tyrone is some four or five miles farther southwest. Old Tyrone was peopled principally by those folks who had established the town of Oak City, a couple of miles northwest of the spot where the railroad penetrated the Neutral Strip. Oak Citians, as Fargo Springs folks had done before them, immediately moved to the railroad. The town of Old Tyrone was just across the line in Kansas, while the stockyards, the loading chutes, and the catch wings were over in the Strip. These stockyards were erected in 1888 and were able to hold many thousands of the wildest Texas steers. Each of the catch-wings that ran out across the prairie was about two hundred yards long, built to envelop the wild and spooky longhorns as they approached the end-of-track where the stockyards had been constructed. The town was promoted chiefly by the railroad officials and was named by a Mr. Watson, after his old home town of Tyrone, Pennsylvania.

When the beef herds from western and central No Man's Land and the Texas panhandle were delivered to the railway at Old Tyrone for shipment in the fall, it presented a never-to-be-forgotten spectacle. Before the viewer was stretched an expanse of buffalo grass prairie to the south and west extending to the horizon. Herds from the Anchor D, from the XIT, from the Backward LX, from the JJ and the JB, from the ranches of the Cators and Tylers came ambling in, each herd sending aloft an announcement of arrival in the form of a great cloud of dust from the cloven hooves. The pall of dust would hang high in the air until the hot south wind carried it over the yards at Old Tyrone and on up across the sandhills on the Kansas range. The herds would be penned, the yards filled with all that could be held in the big pens. A train of 25 or 30 empty stock cars would be standing alongside the seven chutes, a car door at each chute entrance, the beds of the cars well-sanded to keep down disease and provide firm footing for the cattle on their long ride to market. As one train would be loaded, it would depart down the single track to Liberal, and another string of empty cars would be backed down the tracks to Old Tyrone.

At the yards would be heard a tumult of sounds, men shouting at the cattle and yelling to one another as they prodded the cattle into the cars, shut and bolted the car doors, then waited a few minutes while the train was pulled ahead "spotting" seven more cars to loading positions. Occasionally it was necessary to dehorn an animal with an extremely long pair of antlers that would not go through the car doors or might cause other animals to lose eyes during the long trip to market. The bawling of cattle, the neighing of saddlehorses as they they stood, "ground tied" with their dropped reins outside the corral fence, the noise from the busy switch engine, its bell ringing and the steam boiling out sideways from an overheated boiler as it puffed importantly down the tracks, pulling the string of empty cars to the loading chutes, all these sounds contributed to the cacaphony as each man went about his own particular duties, contributing to the day's work at Old Tyrone. Yet out of this seeming discord of noise, came what to the cowboy's and cowmen's ears seemed a symphony of sound, the sound of well-fed, well-drunk, fat cattle being loaded for market, the fruit of their entire year's work or money in the bank to invest in young cattle, or silver in a cowboy's pocket to jingle in the saloons and dance emporiums at Old Tyrone.

The loading never stopped, day or night, as long as the railroad could provide cars and the ranchers had cattle in the yards. When cars were unavailable, the waiting herds would be driven back to a place on the prairie seven miles southwest called "Shade's Well." There they would again be watered and drifted back to the stockyards; for ga'nted livestock shrunk much worse in shipping than stock that had eaten and drunk its fill before being loaded on the cars. Thin and weak stock often got down in the cars and were trampled to death before reaching market, too.

Each night during the beef shipping season there were from twenty to a hundred cowboys and drovers in Old Tyrone. The "town" consisted of three dance halls, two good-sized saloons, a hotel, a general supply store, a blacksmith shop, two restaurants, two card rooms, several "Red Lights," a shoe and boot and saddle shop combined. The post office stood somewhat west of the stockyards and main part of the town, which was north of the yards. Cards were played at the hotel as well as in all the saloons for the games of stud and draw poker, pitch, solo and Old Sledge were more in the nature of a social activity, a form of recreation than they are felt to be in our present age. Over a card table good friends could thoroughly enjoy an evening's entertainment with a bottle or two of bourbon thrown in for elbow exercise. Though Kansas was "dry," this point was considered to be so near the Neutral Strip that no objections arose on the part of Kansas law enforcement officers.

Many of the ladies of the night who operated at Dodge City and other cow towns along the trails, now frequented Old Tyrone at shipping time. There were such as Black Madge, Billy the Bitch, Old Ironsides, Polka Dot, The Mud Hen, Allie and Josie Halm, Banty Legs, Rose of Cimarron, Old Mox-a-dolly, Rowdy Kate, and Pussy Cat Nell. Their procurers and gambler friends, too, infested Old Tyrone for it was a lush spot come shipping time. Texas Slim, Skinny Nose Jim, Bobby Gill, Good Eye, Badger Jack, Lone Wolf, Rowdy Joe Lowe, Tom Small, and the Cimarron Kid held court there at beef harvest time. One of the greatest wrestling-boxing matches ever held in No Man's Land was that between Rowdy Joe Lowe and Dee Hannah on July 4, 1888. But that is another story.

Old Tyrone was as wild as Dodge in her best days—but Tyrone was smaller and newer. Cowboys from the XIT (which shipped

20,000 head one season from Tyrone), the 101, the Anchor D, the JJs and the JBs, the LIT, the Turkey Tracks, the V Bar, and the OX might all be in town on the same night. "Cattle *was* Old Tyrone," grizzled old Bernard Lemert, who had been there, said of the cow town.

West of the stockyards, and immediately ahead of the railway tracks, B. E. Blake squatted on a piece of land, hoping the railway, when it built on southwest, would make his time and land worth while. Blake ran the postoffice at that place, though his hotel was at Old Tyrone. Like most plans that pretend to predict weather in the Southwest or tell where a railroad would go in those days, Blake's forecast gained him nothing. When the railroad did build west, a few years later, it by-passed his holdings. Blake later moved to Liberal and his son, Al E. Blake, became a successful business-man. The elder Blake died in California in 1946.

Liberal, Kansas, was back down the track five miles northwest of of Old Tyrone. The young ladies from Liberal, for want of anything else to do on a dull Sunday, would ride the tops of the stock cars to Tyrone and there watch the cowboys load out the cattle. It made great sport for a community whose social life, to be charitable, hardly existed at all. And the cowboys, many of whom knew the Liberal girls and who later married some of them, enjoyed these friendly visits.

"Myra McDermott's bunch," Charlie Hitch called them, and he spoke with great warmth of those young ladies whose visits offered so much more to the lonesome cowboys than did the painted women of the dance halls.

"Why this shipping of cattle was so attractive to the boys was because they would meet half the cowboys in the world at Shade's Well and half the good-looking girls in the world at the end of trail—Old Tyrone," Hitch wrote years afterward. Charlie Hitch died at age 81, November 30, 1947, at Liberal, Kansas.

The Myra McDermott that Hitch spoke of was the daughter of T. J. McDermott, the railroad hotel operator at Liberal who established the practice that every man eating in his dining room would have his coat on. Most of the cattlemen dined at the Rock Island Hotel, run by McDermott, and it was no easy matter always to slip into a coat while dining there. Once a lively group of cowboys came in and sat down in their shirt sleeves on a hot summer evening. The kindly proprietor smilingly called their attention to his rule. The cowboys nodded their understanding and obligingly left the table to go outside for a few moments to get their garments. When they reappeared each one was attired most correctly in a *coat*, but the coat was their gaudy yellow fishtail slickers, the only coats they carried along! McDermott accepted the *fait de accompli*. To this day shirtsleeve dining is accepted in all hotels and restaurants in Liberal, Kansas.

The "Shade's Well," mentioned previously, is an historic spot on the prairie today, two miles south of present day Tyrone, or 1-5-18, Texas County, Oklahoma. A highway marker on U.S. 54 tells of its history, and passing tourists often turn south at the marker and visit the old site.

J. U. Shade, for whom the well was named, was the livestock agent for the Chicago, Rock Island and Pacific railway when it built over into the Neutral Strip. He was a Philadelphia man and was ordered in 1888 to find a location and prepare a large water well capable of watering the great herds of cattle that were expected from the Texas panhandle, when the stockyards had been completed. Together with H. B. Fore, a helper, Shade found the location for a good well, completed the digging, and put it in operation. Then he looked about for a trustworthy man competent to keep it in operation and handle the watering of the herds.

North, over the Kansas line, was a small rancher and settler, Zachariah (Zack) Cain. He was a man of integrity and good character and was recommended to Shade. So Shade secured Cain's services to operate the well. The well was down in good sand and gravel with a depth of seventy-five feet and water standing in the well twenty-five feet. The well had been located at this point because of the success of some early colonists who had dug wells a few miles south of this point and struck excellent water in ample quantity. The colonists had abandoned their claims during a drought period and these old wells stood open at the top for several years, a hazard to wildlife and to the drovers alike. So the cattle trails approaching Shade's Well came in at

251

angles from the southeast and from the southwest, rather than from the direction of the abandoned wells.

The original plan Shade and Cain developed for watering herds was to build a wide reservoir in a prairie swale, southwest of the well, pump it full, and let the herds drink there as from a fresh-water lake. The reservoir was scooped out by teams and fresnoes, but the plan did not work. The water evaporated too fast; the cattle mired badly, and when pulled out of the mud the animals were choused up and many got on the prod. So the reservoir idea was abandoned and another plan substituted.

A system of wooden troughs was built, the troughs being made about twenty inches high and eighteen inches wide. The troughs were iron-bound to give them added strength. These troughs extended from the well and its supply tank to two points on the prairie, each about 100 yards distant from the well. The troughs fanned out so that a herd of nearly 2,000 head could drink all at the same time. The cattle could easily step over the troughs, drinking from either side. The large, wooden tank that was erected at the well could be emptied into the troughs in a few minutes notice.

The windmill was the largest and latest model, and when a herd's dust was seen high in the air to the southwest or southeast the mill would be turned on. Then great activity would replace the customary peace and tranquility of the place. Water would be let out into the troughs, the womenfolk would light the fires in the kitchen and put the food on the stove to "warm up" for the punchers.

As the demands on the single windmill became greater and greater, a large steam pump was installed to keep the watering troughs filled when the big herds arrived, one after another.

Mrs. Zack Cain recalled later that the first drover to show up with a herd was John Glenn, a Trassas foreman, with a herd of 2,000 steers from a north Texas ranch. He was the kindliest of men, but he arrived dusty and trailworn, frightening little Carrie Cain and her brother Homer and making Mrs. Cain nervous about his presence since her husband was not home. But Zack Cain soon arrived when the big herd watered. When John Glenn left, he placed money under his plate to cover the meals for himself and his men. Though the Cains did not want to take the money, Glenn told them it was the same as though he were buying a meal for his men in Tyrone or Dodge City. So they decided to feed all the cowboys at a charge of 25c per meal. It was hard work to cook for so many right in the hot months of the summer and fall, but the Cains prospered at Shade's Well, and soon the verdant spot on the prairie was also known as "Cain's Wayside Inn." The day following John Glenn's arrival, a big JB herd with Red Cochrum as trail boss arrived—and Cains were well-launched into the restaurant business!

A postoffice was maintained at Shade's Well, and there the Slaughters, J. O. Neighbors, Westmoreland-Hitch, the Cators, and other cattle outfits received mail while on the beef drives. Zack Cain planted trees, bringing cedars from his old home in West Virginia, some of which still stand at the old location and add a touch of green to an uninteresting winter landscape and make appreciated shade for the summer time. Zack Cain once laughingly said, "If they're going to call it 'Shade's Well' we better get some *shade* growing!" Cain also planted fruit trees and shrubs, Mrs. Cain made a garden, and the prairie proved bountiful indeed where a great water reservoir could be depended on for irrigation water!

After the paunches of the trail cattle were filled, they were drifted on slowly to the railhead at Old Tyrone.

Shortly after the turn of the century, the Rock Island railroad built on to Tucumcari, New Mexico. Old Tyrone, Shade's Well, the big shipping pens, all fell into disuse. The stockyards were removed a few years later; the point where Old Tyrone had been located became known only to railroadmen as Stone's Siding and the old town re-grouped and rebuilt farther southwest four or five miles at its present location. When the author saw Shade's Well last, it was filled to within a foot or two of ground level, though it could still be seen in outline. Only one of the original buildings is left at the location, it being occupied today by a Mr. Heacock who farms the area. Homer Cain, son of Zack Cain, accompanied the writer to the site and related events of the happy and carefree days of his youth when the great herds came out of the southwest in a cloud of dust, tongues hanging out, bawling and crowding for water. He told how the cowboys affectionately romped with him, let him ride behind their saddles, and joked his pretty sister, Carrie Cain, then a small girl. Carrie Cain is today Mrs. George Ellison, widow of the late banker of that name at Guymon, Oklahoma. In an hour's tape recording, Mrs. Ellison told incidents of her happy childhood and her many pleasant memories of "Cain's Wayside Inn."

Chapter XIII

It would be difficult to write about the Old West without recording some of its violence. The violence of that age was occasioned by several factors, chiefly by the mixing of all types of men together on a naturally raw frontier immediately following that great fratricidal struggle we call the Civil War. In a lawless land, what order was established was established with a six-gun. The law of the cattle range, that common law of self-preservation, could be defined "You treat me right or we'll have trouble," and was enforced with a gun. Like the stresses in modern life that send us to the psychiatrist's couch for analysis and treatment, the confusions and frustrations of that earlier period sent our grandfathers and their sons to their holsters for their six-guns to "settle-up" with trouble or a troublemaker.

Economic problems that remained obstinate and unsettled often brought about crime, a bank robbery or a murder. The treatment for such sickness on the frontier was hemp—in the form of a rope around the sick man's neck.

Horse theft, cow theft, and murder were collateral crimes, each punishable by death at the end of a rope. In many instances these crimes were perpetrated by men working in pairs or in gangs who devoted their entire efforts toward achieving success for themselves at some other man's expense. But frequently the violence of the hanging of one or more of these men obscured the basic cause of their activities which brought on the violence, turning all eyes away from the root of the trouble. The root of the trouble often was economic, even at it is in our time.

Chief among the economic roots of trouble on the range was "winter joblessness." When Oliver Nelson spoke of Brushy Bush, the Beer City marshal, putting up a "winter job" for himself, he pointed out the simple fact that Bush did not enjoy or relish winter joblessness. That is why the cowboys spoke of it as a *winter job.* It saved them from a winter spent in "riding the grubline," and it gave them even a certain amount of independence to have a few big steers thrown up in some blind canyon where one might be used up from time to time, either as food for the unemployed cowboy or to be sold for cash money in a nearby town. The fact that everyone in the frontier towns bought and ate of this "slow elk," as it was sometimes referred to, shows the general attitude toward the supplier. He was not just a common thief, but was a man who had made a job for himself, a *winter job.*

Once the summer and fall work was completed on the range, many ranchers retired their cowboys simply by paying them off and forgetting them until they needed help on the spring roundup. It would seem that a miserable wage of $25 to $40 per month "and found" could have been paid during three or four winter months by cattlemen who were tax-free and running their cattle on free range belonging to the United States government. But they apparently felt not. So they threw their cowboys on the "grubline," that is, riding the range from ranch to ranch all winter, eking out what existence they found possible through the storms and blizzards.

Now there was no stigma attached to riding the chuckline. Each cowhand who was employed on a ranch during the winter months knew but for the grace of God he would be riding along with the cowhand who came knocking at the cookhouse door, asking for something to eat. All cooks on the ranches accepted the arrangement, for they, too, often fell from grace and were riding the grubline before green grass came. There was a lot of good-natured joshing about the grubline, but they always kept it in fun.

A visit by a grubline rider seldom extended more than a day or two, a week at most if a stormy period. On the Canadian River, in the spring of 1883, a "cowboy strike" against the miserably low wages of $25 per month, after a hard winter of grubline riding, almost stopped the spring roundup work. The cowboys aksed $50 a month, roundup foremen to get $75. Such well-known top hands as Tom Harris, Roy Griffin, J. W. (Waddy) Peacock, J. L. Howard, W. S. Gaton, S. G. Brown, W. B. Borina, D. W. Peeples, Jim Jones, C. M. Hullett, V. F. Martin, Harry Ingerton, J. S. Morris,

Jim Miller, Henry Stafford, William F. Kerr, Bill Davis, T. D. Holliday, C. F. Goddard, E. E. Watkins, C. B. Thompson, G. F. Nickell, Juan A. Gomez, and J. L. Grisson signed the proclamation at Tascosa, Texas, March 31, 1883. The ranches principally affected were the T-Anchor, the LIT, Backward LX, and the LS. After considerable bad feeling, but little violence, the strike was lost. It did, however, help put an end to the hoggishness of the big ranchers, several of the cowboys starting up on their own hook within the larger domains. "Mavericking" became a popular pastime, and it was said that one cowboy, just off the grub line, started with a team of oxen in March 1883 and by July 1884 held 200 head of coming two-year old steers under his own legal brand!

Where a grubline rider found himself at the "home ranch" of his previous summer's employment, he might feel perfectly welcome to stay a few days extra.

One writer, a ranch-born lady, told of a chuckline rider of her youth called Dick the Rover. Dick stayed at her father's ranch one night long ago. She described him as a tall man, spare, but neatly dressed, who knew all the gossip, smiled often, and talked almost continuously. He knew all the gossip of that vast north Texas range.

Dick the Rover was welcomed at the ranch, chiefly for his store of information about the other ranchers and their herds. Dick excused himself just when they had about decided that he was going to stay all night—which is no doubt exactly what he wanted to do! Apparently failing to get an invitation to bed down, after depleting his store of gossip, Dick stated casually, "I want to get over to the LIT in time to put my name in the pot for breakfast." For it was the custom of ranch cooks to provide only for those "who bedded down with the herd."

Undoubtedly, if a social study had ever been made of grubline riding as a breeder of crime on the range, the practice would have stood accused by most fair men and its cause, winter joblessness, would have been convicted.

Often a few of the cowboys would hole up together at an unused line camp or a vacant cabin or soddy on the range, much as the striking cowboys did on the Canadian River, near Tascosa.

257

There, they would attempt to live from a few weeks to a quarter of a year or more without income of any kind. Following the range custom, each would get out and ride the grubline for a few weeks. Later, by some hook or crook, or by some waddy's savings or poker winnings, they would get hold of a bag of flour, a sack of beans, some coffee, and a side of bacon and try to "weather the storm." A few cowchips would be their fuel, maybe a friendly cook would have presented them a sackful of potatoes when the manager or foreman was not looking. There they would remain holed up while the blizzards raged, not in comfort, but alive to do cow punching again come green grass.

With range cattle drifting by all winter, it was not unthinkable to shoot a steer, skin him, and cut out the brands and bury them, then let the meat freeze. "No one eats his own beef anyway," was their saying. As these young men idled away weeks, reading the dime novels about Jesse James and the Dalton Brothers, it was easy to see a bank robbery or a murder as a way to accomplish something, maybe get hold of some money, pay off an old debt, live a little higher on the hog. Just as juvenile minds pick up mayhem, murder, rape, and sadism watching the depressing output of the TV stations today, so did the young punchers of another age make up their minds to try a bank robbery—usually to be shot down by a professional gun marshal or hung by a mob.

Sam Bass was a cowhand as well as a race horse man before turning train robber and outlaw. So were Black Jack Ketchum, Jim Talbot and Billy the Kid as well as several of the members of the Wild Bunch. No doubt some of the members of the Coe Gang had been young cowboys who grew weary of winter joblessness. Most of them had one thing in common with an unemployed man of today, they felt useless to themselves and to society when out of a job. Crime is a concommitant of unemployment, was then, is today. When a society has no use for a man, then the man has no use for society.

Oliver Nelson told the author of the winter joblessness at the T5 in the Cherokee Strip, where he was the cook in 1884. The idleness of the cowboys who were riding the chuckline eventually led to the bank hold-up at Medicine Lodge, Kansas. The robbery ended with Nelson's friend Billy Smith, the wrangler, dangling from the end of a rope fashioned to fit him by a lynch mob. Henry Brown, the town marshal of Caldwell, Ben Wheeler, and John Wesley, a Tredwell & Clark cowboy, were hung alongside Smith. Billy Smith was a fine horseman; John Wesley was a loyal cowboy. But lying around the bunkhouse in idleness that winter and mulling over dime novels about Quantrill and the James Brothers cost those boys their lives. Nelson believed that two other T5 cowboys, John Potts and Ben Franklin, had originally planned to take part in the robbery, but Ben killed John Potts in a gambling quarrel and fled before the boys left for Medicine Lodge. Only Henry Newton Brown, the Caldwell marshal, had any background as a gunman, having played some part with Billy the Kid in the Lincoln County War. Yet he never drank, chewed, smoked, or gambled and was a loving husband of only six weeks time!

Charles Russell, the Montana artist, told of holing up with a few grubline cowboys one winter in Great Falls. They were lucky, for the budding artist sold enough paintings to keep them all in grub—and drink! Charley's picture sales that winter may have saved some of those boys a life of crime or a sudden death in the hangman's noose.

But to counterbalance the few who did resort to crime to avoid the grubline, there were others whom the grubline taught their first lessons in thrift. It was rough to "wonder where your summer's wages went," and a winter or two of grubline riding was a severe teacher. This school of discipline graduated some of the Southwest's greatest cattlemen. Where "light n' eat" was the standard invitation to any homeless man, there was rarely hard feelings between the employed and the unemployed, or between the unemployed and the former employers. "News," at an isolated line camp or at a ranch headquarters, was readily exchanged for a hearty supper of beans, bacon, coffee, and sourdough biscuits, with a black-strap molasses finisher. Having gossip of the range at one's tongue tip gave a man tradin' stock, kept him feeling useful to others.

It was a good feeling for a chuckline rider to unsaddle, turn his tired horse in with the ranch horses for a feed of hay or grain and a good rest, then to drag his suggan into the bunkhouse where there was always an empty bunk or welcome spot on the plank floor near the stove. The ranch hands let him eat his meal in peace, then he was expected to light up his pipe or cigarette and "give out with the news."

One cowboy who started down the outlaw trail for a few years, then turned off onto the straight and narrow, was Jim Herron. Jim worked for many ranches along the Cimarron and Beaver, in the Neutral Strip and in north Texas. He was once sheriff of Beaver County, Texas County, and Cimarron County, the whole Neutral Strip! But along about '93 Jim was accused of rustling. It wasn't a small charge, for they charged him with rustling two trainloads of cattle out of the Strip to be shipped to market from Meade, Kansas. For this, Jim went on trial at Meade in the court of Judge Price. Jim said later that Cape Willingham and P. Doyle did everything to get him to turn state's witness against others they sought to incriminate. But Herron protested his innocence and refused to testify against others. Willingham was the man who shotgunned the LS foreman, Fred Leigh, to death on the street of Tascosa.

A motion for a new trial was made by the defense counsel, and Judge Price adjourned his court for the morning, informing the defense that he would hear their plea for a new trial in the afternoon. Jim Herron, together with another prisoner, Jack Rhodes, was placed in the custody of Sam Givler, a deputy sheriff.

During the recess, Jim learned that Rhodes had a gun concealed on his person. So the two planned to put it to use in an escape plan. Rhodes' part was to pull the gun on the deputy and keep him covered. A Negro attendant at the livery stable was contacted by friends of Herron and was persuaded to have two saddled horses standing by. The prisoners would quickly mount, while Deputy Givler was held off by Rhodes' gun, and head out of town for the Neutral Strip where there was no law to arrest them.

The deputy and his prisoners had just finished their dinner and were walking across the street from the restaurant to the court room. The Negro from the livery stable was leading his

260

riding horses up the street, watching closely to bring about a meeting between himself with his saddle horses and the deputy with his two prisoners. The two groups met about two thirds of the way across the street. There was no crowd around, everything was well-staged for a quick, clean get-away. As the prisoners walked within a few feet of the horses, Herron played his part, which was to pretend to hit the Negro in the stomach, grab the reins and mount his horse, holding the rein of the other until Rhodes could take the deputy's revolver and mount the other animal. But the best laid plans of mice and men gang aft awry, as Burns put it.

Just when Rhodes should have pulled his gun and shoved it into the deputy's face, he lost his nerve. Jim Herron was already aboard his horse. He urged Rhodes to mount quickly, turned his own horse to run into the deputy and prevent him from drawing his gun, then lashed his horse with the reins and sped down the street east, toward Crooked Creek and the Graceland Cemetery. But Rhodes had tarried too long. Though he mounted and dashed after Herron, the deputy took careful aim and fired at Rhodes, hitting him with two bullets in the back and neck.

Rhodes cried out in his pain and Herron held up his horse, permitting Rhodes to draw up alongside him while he held him erect on the horse until they reached Crooked Creek. Seeing that Rhodes was critically wounded and that he could help him no more, Jim Herron pulled the horses up at the foot of the hill on the east side of the stream, dismounted, and helped Rhodes from his horse. By this time Rhodes fell unconscious. The noise down the main street told Herron that it would only be seconds until the deputy and others would be mounted and after him. So he bid Rhodes a hasty farewell, turned his horse down the old Jones & Plummer Trail, and never slowed from a hard run until he struck the state line, twenty miles south. Late that afternoon he rode into Beaver. The posse turned back at the Cimarron River.

Rhodes died of his wounds, and Jim Herron stayed out of Kansas, that is "officially," for many years. After Oklahoma was given statehood, Jim Herron returned voluntarily to Meade, Kansas, and gave himself up for trial. In the meanwhile he had

261

become a valued citizen of old No Man's Land, a capable lawman and a trusted cattleman. The court, after hearing many
testimonials from old timers from the Strip who had known Jim
Herron for many years, showed lenience to him because of the
rectitude of his later years and allowed him his freedom.

Jim Herron lived out the rest of his life in the old Neutral Strip,
was highly respected by all who knew him, and became almost a
celebrity at old timers' gatherings because of his adventurous
youth. "A better man never lived than Jim Herron," Burris
Wright, his personal friend, once told the author.

The violence of the men of the old west and the southwest was
matched in the violence of the weather on the plains. On the
southwest plains, as nowhere else on the north American continent, will you find imposing electrical storms that will bring awe to
the stoutest heart. And here, in a region that seldom receives more
than a couple or three inches of snow at a time, will you find wind
blizzards that will stack that inch or two of snow up into thirty
foot drifts in the canyons and railroads cuts! It was this region,
"about fifty miles south of Dodge," that Charles Russell selected
for the locale of his powerful story of storms and stampedes, which
he titled "Longrope's Last Ride."

Russell could not have chosen a locale more appropriate in
which to depict both storm and stampede and loss of life, both
animal and human, than that hilly area, north of the Cimarron,
where the great hills come down to form the breaks along the
northern edge of the sandy wastes that parallel the river. It was
in this region, "south of Dodge," in 1880 that Otis Ivey, one of
Jim Ellison's trail drivers, and for all we know the inspiration for
the character Longrope, was killed by lightning along with twenty
head of cattle in a stampede. Ellison had Ivey's body returned to
his home at West Fork, Caldwell County, Texas. And it was near
here, too, that Charley Thompson, a southwest Kansas cowboy,
was killed by lightning while holding a spooky bunch of longhorn
cattle on the roundup of 1884 on the Beaver River, in the Cherokee Strip.

Bernard Lemert, old brand inspector for the Southwest Cattlemen's Association, who rode with Thompson on this roundup, told of Thompson's tragic death. Here is Lemert's account of the night, just as he wrote it:

The XI, Figure 4 and LUK wagons were jointly holding their wagons together as their ranges joined each other over northwest of there on the Beaver river. After the evening meal, the night horses were caught and saddled and the men out with the cattle were relieved. The cattle were worked into a large oval formation on the bedground by the first two night guards. While they were humming and singing in a low voice to the cattle to quiet them, a black cloud showed up in the west. It appeared to be one of the many little summer storms we had been having, so no one paid much attention to it. I did ask the cook to let me throw Jim Chaudoin's bed and my own in the wagon under the bows and sheets so they wouldn't get wet until Jim came off first guard. I sat on the bedrolls in the wagon and watched as the storm gathered in the west.

When the first wind blasts ahead of the storm reached us, we realized it was no small storm. The thunder rolled along the prairie sounding like the tread of doom and the lightning crashed in our ears and broke so close that we could hear the sharp, high sizzling noise one hears before the loudest crashes after a particularly bright flash of lightning.

After a time I heard some of the men who were sleeping under a four bed tent (one side anchored to the wagon, three sides staked to the ground). They were up, paddling around in the water trying to get the tent to stay up. The stakes had pulled loose in the rain and the tent was down.

I got out, grabbed my blanket, bridle and saddle, which was laying on the ground, and pulled for higher ground, a few steps east of where the wagon set. The water was getting deeper all around and the Figure 4 men, with the help of some of the XI men, were pulling and tugging at the wagon to get it up on higher ground, to a ridge close to where the XI wagon stood. Several of the night horses had pulled their picket pins and no one got out to relieve Jim until after midnight or later. Jim managed to stay with the herd and got them back close enough to camp so that some of the men got out to help him.

The lightning continued to whine, crack and to break up into a million dazzling streaks in the cloudy sky after which there would be blasts of thunder like field artillery in an engagement.

Now lightning like this will play around the tips of the cattle's horns and on a night like this a cowboy on guard will soon get rid of a pistol, pocket knife or anything else that he believes may draw the lightning down on his own head.

The next morning we ate breakfast at the XI wagon as all the cooking utensils on the wagons and a quarter of beef on the other wagon was all covered with sand and mud and ruined for eating. The cattle had drifted badly in the storm and as we were about in the center of the YL range a good many strays had gotten mixed into our herd and had to be cut out the next day. While getting dried out around the wagon the next morning, a cowboy from the Backward LV (I later learned he was Charles Siringo who was looking up some lost cattle from a trail drive the previous fall) rode into our soggy camp. While drinking a cup of coffee he told us an LIT man, Charley Thompson, had been killed by lightning. The LIT was owned by Col. George W. Littlefield.

Siringo said that Thompson was standing guard over about 60 head of nervous cattle. He was a little distance away from two other cowboys who were also standing guard. The rain had almost stopped, they later told, when a single flash of lightning struck him, killing both Thompson and his horse instantly. They said the smell of sulphur was heavy in the air after the bolt struck.

They needed a wagon to move the body so we unloaded a chuck box on the ground and all the other stuff in the wagon and took the remains over eight miles north on Kiowa Creek, close to the YL ranch. Some of the men got some lumber and made a coffin. They buried Thompson south of the ranch in the horse pasture and we got poles and built a pen around his grave.

There wasn't much of a service, for we were just ordinary cowboys and didn't know much about religion and burying and things like that. Someone said a few words about what a good fellow Thompson had been on the roundup, how he would stand his guard come Hell or High Water, and he asked the Lord to give Thompson consideration for what he was—a good cowboy.

I heard afterwards that Thompson had lived up in Kansas some place and that later his remains were taken back there when the work on the range was finished that year and he was buried again near his folks where he would most likely want to be.

The Charles Siringo mentioned in Lemert's story was indeed the famous cattle detective. Bernard later explained that Bates &

Beal, the Backward LX, had range in the Texas panhandle in 1883, west of the Turkey Track. On their fall beef drive to Dodge they had a bad stampede and lost some of the herd in No Man's Land. Siringo was employed that spring to ride with the roundup for a week or two and look for these lost cattle. He located twenty head or more of big beeves and took them back with him.

Another well-known cattleman killed by lightning "south of Dodge" was August H. (Gus) Johnson. He was killed July 3, 1882, near Mulberry Creek. "The third of July in '82 was the last of August," some of the irreverent cowboys facetiously remarked. But they did so to conceal their real feelings, for Gus Johnson was liked and admired by all the cowboys, for he had been a working cowboy himself, was one until his death.

Johnson was a Texas man who built a "rep" for himself along the old Chisholm Trail in 1874-75-76. He learned the trail business thoroughly, found out how Texas brush longhorns worth five dollars could be converted to a Yankee twenty or more at the northern railheads. He also learned of the free grass in the Cherokee Strip and along the Cimarron and Beaver rivers. He learned how to obtain credit from Kansas City packers, and how to use a part of this to buy cattle. With this knowledge he bought every cow he could pay for that could walk out of Texas.

Johnson sold 49 per-cent interest in one herd of 9,000 head to a Scot syndicate and sold another 49 per-cent interest in a second herd to a group which he organized as the Texas Land & Cattle Company—the T5. He organized another, the Horshoe or Muleshoe, near Mobeetie with another herd of 6,000 longhorn cattle. Early in 1882 he bought the Kennedy interest in the King Ranch (The Laureles) near Corpus Christi.

Gus Johnson was a well-known figure on the streets of Dodge. Probably no other cowman, starting from scratch, achieved more in a few years than did Johnson. Where nerve, decisiveness, and an agressive nature brought quick recognition and fast rewards, men like Johnson prospered. At the time of his death he is said to have been the general manager of at least thirteen large cattle operations in the southwest. Death came to him as it did to many others of that era while he sat his horse on duty, moving up the trail to Dodge.

Deaths from electrical storms and subsequent stampedes brought greater loss of life, both human and animal than any other single cause, reliable cowmen have reported. So it is no wonder that the great bolts from the blue on a dark and stormy night induced frightened cowboys to shed sixshooters, rifles, and knives and any other items of metal in their possession they felt might bring the attention of the Powers from Above down onto their defenseless heads.

In addition to the violence of the great electrical disturbances in the heavens, nature at the opposite turn of the year frequently sent savage blizzards raging across the High Plains. The open plains country in most instances offered no shelter to man or beast, and when they were caught out on the range death might easily come to either. In these unpredictable storms, man was at the mercy of the elements. One man who lived to tell about being through such an experience was J. H. McQuistion of Canadian, Texas.

On January 27, 1891, McQuistion was sent out by his church as a missionary to the cowboys of the ranches along the Canadian River. His task was to go from Canadian to the ranches northwest of there about 32 miles, there to visit with his church clerk. His plans called for him to go east from there down the Canadian to Fort Elliott. McQuistion was riding an exceptionally good horse, a big, rugged roping horse he had traded for the year before and one that displayed superior intelligence upon several occasions. After eighteen miles of riding through the canyons and brakes of the river, he came out upon the high plateau, north of the Canadian. To the north he could see the dark clouds of a storm gathering just as the sun set. As the darkness came on, the chilly blasts struck him and snow started falling. As the mercury began to fall, he untied his heavy coat from behind the saddle, put it on, ate the sandwich he had brought along, and stopped for a short while to rest his horse and let it water at a spring. As he mounted again, he saw a band of wolves that had been tagging along near the spring. They now drew closer to his horse.

As McQuistion continued on in the face of the storm, he found it necessary to dismount and walk every twenty minutes or so to start his blood to circulating and warm his booted feet. When he would walk alongside his horse, holding on to a rein and one stirrup, the wolves would come alongside closer and closer, snarling, snapping, and occasionally darting in to attempt to nip the horse. As the horse tired, the beasts, eleven of them in the pack, grew even bolder. Finally one big male, fully six or seven feet from tip to tip, leaped in, grabbing McQuistion's hand, which held the bridle rein, mangling it badly. It was only with great good luck he was able to beat the attack off by hammering the beast across the nose with the heavy iron stirrup of the saddle, the horse aiding in the struggle by kicking away others of the attacking band that had finally jumped to the attack. McQuistion, though an experienced western man, now realized that he was involved in a battle for his life. His faithful, though weakened saddle horse appeared to be his only hope for survival against the beasts, its endurance and skill at kicking away attackers being their only defense, since he carried no gun.

As darkness closed down, the weary horse staggered on, barely able now to carry the weight of its rider through the drifting snow. Though he felt he should now be at his destination, and the horse knew the place, since he had made the trip several times before, McQuistion now sensed that the played-out horse seemed unable to get them to the first ranch where they usually stopped for the night. The wolves had closed up their ranks and kept so close to the horse that McQuistion could no longer dismount and walk and could only aid the horse in its struggle by kicking at them with his feet when they came close enough to bite the horse's flanks.

As the pack pressed close, forcing the horse to walk almost where they wanted it to go, McQuistion heard a bellowing roar come out of the snowy darkness and a large herd of longhorn cattle commenced to string by, drifting with the storm, bawling at the top of their lungs and with ice-balls forming on their noses almost as large as cannon balls. Suddenly the attention of the wolves passed from his bleeding hand, which they kept sniffing for and crouching to leap upon, to the bawling cattle. As the herd passed by the wolves turned away from the stumbling horse and its worn-out rider, turning to the weakened cattle. Now McQuistion heard a cow bawl out in terror and in pain as the pack leaped upon her and drug her down into the snow. To this cry of distress his weary horse responded, turning almost at right angles and plunging into the teeth of the storm again, then bearing far over to the left. Back behind he could hear the snarling and quarreling of the wolf pack as it fought over the remains of the cow.

Within a half hour McQuistion, now more dead than alive, heard a dog bark. The horse turned directly to the animal's sound. Then a light appeared in the darkness as a man stepped from a cave, pulling a heavy buffalo hide away from the entrance. The hunter, for such he was, quieted the dog, helped both the man and the horse inside the cave. Soon McQuistion had thawed out enough to tell the story of his escape from the wolves.

The next morning the storm had broken and the sun was out. They followed the horse's tracks, saw where the intelligent animal, heading for the cave of the hunter, had twice been turned away by the wolves and how, finally, the animal had found it difficult again to reach the vicinity of the cave for some reason, the dog's barking finally bringing it in.

Only the wolves' attack on the longhorn cow had saved McQuistion from the wolves and only the barking of the faithful dog had finally helped bring the horse to the shelter of the cave. Though fifteen miles off from the ranch he had tried to reach, McQuistion arrived there that next night and held his meeting with his church clerk.

To add to the bad features of the weather in the southwest cattleland, the sandstorms, so frequently referred to by the early-day cowboys, were much closer related to the "dusters" of the 1930's and 1950's than most Southwest chambers of commerce would like you to believe. Some residents of the region today speak of "The Dirty Thirties" as though the dust storms were invented by Nature at that time. Not so. The winds blow over the vast high plains 365 days each year, some days being of greater velocity than others. Since time immemorial there have been sandstorms and dusters in the region of the Cimarron, the Arkansas, the Beaver, and the Canadian. The earliest travelers on the Santa Fe Trail spoke of them; cavalrymen of the 1840's, 1850's, and 1860's rode through them; settlers who arrived in the 1880's and 1890's learned about them; and they were frequent in the years 1904 to 1911. The *Cimarron News* told of a Sunday sandstorm of March 1913:

The dirt was so thick that the sun was shut out. The storm had the appearance of having a heavy cloud between the earth and the sun. The wind was from the southwest and it surely did blow! It stirred up more dirt than any sandstorm since March, 1904, when we had the big one from the north which drifted nearly all the cattle out of the country and was accompanied by much electricity.

A prairie fire accompanied the Sunday duster, nearly burning down some houses . . . but the wind was so strong that the blaze went by so fast the houses did not ignite.

Wind, sand, dust, hail, blizzards, and heat have always been a part of the southwest weather scheme. It is not surprising, when weather changes every fifteen minutes of every day, that the adage has been created, "Only damn fools and newcomers *predict* weather here. Which are you?" As Mark Twain observed, nothing will ever be done about the weather of this violent land. It cannot be wished away, only endured. It is most fortunate for the fine folk who make the Cimarron region their homes that their peaceful and patient dispositions remain unaffected and ungoverned by the violent fits and tantrums of this fickle Nature.

Chapter XIV

One could not select a more appropriate chapter for a book dealing with the many lost trails of the Cimarron than one which dealt with women on the frontier. No trails have been more eroded than theirs. No trails are more difficult to find today than those grassed in or plowed up paths made by the wives, mothers, and daughters of the southwest cattlemen. The nature of woman's work on the frontier kept her at home, out of the limelight frequently enjoyed by a husband, father, or son. Yet her trail was always the loneliest, always the most rock-strewn and difficult to tread. Her lord and master could do little to help her bear her burdens, since his work took him away from the home and actually added anxieties to her lot, worries about the safety and well-being of absent family members.

Though it would make for pleasant reading to relate stories of women's successes on the frontier to match those of her husband it would hardly be factual. For it was woman's place to help make her man successful, not to achieve personal success—though many did! Or we could tell of these major achievements that many women did make, despite the difficulties they had to surmount to do so. But, alas, this, too, is impossible to accomplish. For it was woman's lot to be too busy to leave a single, easily-followed trail, one which would provide a clear, factual record of her activities and accomplishments. So what follows is not intended to present a clear picture of woman's work on the frontier, or even suggest why she was there. The vignettes that follow were selected at large because they are concerned with women who were pioneers, who were vital, who may even be exceptional and not at all like what we picture the Pioneer Woman to have been. But in every case they prove to be women whom some man loved.

Mrs. A. J. Weldon, 719 Washington Place, Long Beach, California, passed her girlhood on a ranch and claim in Clark County,

270

Kansas, down near the old Beeson and Harris range, about twenty miles south of Dodge. It was her task as a small girl to herd the family cows and to prevent them from mixing with trail herds which passed on the nearby Western Cattle Trail. When evening fell she would bring them back to the sod corral and water them at the creek, and they would be ready for milking when her father came in.

One evening as she drove her cows homeward she tarried along the way, then realized that she would not have time to water them at their own creek branch. So she drove them over to the stream where the Texas Cattle Trail crossed the range to water. Because of the fear of Texas ticks she had been forbidden to water them at this trail crossing. Just as she had driven them to the bank of the stream, the "point" of a large herd of Texas longhorns swung down the hill, the thirsty lead steers of the herd sweeping her cows into their midst as they quickly grabbed a few gulps of water and splashed across the stream. When she saw her cows disappear completely into the maw of the great herd, she sat down on a rock and cried bitterly. For she knew her father's cows would go on with the herd and her parents would never forgive her for her disobedience and for losing their cows upon which their very existence depended.

As the distraught child sat weeping, the black-bearded trail boss rode over to her, reined up, and asked, "Why all the tears, child?"

She told him how her cows had been gathered up into the big steer herd and were even now on their way to Dodge where she would never see them again. Though the boss had not seen her cows join the herd, he now called out to one of the Mexican *vaqueros* riding at the point of the herd.

"Ricardo! Let's get this child's cows out of the herd—*pronto!*"

The two point riders rode among the lead steers and quickly cut out the cows, leaving them standing at the side of the trail, abashed at their sudden changes in status from cow herd to steer herd and back to milk cows, all in a space of five minutes.

The trail boss tipped his sweaty Stetson, smiled down at the small girl, and rode away out of her life. She dried her tears on her apron and started her cows homeward again. But she never forgot the kindly trail boss for his splendid action in giving her family back their needed cows, which could so easily have been added to his tally at the shipping pens at Dodge.

When Mrs. Weldon left for college, several years later, she was shocked by the rough language used by the college youths, and took them to task for it. They scoffed at "a girl raised among cowboys" for setting up a fuss about their language.

"The cowboys always mind their tongues when they are around ladies," she told the college boys. "They are far more genteel in their manners than you young men, and they wouldn't stand a minute for the talk from the likes of you!"

Later, Mrs. Weldon and her husband lived in a soddy on the Ludwig Kramer range, near Beaver City. She told of the first jail that was used at Beaver City, when no building for that purpose was yet available.

"It was nothing more nor less than a big, dried steer hide. A fellow who drank too much whiskey or was otherwise out of hand was simply plunked under the hide, which was pegged down to the ground with stakes driven at the edges to hold the hide down upon the prisoner. Sometimes dirt was thrown on top. There was a single hole in the steer hide and the man's head was left outside with his hat carefully set upon it to give him some shade. He stayed there until he sobered up or cooled off!" It could scarcely have been a very cool prison, at least when the mercury was setting at 100 degrees of a July or August afternoon!

That was the southwest cattle country—a land of rough men who could imprison a mean drunk beneath a pegged-down steer hide, yet a land where a dust-covered trail boss would respond instantly to a child's tears.

The name of Mrs. Bob Maple will always be a cherished one in the old Neutral Strip, as will be that of her husband, Bob Maple, who was a foreman on the YL ranch. Her father was Tom Judy, a prominent cattleman in the eastern end of The Strip. When the YL withdrew from the range, Bob Maple acquired some of the land for cattle range of his own as well as appropriating the YL brand, a famous one in that area. The Maples ranched there from the late Eighties, and their ranch bloomed like the proverbial rose. They knew good health, wealth, success. Then came the hard years of the Dirty Thirties and in 1935, at the bottom of their personal depression, Bob Maple's help and strength was lost to her through his murder and Pearl Maple had to pick up her life and go ahead by herself.

It was the worst period the southwest cattle industry had ever undergone, beset as the land was with drought, dust storms, and general business depression everywhere over the land. But Pearl Maple persisted, and through hard work and prayer and astute management she pulled the nucleus of their fine herd of Hereford cattle through the drought and survived the depression.

In addition to riding the range and managing the ranch on Timber Creek, she worked in her spare moments on a hobby project that was dear to her heart. It was the production of an elaborate and beautifully-worked hand-sewn quilt. Upon the vast, white background she carefully quilted in the figures of cattle and saddle horses. Each animal bore the respective brand of the ranch represented, the owner's name, the number of years of his activity in the Strip. Among the brands are those of Otto Barby, a boy who followed a trail herd from Texas to the High Plains at the rate of pay of six dollars per month! The Barby holdings now cover many sections near the old YL range. Another brand that is depicted on the quilt is that of Doc Anschutz, an Englewood rancher who turned the sod in Clark County with an ox team in order to provide winter feed for his cattle in 1877-78. Anschutz was a close friend of Pearl Maple's father, and they rode on the roundups together for many years.

The brand of Perry Brothers appears on her quilt, representing the labors of Colonel Perry who wanted a connecting link between the Santa Fe railway and the Rock Island from Buckland to Dodge City, and a man who had the grit and determination to get it! Will Schmoker's ranch brand appears with the expression, "What Hath God Wrought?" and tells the story of the Schmokers' love of flowers, shrubs, and trees and the bright and lovely spot they fashioned on the prairie where once grew only the sage and the buffalo grass.

Pearl Maple's quilt is like an evening spent with good western friends, pouring over the old Brand Books of the cattleman's associations. Here appear the names and brands of J. O. Miles, John (Toot) Over, Dave and Belle Mackey, Frank Maple, her husband's brother, Henry Drum, Will Rhodes, John George, Ben Steadman, George Healy, Fred Taintor, Doc Day, Will Kelly, Alec Young, B. F. McPherson, E. R. Coffey—and others.

One block of the lovely work is devoted to Old Americus, the favorite cowhorse of her father, Tom Judy. Tom Judy rode this fine cutting and roping horse in the roundups for many years, and Old Americus was known by all the cattlemen of the region and respected for his faithful equine contributions.

Another feature of the quilt is the Chuckwagon, bearing the inscription of the present Kansas state song, "Home on the Range." The buffalo and the coyote are given their appropriate places in the design. This quilt is truly a rich and rare work of art by a person who well understood the subject matter. It faithfully reflects the period of the cattlemen's frontier and preserves for posterity, on museum wall or ranch wall, the heraldry of the southwest plains.

Mrs. Bob Maple's quilt, like her energetic management of the ranch, was a labor of love and should be carefully preserved and cherished in memory of this ranch-woman extraordinary.

There is a little story of unrequited love that originated at the headquarters of the old OX ranch on the Beaver River, northwest of present day Guymon, Oklahoma. At that point, today, stands the ruins of the old stone ranchhouse and the remains of the stone barns and sheds. The site is about a mile west of the old townsite of Optima.

In the years when the OX was withdrawing from the range, a Jimmy McQuillan came into possession of the OX ranch buildings and lived at that place. A friend of McQuillans, a Mr. Clarence McGrath, a Boston man with two lovely daughters, Edna and Emanuela, came out to visit McQuillan's place. Both families were Irish Catholic by faith, both had acquired stock in the OX operation, and they had much in common. While they were visiting at the ranch, which they did for two or three years during the summer months, McGrath had a "Sister's House" erected on a high area, west of the OX ranch house. This stone building is generally what we would call a duplex today, and it, too, is still standing. It has been authoritatively said that McGrath's daughters, Edna and Emanuela, both of whom were teachers, took homestead claims in order to enhance the land holdings of the OX before it withdrew from the range.

While visiting there one summer, Emanuela fell in love with a young cowboy, Ted Luce, who worked at a nearby ranch. Late that summer, after the girls had returned east, Luce took a trail herd to Wyoming or Montana. Word came back that he was drowned in a crossing of the Platte River when his horse failed to swim a flooded area.

Following that information, the two girls never returned to visit with McQuillan's family. But several years later, when the ranch properties were disposed of, Emanuela came into possession of the ranchhouse as her part of the settlement, together with other land which she immediately sold. But she retained the ranchhouse, on an acre or two of land, and had it enclosed with a good barbed wire fence, so the cattle would not rub down the walls.

The years passed and Edna and Emanuela grew old and passed on. The land and the crumbling stone ranchhouse became tied up in the estate where, to the best of the author's knowledge, it may still rest. If not for the sentimental attachment Emanuela held for the old structure, it would now be only a heap of stone. Yet today, after more than eighty years of existence, it still stands, though weatherbeaten and almost denuded of shingles on its roof, staring out through its glassless windows and open doorways toward the placidly flowing Beaver River at its doorstep.

One old cowboy who knew the Boston girls and had danced with them said, "Yes, many a man among us led in a gentle horse for Edna or Emanuela to ride up to Old Buffalo when a dance was held there in the bygone days."

So came to its close the era of the "Buffalo Girls," with the deaths of Edna and Emanuela. But the standing rock walls of the OX ranchhouse still testify to the undying love of Emanuela.

At a camp that adjoined the T5 range in the Cherokee Strip lived a ranch foreman and his new bride whom he had brought back with him from a small Kansas town. Her name was Molly Snow. Now, Molly, according to the way Oliver Nelson told the story, had a streak of meanness in her system that soon commanded the attention of all the ranch hands.

One day an innocent colored puncher rode up to the ranchhouse, dismounted, and, hat in hand, knocked on the front door of Molly's soddy. Molly refused to answer. Seeing her plainly standing at her ironing board, the cowboy asked politely, "Lady, will yo' all give me sumpin' to eat?"

Molly kept running her iron. Again the colored man entreated her, "Lady, can yo' please fin' me sumpin' to eat?" He waited a moment and added, "I'se hongry."

It was a simple enough request, one that would have been promptly honored at any other ranchhouse in the Strip. But Molly only broke for the east room where her man's six-gun hung in its holster from a wall peg. Her fast movement alerted the Negro, who ran to the west window for a better view to see what caused Molly's actions. The sight of the big 45 revolver in her hand quickly convinced him that she was going to feed him lead, if anything, and all of it he could handle. So the cowboy scaled a four-wire fence at the rear of the house like a bobcat, turned west, where a patch of plum brush covered his retreat.

Molly now was compelled to run to the east gate to get him in her gunsights, then she started blasting—boom! boom! boom!

The Negro puncher ran west, then turned south across a draw, Molly all the while trying to get in a better shot at her victim— boom! boom! Running so fast, Molly stepped on the hem of her long skirt, went down with heels flying in the air, which was all to the colored man's favor. He now make a quick turn back to the house, leaped on his ground-tied horse, and left the place on the dead run before Molly could get back to the soddy and reload the six-shooter. Molly and that colored cowboy never crossed

276

trails again; in fact, it is unlikely that he ever returned to that range after such an experience.

Later Molly became a widow. The ranch hands gathered at their foreman's bier and with all the sympathy they could muster sat out the night in a wake, as was the custom of the range. About daybreak, the night wrangler came in the house to pay his respects to his departed leader. He looked down upon the calm, sad but serene face of the dead man, then said, "That's the first night's rest he's had since he married Moll' Snow."

Flory Dunlap, whose husband was a railway section boss, told of an experience with a band of Mexican vaqueros who trailed a big herd of cattle north through Colorado in the early Eighties and nearly scared her out of a year's growth.

They came to her house alongside the railway tracks east of Denver on the Burlington railroad one day in the month of July. It was extremely hot, and she had a sick baby on her hands as well as the twelve section hands to feed when they came in from their work several miles away. There were ten of the Mexicans, and they gesticulated, spoke loudly in Spanish, and finally pushed past her right into the house. The baby was only a few months old, and she hurriedly took it from its cradle and put it in the bedroom, fearing for its life as the men strode around through the house, looking through everything, talking to each other, pointing and questioning.

She tried to allay their tempers by offering them food, but they only spoke more wildly and continued their search through the house. Flory Dunlap was almost frozen with fear by now and thought of offering them the cash box which she kept to pay for supplies at the station when foodstuffs arrived.

Finally a very dark vaquero with a black mustache, apparently their leader, pushed the kitchen door shut. The woman threw herself across the bedroom door to shield the baby from whatever hidden danger might come, ready now to sacrifice her own life if necessary to protect her child. But now all the vaqueros began to laugh and shout. They had finally found what they sought—

the water pail, sitting on its little stand behind the kitchen door where it was always kept out of the way!

Flory Dunlap now hurried and brought cups and glasses, seeing what is was the men wanted. They drank and drank until the pail was empty, all the while bowing and smiling to show their gratitude and repeating over and over, *"Gracias, amigo; gracious, senora; gracias, gracias!"*

She then pointed to the well at the water tower, a short distance down the tracks, and the vanqueros took the pail and watered their horses. They then spread out their food on the ground beneath the big water tank, built a campfire, and cooked their dinner. The leader soon returned to the house, his big sombrero in his hands. Bowing and smiling, he tried to welcome Flory Dunlap to partake of their food with them. When she declined with a smile, he departed, later to return with a bottle of chili, the first she had ever eaten—and oh, so hot!

"When they left," Flory Dunlap said years later, as she told this story, "they all bowed gracefully from their saddles. They passed by, each one taking off his big hat and waving it to me and the baby and saying, *'Adios! Buena esta! Hasta la vista!'*

"From that day on, I was never afraid of men who worked with cattle, and I always found them to be perfect gentlemen, regardless of creed or color," she said.

On the frontier houses were scarce, bedrooms, at a premium, and every sleeping space was expected to serve at full capacity. Out of this situation grew amusing stories, while, if not entirely true in all instances, bear enough similarity in their retelling to warrant belief in the actual occurrence of something very similar at some time or other in the opening days of the West and Southwest.

The Prairie Owl, the first newspaper in Seward County, Kansas, was established at Harwoodville, the old Harwood Ranch, or Fargo Springs, as the community came to be called. In its columns of January 14, 1886, it reveals the theme suggested above, a situation that was considered very amusing to the people on the frontier at that time. The story follows:

278

GARDEN CITY SPECIAL TO THE CRUSADER: About eight o'clock yesterday evening a tall, lean, lank smoothface bashful youth with a blushing damsel on his arm stepped into Squire Smith's office and asked if His Honor was present. Upon being informed by the Clerk that Justice Smith had departed for the evening and would not return until 9 o'clock the next day, the countenance of our Kansas granger sank two degrees below zero, and he stood fumbling with his hands in such a distracted manner as to make him the object of real pity. His fair companion evidenced her sympathy by shedding a few tears which she wiped away with the corner of her calico apron. Observing their embarrassment, the Clerk politely asked, "Is there something I can do for you?"

After some hesitation the youth replied, "You see, sir, we cum tew get married, sir, Jinny and me, and we want to see the Squire." The Clerk again explained to them that the Justice was gone for the night and that at that hour all other offices were closed, and suggested that they return early the next morning to have the ceremony performed. With this the courage of our hero sank lower than before and whispering some tender words into the sunburnt ear of his dulcinea, they withdrew for consultation. Presently they appeared, crestfallen and disconsolate.

"Shall I show you to a hotel," asked the Clerk.

"Now that's the p'int," said the youth, taking courage. "We've only got fifty cents between us, jes' 'nuff fer one bed—an'—an'—an' Jinny don' like to stay alone—ah-h-h—and you see we thought we could get married an—an—an. . ."

"Oh, I see," said the Clerk, and then with characteristic Kansas enterprise he proposed a way out of the difficulty.

"You understand," said he, "That I'm no Justice but I am a Justice's clerk and can perform the ceremony for you *de-bene-esse,* and can join you in marriage *nunc-pro-tunc,* but, by the Eternal, you must promise to come back in the morning and let the Squire do the thing all over again or it won't hold."

The pair promised, and the Clerk officiated and the twain were soon as happy as if the *de-bene-esse-nunc-pro-tunc* ceremony had been a genuine *bona-fide ne-plus-ultra* clincher!

So intriguing was this old theme to the pioneers, it was related in various forms, but always ended up getting the young couple legally married and acceptable to the mores of frontier society.

Frank Sullivan, for example, told it this way in his *History of Meade County, Kansas* (Crane & Co., 1916) :

THE OLD CALABOOSE

He (an informant) recounted a romance in which the participants were a man and woman convicted on the same day—he of disorderly conduct, she of vagrancy. Both were fined and sentenced to stand committed until fine and costs were paid. Neither party having the necessary funds, the Court was in a dilemma, for the jail was not provided with suitable accomodations for lady guests.

The defendents relieved the situation and solved the Judge's quandary by offering to get married. A collection was accordingly taken up, the license procured, the Judge performed the ceremony and the honeymoon was celebrated in the old calaboose.

There are many variations of this old story, where revelers are snowed in by a bad blizzard, all couples having spouses, of course, and the proper number of beds, except the unmarried couple which it takes to complete the story. The scene changes, from Nebraska to Texas, but the theme remains the same. There may be a moral to the story, but as the pioneer editors would put it, "the author knoweth not what it is." That it provided entertainment for those folks of that day was reason enough for its popularity and appeal.

Though women are generally credited with great skill at baking hot rolls and fine-textured bread, there were roundup cooks who produced the tastiest biscuits man ever consumed. Their successes lay in the single word—"sourdough." Sourdough bread still remains the tastiest morsel of food produced on the High Plains. And the most talked-about bread in the Oklahoma Panhandle is that of Mrs. Rome Jennings and her daughter, Mrs. Ray Jennings of Adams, Oklahoma. Their success story has a long history.

When Anna Dibbens left London in 1872 to sail for America, her mother handed her a small gray jug, filled with sourdough from a starter that had been in the Dibbens household for many years.

"Take this with you and you will always have good hot bread

for your family," her mother advised her. Anna followed the advice and brought the starter to the Neutral Strip with her. Anna Dibben raised a good, healthy family on the sourdough bread made from this starter.

A few years ago, H. T. Whitmer of Kinsley, Kansas, a son-in-law of the Anna Dibbens of the story, was asked by his son, Ray Whitmer of Hooker, Oklahoma, the age of the sourdough. The elder Whitmer reflected a moment, then said, "Well, I am 83 years of age and that starter is many years older than I."

Ray Whitmer can claim another historical first for his family. His mother, he states, was born in the first frame house in Wichita. That makes her trail one of the longest and best defined along the Arkansas River valley!

The cowboys called her Frenchy, though she was actually of Irish extraction. When she died at Channing, Texas, a few years ago, she was Mrs. Mickey McCormick.

Frenchy was really Elizabeth McGraw of Baton Rouge, Louisiana, born in 1853. By the time she was fourteen she was working in a St. Louis dance hall. In 1873 she showed up at Dodge City, stylish in her fine clothes, a beautiful girl with a fine figure, corseted into a wine glass. There, she worked for the dance halls below the deadline.

By 1875 Frenchy was in Mobeetie, following the "buffalo trade" south as the hunters killed off the remnants of the southern herd. When the shooting was about over, Frenchy packed up and took the stage to Tascosa, the burgeoning cow town westward, up the Canadian River about a hundred miles. Tascosa was about "trail's end" for a woman of virtue in those days, though many of the Mexican *pastores* who had previously controlled the grazing lands maintained their families in that area. But Frenchy was there to "work the cattle trade," not to pasture sheep. And there she worked, and in 1881 met and married Mickey McCormick.

Mickey was a Tascosa gambler. Later in his life he operated a livery stable there. When he met Frenchy she was a mature woman of twenty-eight years who had been boozing, bustling, and blarneying buffalo hunters and cowboys for more than ten years with the "buy me another drink" routine. Though she still had a lovely figure and dressed the part of a woman of wealth and breeding, her beauty was fading. Within, the still, small voice told her how fortunate she had been to find, at the end of her trail of degradation, a man whom she loved and who, in turn, loved her. It was a great deal more than she had learned to expect from her sort of life.

Frenchy quit the dance halls when she married Mickey, and she set out to make him a good wife. Like many women of easy virtue before her, she succeeded. Together with Mickey, she pledged never to leave Tascosa without the other. And there, in the little town nestled beneath the giant cottonwoods on the north bank of the Canadian, Mickey and Frenchy lived together in happiness for many years. Then in 1908 Mickey died.

Frenchy laid Mickey away beautifully in the little Romero Cemetery to which he was carried by Louis Bosman, an old chum of Mickey who had participated in the last gun fight at Tascosa, and other younger men. Mickey had requested that he not be buried on the Boot Hill west of the town where other booted friends were put away. Frenchy told friends that she would never leave Tascosa, now that Mickey's remains rested there. So for more than thirty years she lived in their little adobe home under the cottonwood trees that had grown straight and tall since she planted them many years before.

In 1939 Frenchy was 86 years of age, feeble and ailing. She was eligible for old age assistance and the pension helped out greatly. She went to Channing to live, since friends had agreed to care for her in her last days. But she made them promise that when her time came, she would be buried beside Mickey.

In 1941, Frenchy told her friends that she felt she would soon be called to make her Peace with the Lord. She confided in Mrs. Lona Blackwell, with whom she stayed, that she had joined the Catholic Church in St. Louis when she was a girl. But she never fully revealed who her family were nor where they lived, and it was only later that friends learned.

When she died, Frenchy was laid beside her Mickey under the buffalo sod along the Canadian, "the last of the Girls of the

Golden West." There, in the shade of the cottonwood trees the pair will now sleep through until their Judgment Day. They had contributed nothing of lasting value to the Southwest or its people, neither to its mores nor its morals, unless it be further proof of that one eternal fact, so often overlooked—that 'tis Love and Love alone that rules, always.

Chapter XV

"The Old West is dead," wrote Charlie Russell not too many year ago. "You may lose a sweetheart, but you will never forget her." Likewise are the lost trails of the old cowmen faded and gone—gone the old cowmen, gone even the trails he left behind him for so short a while. The cowboy now remains only as a memorable character of history.

The cowboy, in his day, was a strange creature and so much so that his contemporary newspapers and magazines saw him as such. They made of him a symbol of the adventurous spirit of the west, a man of great courage, living under the code of derring-do, strong-willed, with a strong stomach and a backbone of steel. He is today portrayed much that way on television screen, in motion pictures, and in the writings of most writers of western fiction. To those of us who have known him more intimately, sometimes as father, uncle, perhaps as old friend, the American cowboy was a much more understandable and likeable human than the shadows that are reflected back to us from the screens and pages of fiction.

What was he really like? He was much like his descendents would be under the circumstances which gave him his character and his niche in history. But since those circumstances will never again be repeated on this continent, we shall never again know his like.

The range land cowboy was basically a herdsman, concerned first and last with the animals under his care. He lived in the open, under the sun and stars, many weeks out of the year. He lived close to and in harmony with live animals, a mode of life denied most of us today and one we can ill-afford to suffer as human beings, if we desire to live a full and complete life.

A cowboy's life was one of activity, which kept him in reasonably good health so that he fully enjoyed living. He was usually a young man, whose livelihood kept him from the company of good women, so he held womankind in a sort of awe, judging them as he would judge his own mother. The women he met in the dance halls and red lights he quite frequently married and took them away from a life of vice; and strange though it may seem, these women in many instances, most instances it may be said, made good, loyal, and affectionate wives and good mothers to their children.

About the cowboy's inner feelings, there will be as much speculation as there would be about any comparable group of men working in the livestock industry. No doubt as the cowboy of the Cimarron range sat his horse on the high plains cattle range at night, watching his herd as other herdsmen had done two thousand years before him, he felt a closeness with those ancestral characters that we, who rarely spend a night out in the open, never have felt for them, their age of history or their ideas. As a result, the cowboy undoubtedly became a better Christian for it, though he was quick to deny any particular awareness of religion in its orthodox sense or admit any attachment for the "sky pilots" who traveled the missionary routes around the ranches, attempting to foist their brand of religion upon men who had been living a deep and full brand of work-a-day Christianity every day, month in and month out, for years.

Most of the cowboys were inarticulate when it came to expressing philosophical or religious thoughts, but in the doggeral verse that passed for poetry on the cattle range there is an indication of their innermost beliefs.

Allen McCandless, a Crooked L cowboy, summed up the inner thoughts of at least some cowboys when he penned his widely quoted and preserved "Cowboy's Soliloquy" on a scrap of paper and submitted it to the Dodge City and Trinidad newspapers in 1885. This verse was clipped and carried in many a cowboy's warbag, and an old cowboy, more than eighty years old, once pulled the tattered clipping from his purse and made the writer a present of it. The last lines of McCandless' verse declares:

> Abraham emigrated in search of new range,
> When water got scarce and he needed a change;

Isaac had cattle in charge of Esau,
    And Jacob ran cows for his father-in-law;
He started in business clear down at bed rock,
    And made quite a fortune by "watering stock;"
David went from night-herding and using a sling
    To winning a battle and becoming a King.
And the Shepherds, while watching their flocks
                                    on the hill,
    Heard the Message from Heaven, of Peace and
                                    Good Will.

Despite the violence of their time, the message of Peace and
Good Will came through to the American cowboys as the only
well-defined trail that could lead humanity to a tranquil future.
And despite the violence that has marked our own more recent
period, that Message still comes through, sharp and clear, to those
that will hear. We may sympathize with the Biblical Esau in the
loss of both his birthright and his father's blessing. But how much
more tragic if Mankind should lose its Father's blessings by following a false and crooked trail today, a trail that may be sublimated
and obscured by atomic fire, even as the more orderly and gentle
forces of Nature have washed away and obscured these many old
trails of the Cimarron.

Appendix

BRANDS FROM THE BRAND BOOK OF APRIL 7, 1885
THE WESTERN KANSAS CATTLE GROWERS ASSOCIATION
Dodge City, Kansas

(Key: *O*-wner; *M*-anager; *F*-oreman)

No.	Name of *O*-wner, *M*-anager, *F*-oreman	Brand	
1.	American Pastoral Co. James Campbell, *M*.	Backward LX (Connected)	X
2.	Arnold Brothers	Triangle Z	ΔZ
3.	Arkansas Valley Land & Cattle Co. R. C. Blumfield, *M*	Bar SS	¬SS
4.	Anderson, George	A	A
5.	Beeson & Harris N. J. Atteberry, *M*	COD	COD
6.	Beverly Brothers Wm. Beverly, *M*	V under B or VB	ᵛⱽᵇ
7.	Barton, Clay Henry Barton, *M*	TO Bar	TO
8.	Barton, D. W. Henry Barton, *M*	OS Bar	OS– OS
9.	Barton, Al Henry Barton, *M*	Lazy SH Connected or S Cross H	ᴄH⊃
10.	Bullard, S. A.	O Cross O	O+O
11.	Brown, Wm. S.	Diamond L Connected	⬦
12.	Buffalo Ranch Co. (Word, Byler Co.) J. H. Mussett, *M*	R Bar S	R–S
13.	Biggs, J. E.	7HK Connected	7HK
14.	Clark, R. B.	Two Bar (Horizontal Bars)	=
15.	Cattle Ranche & Land Co., Ltd., Spencer & Drew, *M's* A. U. Young, *F*	777	777

No.	Name of O-wner, M-anager, F-oreman	Brand	
16.	Cattle Ranche & Land Co., Spencer & Drew, *M*'s Tom Baldwin, *F*	YL Connected	Y
17.	Cimarron & Crooked Creek Cattle Co. R. E. Steele, *M*	L (Crooked L)	L
18.	Davis, F. M.	Cross	+
19.	Davis, F. M.	Backward FD Connected	ꟼD
20.	De Cordova H. M. DeCordova, *M*	HM Connected	HM
21.	Dudley, E. C. & Co. C. H. Bagbee, *M*	Anchor D	ED
22.	Day, J. M. Jno. T. Edgar, *M*	DD	DD
23.	Day, J. M.	D Cross	D+
24.	Drake & Telfer Adam Telfer, *M*	TE Half Bar	TE
25.	Dutchess Cattle Co. Percy B. Russell, *M*	Horshoe H Bar	ꓵH
26.	Evans & Harper	Lazy H	ꓱ
27.	Emporia Cattle Co. S. R. Taylor, *M*	T Bar T	T-T
28.	Eno & Russell	BK	BK
29.	Eno & Russell	Muleshoe Bar H	ꓵ-H
30.	Farrar, S. H.	18 81	18 81
31.	Fonda, Frank	JNP Connected (Written)	ꝰ
32.	Ford County Land and Cattle Co J. H. Wright, *M*	WC Bar	WC- WC
33.	Fares & Lewis Henry Fares, *M*	H Inverted L Connected	HꓶΓ
34.	Gorham, Arthur	Three Ovals (Catspaw) or Three Rings	°₀°
	" "	Quartercircle Box	
35.	Given, James I.	444	444
36.	Gluck & Myton A. Gluck, *M*	A Bar M	A-M
37.	Grimmer, C. F.	IB or JB	JB

No.	Name of O-wner, M-anager, F-oreman	Brand	
38.	Harwood Cattle Co. W. I. Harwood, *M*	Circle Cross L Connected	
39.	Holstein, Sim	Cross H7	
40.	Harbough, Wm.	OV Bar	
41.	Hungate Bros. D. B. Hungate, *M*	Quartercircle 7HL Connected	
42.	Hardesty Brothers Tom Hungate, *F*	Inverted S Quartercircle	
43.	Hardesty Bros.	Backward LF	
44.	Harvey, Fred	XY	
45.	Hightower, M. R.	T (in a) Circle	
46.	Healy Bros. George Healy, *M*	KK	
47.	Imel, James M.	JI	
48.	Irwin Cattle Co. James C. Irwin, *M*	P (Flag)	
49.	John, D. S. R. R. Ewing, *M*	V Bar Connected (Called "VK")	
50.	John, D. S. R. R. Ewing, *M*	VV	
51.	Kollar, Hi	Half Circle Reverse J Connected	
52.	Lee Summit Cattle Co. H. A. Latham, *M*	IV	
53.	Lemert, Laban	Half Circle L (Called Crutch L)	
54.	Langton & Walker Wm. Walker, *M*	VK Connected	
55.	Lee Scott Cattle Co. J. E. McAllister, *M*	LS	
56.	Latham, R. B.	KL	
57.	Leuthstrom, C. A.	LC Connected	
58.	Mills, C. C. & Bro.	Running W5 Bar	
59.	McCoy Bros. & Co.	XI 11 (Eks I Eleven)	
60.	McCoy Bros. & Co. A. H. McCoy, *M*	XI Bar	
61.	McCoy Bros. & Co.	UV	
62.	McKinney, Over & Co. John E. Over, *M*	Running M Bar	

No.	Name of O-wner, M-anager, F-oreman	Brand	
63.	McCarty, T. L.	SIS	SIS
64.	Muscatine Cattle Co. A. J. Streeter, Gen. Supt., Trinidad Thos. A. Lee, Gen. Agt., Kansas City	Z Lazy H	ZH
65.	Marselus Bros.	17 Bar	17- 17
66.	O'Loughlin & Company Richard Joyce, F	Open A7 Half Bar	A7
67.	O'Loughlin, John Richard Joyce, F	Pigpen 7	#7
68.	Pierce, Brown & Co. J. S. Simpson, M Lafayette County, Mo.	"Seventy Six"	76
69.	Perry, R. K.	E	E
70.	Perry, R. K.	Reverse J	J
71.	Roberts and Evans A. K. Chilcott, M	IL	IL
72.	Reighard, Geo. W. & Co.	JFH	JFH
73.	Ryan, Pat	Bar R	-R
74.	Rhodes and Aldridge D. Hargrave, M	Quartercircle U	U
75.	Riley, Wm.	LT	LT
76.	Rafferty Cattle Co. C. B. Wiser, M	XK Bar	XK
77.	Southwestern Land & Cattle Co. C. A. Brelesford, F S. A. Bullard, M (?)	KH	KH.
78.	Spencer, H. F. William H. Jay, F	TV Bar	TV- TV
79.	Sitler & Langton Robert A. Harper, F	SL	SL
80.	Steele Bros., Woodward, Warren & Co. C. E. Woodward, M	L Small Cross	Lt
81.	Taintor, Fred	GG	GG
82.	Tilghman & Brown	A	A

No.	Name of O-wner, M-anager, F-oreman	Brand	
83.	Towers & Gudgell	OX	OX
84.	Towers Bros.	V (over) Bar Connected	V
85.	Threlkeld, John	X (Crossed Rifles)	X
86.	Thompson, Wm.	Rafter Cross	
87.	Tatum, B. F.	TT Bar	TT
88.	Tyler, S. C.	ZV Connected	V
89.	Tyler, S. C.	JHA	JHA
90.	Weeks Bros.	EH Half Bar	EH
91.	Wright, R. M. John Folley, M W. B. Rhodes, F	Quartercircle W (Or Crescent W)	W
92.	Wettick, A. D.	L Bar 4	L-4
93.	Wettick, J. T.	L Bar 7	L-7
94.	W. L. Ranche Co. Shed. N. Rose, M	WL	WL
95.	Washita Cattle Co. Frank Biggers, F	7K Connected	K
96.	Washita Cattle Co. F. B. York, Gen. Mgr. Wm. Ragland, F	7V Connected	V
97.	Walsh, T. E. John P. Ryan, M	SL	SL
98.	Watson & Fullington T. J. Sidener, F	TWT Connected	TWT
99.	Wettick, J. T. A. D. Wettick, M	L Bar 7	L-7
100.	Westmoreland, Hitch & Co. Wm. Westmorland, M	LV	LV
101.	Young, A. M.	Cross Muleshoes up and down Y	+∩∪y

COMANCHE POOL BRANDS

A. G. Evans, R. W. Phillips, R. Kirk, Directors

No.	Name	Brand	
102.	Blair, Wm.	WIL	WIL
103.	Carter, W. H.	XX	XX
104.	Colcord, W. R.	Jug	
105.	Comanche Horse Brand	Backward PC	CP Ͻꟼ

291

No.	Name of Owner, Manager, Foreman	Brand	
106.	Doyle, J. B.	JB Connected	
107.	Eno & Russell	Muleshoe H Bar	
	W. L. Hobbs, M		
108.	Evans, Hunter & Newman	Heart	
109.	Gregory, R. I.	Inverted LX Connected	
110.	Gregory, R. I.	4B Connected	
111.	Kirk & Co., E. B.	7K Connected	
112.	Mather, Wm.	J J	
113.	Payne, E. W.	P HP Connected	
114.	Phillips, R. W.	UL Bar	
115.	Rawlins, J. M.	Diamond R Connected	
116.	Wilson, John	JON	

Officers of The Western Kansas Cattle Growers Association for the years 1882-3-4 were as follows:

A. H. McCoy, Dodge City............President
Arthur Gorham, Kinsley............Vice-president
C. W. Willett, Dodge City............Secretary
F. B. York, Dodge City............Treasurer

Executive Committee:

R. J. Hardesty, Dodge City   E. W. Spencer, Kansas City
J. M. Coburn, Kansas City

For the year 1885, officers were as follows:

Arthur Gorham, Kinsley............President
A. H. McCoy, Dodge City............Vice-president
C. W. Willett, Dodge City............Secretary
F. B. York, Dodge City............Treasurer

Executive Committee:

Hi Kollar, Dodge City   W. I. Harwood, Dodge City
J. M. Coburn, Kansas City

Round-up Captains elected for 1885 were:
    Beaver Division, Sim Holstein
    Cimarron Division, Wash Mussett.

RECEPTION COMMITTEE
FOR CONVENTION 1885
March 21-22-23

Martin Culver
I. P. Olive
R. J. Hardesty
R. M. Wright

INVITATION COMMTTEE

W. H. Harris
D. W. (Doc) Barton
Arthur H. Gorham
J. Edward Dudley

FLOOR MANAGERS

Sim Holstein
Bake Hungate
Fred Taintor
R. E. Steele
Chalkey M. Beeson

Index

(Note: The word "Old" following town names indicates abandoned townsites. Town of same name may presently be established elsewhere.)

Bent, William, 20, 58
Bernard Brothers, 75
Beverly, H.M., 177-78-79, 202
Biggers, Frank, 106
Bigham, Sol, 117
"Billy The Kid," 258
Bivens, Lee, 78
Black, Gus, 70
Black Kettle, Chief, 22, 59
"Black Sam," 192, 201
Blackwell, Lona, 282
Blake, Al E., 250
Blake, B.E., 250
Bland, Mrs. Cora, 222
Bland, Willie, 22
Blocker, Ab, 70, 85-6, 165
Blocker, John R., 85
"Blue Belly," 38
Boggs, Thomas O., 58, 83
Boise City, Okla., 76
Boles, John L., 69
Bolton, A.J., 69
Bond, Brick, 19
Borders, Kan., (Old), 213
Boss, Isaac, 74
Bosman, Louis, 282
Boyce, H.S., 83
Boyd, Okla. (Old), 84, 142
Brennan, Matt, 192
Briggs, Charley, 87
Bright, Perry, 200
Brooks, Ed, 37
Brown, Court, 156
Brown, George W. (Hoodoo), 18-19,
    22-23-24-25-26, 33, 39, 63, 65, *126*,
    221
Brown, Grace (child), 24
Brown, Nellie (child), 24
Brown, Sonny (child), 24
Brown, Henry Newton, 259
Brown, Joe, 160
Brown, Marvel, 81
Brown, Neal or Neil, 37, 175
Brown, Pvt., 39
Brown, Sarah E., 24
Brown, S.G., 256
Brown, William, 95
Bryson, Mrs. John, 34

Buchanan, Al, 69, 93, 150-51, *194*
"Buck," a vigilante, 119
Buckland, Beatrice, 156
Buffalo, Okla. (Old), 171
Bugby, T.S., 69, 163
Bull, Bear, 27
Bull City, Kan. (Old), 203
Burnett, T.H., 75
Burns, Mrs., 140-41
Bush, Lewis (Brushy), 171, 255
Bush, "Mexican Joe," 78
Butler, Fayette, 70
Butler, Pleas, 70
Butterfield Stage Route, 45
Buttons, Bill, 106
Byram, Wiley, 87

—C—

Cain, Carrie, 252
Cain, Homer, *55*, 252
Cain, Zachariah, *55*, 251-52
Cain, Mrs. Zack, *55*, 252-53
Caldwell, Kan., 116, 135, 228, 229
Calvert, Miss Edith, 170
Camp Supply Military Road, 43
Campbell, Bob, 87
Campbell, Frank, 95
Campbell, George, 95
Campbell, 2nd Lt. George J., 57
Canadian, Texas, 39, 266
Carr, General, 22
Carson, Kit, 47, 57, 58 74
Carson, Victor, 225, 226
Carson, Walter, 226
Carter Claude, 192
Cartwright, W.J., 77
Carver, Dr. George Washington, 208
Catalpa, New Mex., 76-7
Cator, Jim and Bob, 17-8-9-20, 41,
    54, 69, 253
Catron, Tom, 182-83-84
Cattleman's Magazine, The, 216
Cavanaugh, F.E., 74
Channing, Tex., 281-82
Chapman, Amos, 39
Chapman, Frank, *123*
Chase, "Judge" O.G., 111-12-13-14,
    116, *125*

295

299

302

304

3 5132 00238 2398
University of the Pacific Library

WITHDRAWN

1ST ED.
SIGNED.

ZOLX
5⸺

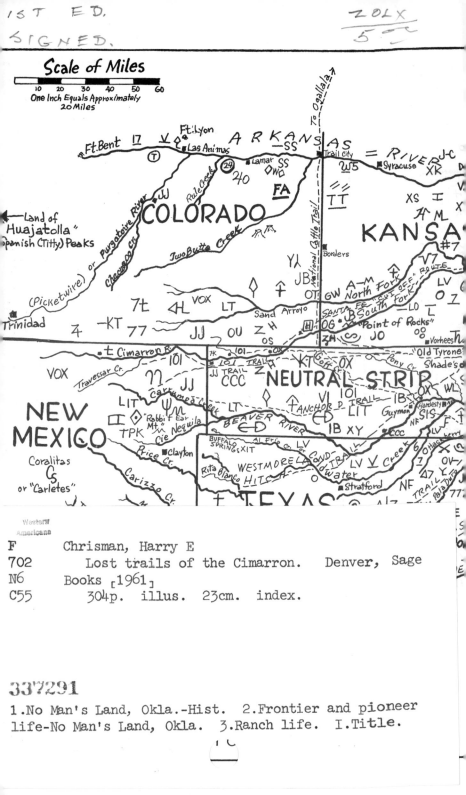

Western
Americana

F   Chrisman, Harry E
702   Lost trails of the Cimarron.   Denver, Sage
N6   Books [1961]
C55   304p. illus. 23cm. index.

337291

1.No Man's Land, Okla.-Hist. 2.Frontier and pioneer
life-No Man's Land, Okla. 3.Ranch life. I.Title.